Social Media

Chandos
Social Media Series

Series Editors: Geoff Walton and Woody Evans
(emails: g.l.walton@staffs.ac.uk and kdevans@gmail.com)

This series of books is aimed at practitioners and academics involved in using social media in all its forms and in any context. This includes information professionals, academics, librarians and managers, and leaders in business. Social media can enhance services, build communication channels, and create competitive advantage. The impact of these new media and decisions that surround their use in business can no longer be ignored. The delivery of education, privacy issues, logistics, political activism and research rounds out the series' coverage. As a resource to complement the understanding of issues relating to other areas of information science, teaching and related areas, books in this series respond with practical applications. If you would like a full listing of current and forthcoming titles, please visit our website www.chandospublishing.com.

New authors: we are always pleased to receive ideas for new titles; if you would like to write a book for Chandos in the area of social media, please contact George Knott, Commissioning Editor, on g.knott@elsevier.com or telephone +44 (0) 1865843114.

Chandos Publishing Social Media Series

Social Media

The Academic Library Perspective

Edited by

NINA VERISHAGEN

ELSEVIER

CP
CHANDOS
PUBLISHING
An imprint of Elsevier

Chandos Publishing is an imprint of Elsevier
50 Hampshire Street, 5th Floor, Cambridge, MA 02139, United States
The Boulevard, Langford Lane, Kidlington, OX5 1GB, United Kingdom

British Library Cataloguing-in-Publication Data
A catalogue record for this book is available from the British Library

Library of Congress Cataloging-in-Publication Data
A catalog record for this book is available from the Library of Congress

ISBN: 978-0-08-102409-6

For information on all Chandos Publishing publications
visit our website at https://www.elsevier.com/books-and-journals

Publisher: Glyn Jones
Acquisition Editor: Glyn Jones
Editorial Project Manager: Joshua Mearns
Production Project Manager: Swapna Srinivasan
Cover Designer: Victoria Pearson

Typeset by MPS Limited, Chennai, India

CONTENTS

LIST OF CONTRIBUTORS

Becca Billings
UAB Libraries, University of Alabama at Birmingham, Birmingham, AL, United States

Matthew Blaine
Fairfield University, Fairfield, CT, United States

Lauren Valentino Bryant
Shoreline Community College, Shoreline, WA, United States

Sarah Christensen
University of Illinois Urbana-Champaign, Urbana and Champaign, Illinois, United States

Emy N. Decker
Georgia Institute of Technology Library, Atlanta, GA, United States

Alexander S. Di Iorio
Panel Research Coordinator, Simmons Research

Heather Domenicis
Outreach Librarian and Heather Domenicis, Student Social Media Representative, College of the Holy Cross, Worcester, MA, United States

Joanna Ewing
University of Central Arkansas, Conway, AR, United States

Monica Fazekas
Western Libraries, Western University, London, ON, Canada

Steve Fowler
Assistant Librarian for Access and Outreach Services, Mount Saint Mary College, Newburgh, NY, United States

Stephanie Henderson
Reference Librarian, Northeast Ohio Medical University, Rootstown, Ohio, United States

Dana Hettich
UAB Libraries, University of Alabama at Birmingham, Birmingham, AL, United States

Michael Holt
Valdosta State University, Valdosta, GA, United States

Brandy R. Horne
University of South Carolina Aiken, Aiken, SC, United States

Katie Hutchison
Student Engagement & Archival Services Librarian, Walsh University, North Canton, Ohio, United States

Emily Jack
University Libraries, University of North Carolina, Chapel Hill, United States

Sheeji Kathuria
Mississippi State University, Starkville, MS, United States

Jacalyn Kremer
Fairfield University, Fairfield, CT, United States

Ann Liang
Saskatchewan Polytechnic Library, Saskatchewan Polytechnic, Moose Jaw, SK, Canada

Nicole Maddock
Western Libraries, Western University, London, ON, Canada

Molly Marcusse
American Heritage Center, University of Wyoming, Laramie, WY, United States

Laura MacLeod Mulligan
Head of Access Services, Ball State University Libraries

Alejandra Nann
Copley Library at the University of San Diego, San Diego, CA, United States

Jen Park
Assistant Librarian for Access and Outreach Services, Mount Saint Mary College, Newburgh, NY, United States

Samantha Paul
Valdosta State University, Valdosta, GA, United States

J.J. Pionke
University of Illinois Urbana-Champaign, Urbana and Champaign, Illinois, United States

Mark Aaron Polger
Department of the Library, College of Staten Island, City University of New York (CUNY), New York, NY, United States

Amanda Clay Powers
Mississippi University for Women, Columbus, MS, United States

Karen Pruneda
University of Central Arkansas, Conway, AR, United States

Dan Sich
Western Libraries, University of Western Ontario, London, ON, Canada

Morgan Swan
Rauner Special Collections Library, Dartmouth College, Hanover, NH, United States

Kevin Tanner
Reg Erhardt Library, Southern Alberta Institute of Technology, AB, Canada

Nina Verishagen
Saskatchewan Polytechnic Library, Saskatchewan Polytechnic, Saskatoon, SK, Canada

Amber Wilson
University of Central Arkansas, Conway, AR, United States

Laura Wilson
Outreach Librarian and Heather Domenicis, Student Social Media Representative, College of the Holy Cross, Worcester, MA, United States

ABOUT THE AUTHORS

Becca R. Billings received her bachelor's degree in English writing with a minor in Small-Press Publishing in the fall 2011 from Southeast Missouri State University, and then graduated with her MLIS from the University of Alabama in 2015. Immediately after receiving her degree, she became a reference librarian at Lister Hill Library of the Health Sciences, part of UAB Libraries at the University of Alabama at Birmingham. She currently works as the liaison to the UAB Schools of Nursing & Optometry teaching skills in effective searching, evidence-based practice, critical appraisal, APA, and predatory publishing.

She serves on numerous library committees and professional organizations within the field of health sciences librarianship including ALLA, ALHeLA, and SC/MLA. As co-chair to UAB Libraries Marketing Committee since 2016, she has gained a new perspective on the importance of library outreach and the promotion of resources by way of marketing.

Matthew Blaine is a Reference and Outreach Librarian at Fairfield University's DiMenna-Nyselius Library. He received his MLIS from San Jose State University in 2017 and has previously worked in the archives of Travelers Insurance, the Connecticut Historical Society, and the Mark Twain House. While his background is primarily in archives and records management, his current role as an outreach librarian has led him to thinking about innovative ways to use social media to promote and encourage information literacy.

Lauren Valentino Bryant is an Associate Librarian at Shoreline Community College in Washington state. She manages the website for the Ray Howard Library and uses her web development skills to keep their LibGuides looking snazzy. When she is not working the reference desk or designing online courses, she spends her time playing video games and reading graphic novels. Visit Lauren's website at www.LaurentheLibrarian.com

Sarah Christensen is the Visual Resources and Outreach Specialist at the University of Illinois Urbana-Champaign. Her professional practice includes support for digitization projects, visual literacy instruction, general reference, social media management and practices, and outreach and engagement events. Her research interests focus on the role of academic libraries in supporting the public engagement mission of land-grant universities. She holds a B.A. in art history from the University of Massachusetts at Amherst, an MLS from Simmons College in Boston, MA, and is currently in the graphic design program at the U of I.

Emy Nelson Decker is the NextGen Public Services Manager for the Georgia Tech Library. She holds an MLIS from Valdosta State University and an MA in art history from the University of Chicago. Her current research interests are centered on leadership and team building, professional development, and reimagining library services toward a greater focus on user engagement and the needs of digital thinkers. In addition to presenting in venues such as the American Library Association and the Association of College & Research Libraries, she has published numerous refereed journal articles and book chapters within the library field. She is also the co-editor of the *Handbook of Research on Disaster Management and Contingency Planning in Modern Libraries.*

Alexander Di Iorio is Panel Research Coordinator for Simmons Research, a market research company in Deerfield Beach, Florida. He brought his knowledge of research methods to Simmons after graduating with a Master of Arts in Cognitive and Social Processes from Ball State University in 2017, where he also worked as a Graduate Assistant for the University Libraries. In this position, he facilitated reference service to library patrons, assisted with instructional service, and used his talents in graphic design to create informational and promotional materials—including one Snapchat geofilter. Even in his current position at Simmons Research, he has designed mailing invitations, flyers, and webpages. As his career progresses, he hopes to enter the field of user experience, where he can focus his skills in research and visual design.

Heather Domenicis, a Worcester native and student at Holy Cross, majors in English with a concentration in Creative Writing. She expects to graduate in 2019 and plans to pursue a creative writing M.F.A after graduation. She is a student library assistant in Holy Cross' music library as well as the student social media intern for Holy Cross Libraries. Outside of school and work, she enjoys playing guitar, singing in an A Capella group, and performing in and building sets for Holy Cross' theater productions.

Joanna Ewing is the Head of Cataloging at the University of Central Arkansas Torreyson Library. She has worked at UCA since 2013 and professionally in libraries since 2007. She earned a Master of Library and Information Studies from the University of Alabama in 2006 and an MS in Community and Economic Development from UCA in 2017. In addition to her cataloging responsibilities, she also actively participates in the library's education and outreach activities, including providing reference services and teaching library instruction sessions.

Monica Fazekas is the Student Engagement and Outreach Librarian at Western University. Her research interests reflect current and past roles and include social media use in academic libraries, Wikipedia edit-a-thons as a community-building tool, copyright issues within music librarianship, and library user experience. She has masters degrees for both Library and Information Science and Musicology. She is currently serving as an editor for *The Canadian Journal of Academic Librarianship.*

Steve Fowler worked at the Mount Saint Mary College Writing Center for 2 years. He now works as Assistant Editor of *Hudson Valley* magazine.

Stephanie Henderson is a Reference Librarian at Northeast Ohio Medical University's Aneal Mohan Kohli Academic and Information Technology Center. She is also an Adjunct Graduate Faculty member in the College of Graduate Studies, where she gives scholarly communication lectures. As the solo reference librarian, she provides instruction, consultation, and literature search assistance to the Colleges of Medicine, Pharmacy, and Graduate Studies. Previously she has worked at Walsh University as the instructional services librarian. She holds a BA in Biology from Berea College and an MA in Library and Information Science from the University of South Florida.

Dana Hettich is an Assistant Professor at the University of Alabama at Birmingham where she works as the Student Success Librarian with UAB Libraries. As liaison to the Academic Student Success Center, student organizations and nonacademic departments, she frequently comes into contact with the continued struggle to market the library, its people, and its services to a wider campus audience. Prior to coming to UAB Dana worked as a Collection Development Librarian at a community college where she taught and helped create credit bearing courses on research and design. She holds Master's degrees in both History, with a focus on medicine in the new south, and Library & Information Sciences. Her research interests include the crossroads of librarianship with universal design, library as third place, marketing, and international students.

Michael Holt currently serves as an Associate Professor and the Marketing and Assessment Coordinator at Valdosta State University's Odum Library. His research interests include the academic library's role in student retention, social media assessment, and the relationship between higher education administrators and academic libraries. He has master's degrees in both Library and Information Science and History.

Brandy R. Horne is an Instruction/Reference Librarian and Associate Professor at the University of South Carolina Aiken. Having primary responsibility for her library's outreach and promotional efforts, she has written and presented on various related topics including library displays and social media, using social media for fundraising, and creating professional marketing materials. Her other primary research areas include undergraduate citation support and information access in a digital environment. She holds an MLIS from Valdosta State University and a BA in English and Political Science from Georgia College and State University.

Katie Hutchison is the Student Engagement and Archival Services Librarian at Walsh University, in North Canton, Ohio. She has presented at various conferences on the topics of student engagement, outreach programming, and personal librarian programs. At Walsh University she is responsible for coordinating library events, social media, and outreach initiatives. She received her master's in Library and Information Science from Kent State University in 2009.

Emily Jack is the Community Engagement Librarian for the University of North Carolina at Chapel Hill, where she manages the library's social media presence, cultivates brand identity, and awareness for the special collections library, and coordinates efforts that engage the UNC community with the library in research and learning activities outside of the curriculum. In previous positions, she has developed digital projects for a small regional museum and created a free digital textbook of North Carolina history. She is passionate about the open culture movement and is one of the founders of a regional Wikipedia user group.

Sheeji Kathuria is an Assistant Professor and Social Sciences Librarian at Mississippi State University (MSU). As of 2016, she is also MSU Libraries' Social Media Research Librarian, where she chairs the library's social media committee as well as teaches workshops and provides research support related to effective online presence and social media. Before coming to Mississippi State University, she was an instruction librarian at the University of Alabama in Huntsville and a Reference Librarian at Georgia Perimeter College. She received her MLIS from the University of Tennessee, Knoxville in 2011, and Bachelor of Arts in Sociology from the University of Georgia in 2006.

Jacalyn Kremer is the Dean of the Amelia V. Gallucci-Cirio Library at Fitchburg State University in Fitchburg, MA. Prior to coming to Fitchburg State, she was Library Head of Assessment and Partnerships at Fairfield University, Fairfield, CT, where she led the assessment team and the liaison team. She managed multiple assessment projects with colleagues across the university with the goal of identifying and communicating the value of the academic library in student learning. Jacalyn is also committed to promoting the academic library as a partner in academic integrity initiatives and working collaboratively with faculty to explore the complex issues of academic dishonesty. Her research areas include academic integrity, assessment, and social media. She has a Master's in Library Science from Southern Connecticut State University. She also has a Certificate in Higher Education Leadership & Management from UMASS Amherst.

Ann Liang is the User Experience and Business Librarian at Saskatchewan Polytechnic, Moose Jaw Campus. She has worn many hats in her short time at Sask Polytech, from Marketing Liaison to overseer of digital and in person user experience as well as the library's biennial user survey. Her current research interests include marketing, service design, and addressing international student's information literacy needs. She has earned a BA in Archeology and a BSc in Biology from the University of Saskatchewan, and a Master's in Library Science from Western University in London, Ontario.

Nicole Maddock is the User Services Manager, Information & Public Service and Outreach & Events, at Western Libraries. Her research interests include user experience, service design, and academic library marketing, with an eye to finding innovative ways to engage with users. She has spoken about library marketing in many contexts, academic, public, and even hospital libraries. She is currently sitting a two year term on the organizing committee for the Ontario Library Association Marketing Think Tank.

Molly Marcusse is a Reference Archivist at University of Wyoming's American Heritage Center in Laramie, Wyoming and currently serves as chair of the marketing committee. She enjoys working with researchers of all varieties, from the general public to established scholars, but has a particular passion for providing instructional support for fourth grade through graduate students from schools across the state of Wyoming. She has a Master's of Library Sciences with a concentration in archives, records, and information management from University of Maryland and a BA from University of Michigan in Near Eastern Studies with a minor in Museum Studies.

Laura MacLeod Mulligan is Head of Access Services at Ball State University Libraries in Muncie, Indiana, where she leads the Libraries in circulation, course reserves, stacks management, and resource sharing. Previously, she worked as Information Services Librarian at Ball State University Libraries, where her role included reference assistance, liaison work and outreach to academic departments and faculty, and instruction to students. In addition to her regular duties, she coordinates a team to manage the Libraries' social media presence, which currently includes Facebook, Twitter, Instagram, and Pinterest accounts, as well as a foray into the world of Snapchat. She earned her Master of Library Science from Indiana University–Bloomington in May 2010 and a Bachelor of Arts in English and Anthropology from Dickinson College in May 2004. Prior to her career in librarianship, she worked for several years as a book editor for academic presses located at Indiana University and Dartmouth College.

Jen Park is the Assistant Librarian for Access and Outreach Services at Mount Saint Mary College in Newburgh, NY, where she enjoys working with the students, faculty, and staff in all aspects relating to access services, marketing, and outreach with regards to the library. Prior to MSMC, she was Head of Circulation at Thomas M. Cooley Law School in Lansing, MI. She holds her masters in Information and Library Science from Wayne State University.

Samantha Paul is a Reference Librarian and the Virtual Services Librarian at Valdosta State University. She has a BA in Linguistics from the University of Georgia. She received her MLIS from Valdosta State University. Her research interests include marketing, LibGuide design, and language usage in instruction.

JJ Pionke is the Applied Health Sciences Librarian and the University of Illinois at Urbana-Champaign. His research focuses on disability and the library.

Amanda Clay Powers is the Dean of Library Services at Mississippi University for Women. Previously, she worked as the Research Services Coordinator at Mississippi State University. She received her bachelor's degree from Wellesley College in Wellesley, MA, and she received her Master's in Library and Information Science from Simmons College School of Library and Information Science. Her research interests include library management, virtual reference, and assessment of library services.

Mark Aaron Polger is the First Year Outreach Librarian at the College of Staten Island, City University of New York (CUNY) and an Information Literacy Instructor at ASA College. His research interests include library marketing, outreach, and user experience design. He has written and presented on topics such as library marketing strategies, faculty outreach, information literacy campaigns, library jargon, and library signage.

Currently, he is founder and editor-in-chief of the open-access, peer reviewed journal *Marketing Libraries Journal*, which was launched in 2017.

He holds a BA in Sociology from Concordia University, an MLIS from the University of Western Ontario, an MA in Sociology from University of Waterloo, and a BEd in Adult Education from Brock University. He is in his third year of his PhD in Curriculum, Instruction, and the Science of Learning at SUNY University at Buffalo. Originally from Montreal (Canada), he moved to New York City in 2008.

Karen Pruneda is the Library Technician for Education and Outreach at the University of Central Arkansas Torreyson Library. She has worked in libraries for three years and secondary schools at the middle and high school level for seven years. In 2014 she received a Master of Education in Special Education from Waynesburg University. Currently she manages day-to-day social media outreach, works to increase student engagement with the library, and teaches a few research classes. She has taken on a leadership role in the Arkansas Library Paraprofessionals Division of the Arkansas Library Association by managing their social media accounts.

Kevin Tanner is the Coordinator of Library Instruction at the Southern Alberta Institute of Technology (SAIT) in Calgary, Alberta. In addition, he is also responsible for communications at the SAIT Library. Previously, he worked as a Research Assistant at Western Libraries in London, Ontario, investigating how Snapchat could be leveraged in an academic library setting to connect with students. He received a Master's of Library and Information Science from Western University, and a Bachelor of Arts, English Language and Literature from the University of Windsor.

Dan Sich is the Teaching and Learning Librarian, E-Learning at Western Libraries at the University of Western Ontario in London, Ontario, Canada. He began his library career as a Liaison Librarian at the University of Waterloo Library, Waterloo, Ontario, Canada (2000–2008) and was a research and instructional services librarian at Western Libraries (2008–2018). He has been involved in the creation of video tutorials since 2011. He holds a BSc in Physics, a Diploma in Honors Standing in Philosophy, and an MLIS all from the University of Western Ontario.

Laura Solomon is the Library Services Manager for the Ohio Public Library Information Network. She has been doing web development and design for 20 years, in both public libraries and as an independent consultant. She specializes in developing with Drupal. She is a 2010 Library Journal Mover & Shaker. She has written three books about social media and content marketing, specifically for libraries, and speaks nationally on both these and technology-related topics. As a former children's librarian, she enjoys bringing the "fun of technology" to audiences and in giving libraries the tools they need to better serve the virtual customer.

Morgan Swan has served as the Special Collections Education and Outreach Librarian at Dartmouth College for six years. His duties include teaching, supervising the Reader Services department at Rauner Special Collections Library, and coordinating outreach efforts via public programming and social media. Before coming to Dartmouth, he worked in Public Services at the Beinecke Rare Book & Manuscript Library at Yale University for nearly five years. He has a PhD in English Literature from Yale and an MLIS with a concentration in Archival Studies from the University of Wisconsin-Milwaukee.

Laura MacLeod Mulligan is head of Access Services at Ball State University Libraries in Muncie, Indiana, where she leads the Libraries in circulation, course reserves, stacks management, and resource sharing. Previously, she worked as Information Services Librarian at Ball State University Libraries, where her role included reference assistance, liaison work, and outreach to academic departments and faculty, and instruction to students. In addition to her regular duties, she coordinates a team to manage the Libraries' social media presence, which currently includes Facebook, Twitter, Instagram, and Pinterest accounts, as well as a foray into the world of Snapchat. She earned her Master of Library Science from Indiana University–Bloomington in May 2010 and a Bachelor of Arts in English and Anthropology from Dickinson College in May 2004. Prior to her career in librarianship, she worked for several years as a book editor for academic presses located at Indiana University and Dartmouth College.

Nina Verishagen is the Marketing Librarian at Saskatchewan Polytechnic Library. She is passionate about developing connections with library patrons and does this through her work managing events, developing promotional materials, and chairing the library's social media committee. For the past six years, she has been developing and fostering important relationships with her colleagues in various student support services including Indigenous Student Success Strategy and International Education. She is also actively involved in library instruction, focusing her efforts on developing a programming for students enrolled in academic upgrading. She holds a BA in History from the University of Saskatchewan and an MLIS from McGill University in Montreal. Her research interests include adult instruction and social media in the academic library.

Laura Wilson is the Outreach Librarian at College of the Holy Cross in Worcester, MA. Her professional duties include marketing the campus libraries and their services, organizing outreach events, and managing the libraries' social media accounts. She also teaches library instruction sessions, answers reference questions, and serves as library liaison to the Spanish, Modern Languages, Sociology, and Anthropology departments. She holds a Master's degree in Library Information Science from Simmons College, and a Master's degree in French from Boston College. Her recent publications include several book reviews as well as a chapter on the library orientation at Holy Cross in *Planning Academic Library Orientations*.

FOREWORD

I have an ongoing horror of the broad overview.

Ditto for high-level perspectives, foundational works, and introductory texts. Granted, these kinds of writings have a place. However, for me, these have always represented obstacles to getting to the "stuff I actually need to know right now." When I am searching for practical advice or a concrete road map, concepts are rarely helpful.

Perhaps you have felt the same way, when you have gone to a conference session, hoping to find actionable ideas, only to come away disappointed when they never materialized. Maybe you jumped to another session, or even gave up altogether, going in search of a drink, instead. Too many times, I have been itching to get my hands dirty in the logistics of a topic, only to find that the logistics never even came up in the discussion.

When I was first asked to write this foreword, and before I actually got to read the manuscript, I had an underlying fear that this would be yet another sweeping, bird's-eye view of social media in libraries. From my own viewpoint, we are well beyond needing to convince libraries to participate in social media. The vast majority of libraries are already there. . .and they are looking for actionable ideas and practical advice. We do not need to be told *why* to be doing this work: we need to know more (a lot more) about the *how*.

I will be frank; I was more than pleasantly surprised to find that this book was not what I had dreaded. I was elated that every single chapter gave solid recommendations for tools and strategies that worked for academic libraries. Even more wonderful was a refreshing, brutal honesty about what *did not* work for them. Knowing that "here be dragons" is perhaps even more valuable for creating our own campaigns.

A large portion of this volume is devoted to case studies. This is where libraries put the pedal to the metal, and clearly report on process and results. Hindsight is 20/20; each case study not only examines the details of what the library did on a particular social media platform but also gives us recommendations for what it would change if it was to do it again.

Guidelines for the murky area that is social media marketing are priceless, but this book offers far more. Sometimes, a picture says a thousand words. You will find post and survey samples. Seeing the questions that a library actually used in a survey, or how it decided to format a photo for a post on Instagram, may give you guidance you did not even know you were searching for. You will also see samples of print campaigns and letters. Charts and graphs show survey results and workflows. In putting this together, many of the writers clearly understood what we really wanted to see.

To sweeten the pot, each chapter is eminently readable. This is also of great import to me, as I have an additional dread of reading most nonfiction. Long, wordy paragraphs make information difficult for me to absorb. I am happy to report that this was a nonissue in this instance. You will find this to be a very practical, straightforward guidebook that is broken down into understandable chunks and lists. Planning your own library's social media promotions will be made easier, with no need to wade through large swaths of text.

I have always had a love/hate relationship with social media. While I love the potential for communication, I have never been a fan of how nebulous the work can be. Making sense of social media marketing has always been a challenge. There seem to be very few absolutes and success is continually elusive. I am always looking out not only for the "next big thing," but also for real-world examples that I can actually learn from. (Even experienced pros can gain insights from this book; I will be using "camel case" in my hashtags from now on, thanks!)

Allowing the reader to get up close and personal with the inner workings of what these libraries did provides an invaluable look behind the scenes, one that is rarely available to us folks in the social media trenches. The fact that these glimpses include dives into rarely covered subject areas such accessibility, copyright, committees, and scheduling tools make this unique collection a vital read for those of us trying to figure out what the heck we need to be doing, in an environment that seems to have only quicksand as its foundation.

This *is not* a broad overview. This is where you are going to get your hands dirty in the process of social media. Go forth, without trepidation, and benefit from the level-headed advice your colleagues have to offer.

Laura Solomon

ACKNOWLEDGMENTS

Throughout this process I have received personal and professional support from many individuals.

First, I must acknowledge the chapter contributors who helped realize a vision. We have created something useful, interesting, and, at times, amusing. It has been a very positive experience and I have learned a great deal from this collaboration.

Second, to the colleagues who listened to my thoughts, read drafts, and counseled me every step of the way. I appreciate your patience, generosity, and support.

Finally, to my family. To my parents who provided unending support and excitement; to Kevin, for always encouraging me to strive for more; and to Reese, my newest reason to pursue lofty goals, thank you.

INTRODUCTION

Academic libraries today are filled with Millennials and post-Millennials, spanning the age range of 18–37, these generations were seemingly born with smartphones in their hands (Dimnock, 2018). Whether faculty members, professional staff, or students, most use their phones for a variety of online activities, including social media. A primary goal of any academic library is connecting with students to halt library anxiety and facilitate educational success. Marketing and outreach librarians are often tasked with initiating these meaningful connections. But how do we connect with patrons who don't attend our library orientations? How do we do it when there are institutional barriers to sending mass email communications? What about the patrons who've never stepped through our doors? Or those sitting in cubicles, not wanting to approach a service desk for help?

Enter social media. In early 2018, two reports were released, both of which shed light on social media use among adults (18 +) in North America. The Social Media Lab at Ryerson University reports on Canadian usage, while the Pew Research Center's report focuses on American usage. Both studies show a large number of adults engaging with Facebook (68% United States; 84% Canada) and YouTube (73% United States; 59% Canada) (Grudz, Jacobson, Mai, & Dubois, 2018; Pew Research Center, 2018). A large majority of the younger generations (ages 18–28) report that they use at least three of the eight major platforms measured. Also notable, the youngest age group in the United States, those aged 18–24, are more likely to use Snapchat, Instagram, or Twitter (Pew Research Center, 2018). The youngest in Canada maintain a usage rate above 50% on all of these platforms, with Pinterest coming in close at 45% (Grudz et al., 2018). So it seems, social media adoption and usage among the Millennial and post-Millennial generations is remaining stable. Over the past decade librarians have been observing these trends and trying to evolve with them.

This book is a practical guide for librarians and others in the education field. Whether you are looking for new social media ideas, hoping to reinvigorate a platform or adopting for the first time, you will find something valuable within. The chapter authors are experts in their fields, all currently engaged with social media work in the postsecondary environment. Unsurprisingly, each chapter discusses connecting with a common patron group shared by the academic institution: students. The anthology includes two sections, the first section (Chapters 1–5) provides guidance on how to administer social media in an academic setting; the second (Chapters 6–11) presents a series of case studies that highlight the experiences of academic librarians with specific social media platforms and the lessons they have learned.

I.1 PART I: THE SOCIAL MEDIA LANDSCAPE AT THE ACADEMIC LIBRARY

In *How to Assess Students' Social Media Preferences: A Comparison at Two Academic Institutions*, Dan Sich and Mark Aaron Polger highlight their experiences assessing the social media preferences of students at two different academic libraries. They provide a workflow aimed at answering the big question in every social media librarian's mind: Am I posting the right message in the right place?

In *Social Media Committees: Sharing the Library's Voice*, Alejandra Nann and Nina Verishagen discuss their experiences developing social media committees at two different academic libraries. They provide insight into efficient workflow, discuss common issues such as member roles and scheduling and provide a series of tips that can be adapted by any social media committee.

Next, Morgan Swan provides a five-point framework for selecting the best social platform for your library in the aptly titled *The Right Social Media Platform for Your Library.*

Social Media Best Practices: Implementing Guidelines for Disability and Copyright, by Sarah Christensen and J.J. Pionke, provides insight into social media management for a very large academic library—one with over 50 social media accounts! They focus on copyright and accessibility, critical issues that should be addressed by all libraries in the social media world.

Finally, Samantha Paul and Michael Holt provide an overview of third-party scheduling apps. Their analysis *Using Scheduling Apps to Streamline a Social Media Workflow* includes common themes and trends, pricing, features, and benefits.

I.2 PART II: TRIED AND TESTED BY LIBRARIANS: SOCIAL MEDIA CASE STUDIES

Part II covers specific social media platforms including Instagram, Twitter, Facebook, YouTube, SnapChat, and Pinterest. Each case study provides a list of challenges and successes with recommendations for those considering similar social media campaigns.

I.2.1 Instagram

The first case study, *Using Instagram to Engage Students During Library Orientation* by Katie Hutchison and Stephanie Henderson, covers a successful Instagram scavenger hunt that takes place during a library orientation and welcome event offered to incoming first-year students at a small liberal arts college in Ohio.

Next, in *Enhancing Your Instagram Following Through Interdepartmental Collaboration*, Jen Park and Steve Fowler discuss an interdepartmental collaboration, between the Library and the Writing Center. Partnering with other departments to develop an Instagram contest enabled them to extend their reach beyond their service areas and develop meaningful relationships with their colleagues.

Student Social Media Representatives and Instagram: Connecting With the Campus Community Through Library Student Workers takes readers through Laura Wilson's experience hiring a student worker, Heather Domenicis, as a social media representative. The authors share their experiences with this new initiative and describe a series of successful campaigns.

Authors Matthew Blaine and Jacalyn Kremer examine their library's Instagram account with a critical eye in *Are We Failing at Instagram?* This study examines the effective (or ineffective) use of the platform by a library serving a medium-sized university. The authors provide a model to analyze likes, comments, and views and recommend how to use various features of the platform, including still images, videos, and Instagram stories for maximum impact.

I.2.2 Twitter

In our first look at Twitter, a librarian at a large university attempts to engage students during the ALA-sponsored International Games Day. In *Tweeting to Success: Managing an Academic Library's Twitter Campaign to Enhance User Engagement*, Emy N. Decker discusses the fine line libraries must walk in the social media world—a world in which students are often amenable to following, but do not want a flood of promotional messages. How do you avoid "getting old" or "being annoying" on this platform? The author emphasizes live tweeting during an event to build hype and engage users in the online environment.

Case study two focuses on the use of Twitter to promote a Drop Everything and Read (DEAR) campaign at a middle-sized university. In *Drop Everything and Tweet: Building Community on Your Campus*, Joanna Ewing, Amber Wilson, and Karen Pruneda explain how they engaged with an entire collegial community by inviting a wide array of people to participate in various ways. This resulted not only in extending the libraries outreach, but also in book-led community building throughout the campus.

In our third case study, *What Do You Do When They Start Talking Back? Training Librarians for Next-Level Twitter Engagement Using Springshare's LibAnswers*, librarians at a large university emphasize that building a huge social media following is not the end of the line. Once your community starts using Twitter to ask questions, how do you keep track? Sheeji Kathuria and Amanda Clay Powers describe the adoption of a new workflow that allowed them to route their tweets through LibAnswers—and the lessons they learned along the way.

In our final look at Twitter, *Rising Above the Noise: Increasing Local Engagement Through a Global Hashtag Campaign*, a librarian at a large academic library explains how to participate in a global hashtag campaign that aligns with your institution's vision. Building on a preexisting athletic rivalry, Emily Jack and her team challenged librarians at another institution to participate in a Wikipedia-centered competition. She describes the clever way in which they used—but did not to overuse—newsjacking to express a strong library voice amid all the other online campus chatter.

I.2.3 Facebook

Dana Hettich and Becca Billings, the authors of *Breaking Up Is Hard to Do: UAB Libraries and Facebook's Mis(sed)connection*, ponder their library's relationship with Facebook. Unsure of its value as a promotional tool, the Libraries Marketing committee develop a targeted campaign to promote a specific resource through a variety of media, including Facebook, to see which, if any, generated increased resource use. Campaign results were used to decide whether or not the library would stay in a relationship with Facebook.

Next, Nina Verishagen and Ann Liang, librarians at a polytechnic institution, share their experiences running a monthly Facebook contest targeted at students. *Buying Likes: How Our Library Jumped From 200 to 1000 (Student) Likes in 5 Months* examines the key steps in creating and promoting any online contest and provides a step-by-step guide, key takeaways, and lessons learned.

In *So You Have Been Given the Social Media Passwords. Now What? A Trial-by-Fire Case Study in Facebook Marketing*, Molly Marcusse describes a social media campaign that aimed to connect the library with residents of the surrounding community rather than just the library's academic community. The study covers two campaigns, one successful, one not, and emphasizes the fact that focusing on content for a target audience is the most effective way to increase engagement.

I.2.4 YouTube

In *Thousands of Views: Why Three Simple Library Videos Have Done So Well*, a librarian at a large Canadian university discusses his success with YouTube. By focusing on three videos that have received thousands of views and continue to do well, Dan Sich describes the factors that contributed to this success. He provides not only an overview of technical and promotional considerations, but also perspectives on assessment.

In our second look at YouTube, *Show Me: Getting YouTube Videos to Your Students Through SEO*, Lauren Valentino Bryant reflects on her examination of student information seeking behavior and her use of Search Engine Optimization to connect students to the library's YouTube page. The case study includes a technical checklist covering concepts such as evaluating, boosting, and increasing traffic, profile optimization, and content-rich descriptions.

I.2.5 Snapchat

How can a library combine its social media efforts with those of the larger institution? Nicole Maddock, Monica Fazekas, and Kevin Tanner answer this question in *Snapchat and Academic Libraries: We ain't Afraid of No Ghost*. Covering their experiences collaborating with Western University's Institutional Communications and Marketing Department, the library effectively reached students on Snapchat by pushing library "Stories" through their account, which already hosted a large and engaged audience.

Another effective use of Snapchat to engage students is through geofilters. In *Snap to It: Reaching Users Where They Are With Snapchat Geofilters*, Laura MacLeod Mulligan and Alexander S. Di Iorio describe how to create an effective Snapchat geofilter. This technology can be used by libraries that want to engage with the Snapchat world but are hesitant to develop their own accounts.

I.2.6 Pinterest

The final case study of this anthology is *Extending the Library's Presence Into the Virtual Space Using Pinterest.* Author Brandy R. Horne describes one library's use of Pinterest to expand physical displays into the digital space. The resulting Pinterest boards continue to grow and can be reused over time.

REFERENCES

Dimnock, M. (2018). *Defining generations: Where Millenials end and post-Millenials begin.* Retrieved from <http://www.pewresearch.org/fact-tank/2018/03/01/defining-generations-where-millennials-end-and-post-millennials-begin/>.

Grudz, A., Jacobson, J., Mai, P., Dubois, E. (2018). *The State of social media in Canada 2017. Version: 1.0.* Ryerson University Social Media Lab. Retrieved from <https://doi.org/10.5683/SP/AL8Z6R>.

Pew Research Center. (2018). *Social media use in 2018.* Retrieved from <http://assets.pewresearch.org/wp-content/uploads/sites/14/2018/03/01105133/PI_2018.03.01_Social-Media_FINAL.pdf>.

PART I

The Social Media Landscape at the Academic Library

CHAPTER 1

How to Assess Students' Social Media Preferences: A Comparison at Two Academic Institutions

Dan Sich[1] and Mark Aaron Polger[2]
[1]Western Libraries, University of Western Ontario, London, ON, Canada
[2]Department of the Library, College of Staten Island, City University of New York (CUNY), New York, NY, United States

1.1 INTRODUCTION: REASON FOR STUDY

This chapter will outline our experiences conducting an assessment of a specific patron group's social media (SM) preferences. The main goal is to provide a framework that can be adapted and utilized by other academic librarians. We will touch on the findings of our study, but focus mostly on our experience conducting it.

We ran a study of the SM preferences of students in relation to their libraries, at two separate institutions. At both libraries we thought it necessary to conduct the study because we noted the potential for investing too much time in the libraries' SM presence. We also saw potential for tool creep—multiple SM accounts (including Facebook, Twitter, and Snapchat, to name a few) for various libraries. Tool creep could lead to a situation where there are too many SM accounts for users to choose from, leading to confusion. It is also more difficult for the library to manage. We wanted to make sure that the time and effort our libraries were investing in their SM presences was worthwhile. Were we posting the right messages in the right places? Our study was intended to help address this concern.

The results we obtained provide a snapshot of our students' use of SM tools vis-a-vis the library. The SM use landscape changes from year to year and so this type of research should ideally be run on a continual basis. It can provide 'snapshots' of student use of SM tools that can be used to tweak a library's SM strategy.

Social Media
DOI: https://doi.org/10.1016/B978-0-08-102409-6.00001-8

Understanding our students' SM preferences is important. Evaluation of our data will help improve our libraries' SM tool choices, posting behaviors, and thus our efforts to inform and educate our users. For example, we might consider changing the emphasis on which SM tools we are using, reconsider the type of content to post, and customize posts to target specific audiences. Throughout, we must assess whether we are successfully engaging with students, or are merely engaged in marketing.

1.2 SOME BACKGROUND

The literature provides further context for a study of this sort. Gerolimos (2011) suggests that rather than overloading Facebook with posts, we attempt to engage 'fans' by carefully crafting posts of interest. He concludes that while librarians put much effort into developing Facebook pages, they fail to assess whether their users are seeking information via these pages. Surveying users, as we have done, will help libraries understand how their users access information about the library.

There are many factors that influence students' SM preferences. Brookbank (2015) notes that SM tool preferences can vary from campus to campus. We wanted to learn something about how students' SM use varies between institutions. Our institutions are quite different (see later). We were interested in whether or not these differences might lead to differences in our data. If we could highlight how our respective students' SM use differs from those at the other institution, we could then focus our SM campaigns on tools and topics that appealed to our users in particular.

Our results show clear preferences at both institutions, which will be used to help inform our libraries' choice of SM tools. We now know more about the type of information students would like to see from us via SM, and a bit about what they do not want to see. These findings regarding what make our student populations different will be used in tailoring future SM posts.

1.3 OUR INSTITUTIONS

Our two institutions differ in a number of ways.

The University of Western Ontario (UWO) in London, Ontario, is a Canadian public university with three affiliated University Colleges. UWO has a total of 38,335 Full Time Equivalents (FTE), with 32,529

FTE on our main campus (Office of Institutional Planning & Budgeting—Western University, n.d.). At the time of this research, Western Libraries had several Facebook and Twitter accounts. These accounts are administered by various teams and individuals. UWO has SM guidelines regarding use of appropriate perspective, verbiage and hashtags, and on how to reply to user comments.

The College of Staten Island (CSI), City University of New York (CUNY), is a public, comprehensive college, providing associate degrees, bachelor, master, and PhDs. CSI is part of the City University of New York, which comprises 24 campuses. CSI has 14,000 students, mostly 1st and 2nd year undergraduates. The CSI Library has been actively using SM tools to promote library services and resources since 2010. Currently, the CSI Library manages SM accounts for Facebook, Twitter, Instagram, and Google+ (Google Plus). All SM accounts are administered by one librarian (Polger) and assisted by the Web Services Librarian. There is a SM policy document in place and a SM scheduling calendar that is populated with content through consultations with the Library's Marketing and Outreach committee (chaired by Polger).

1.4 SURVEY QUESTIONS

The survey included six questions (see Fig. 1.1).

We felt that the questionnaire was effective at providing the data we were seeking. See our Recommendations and Limitations section for advice on composing survey questions.

In order to be able to compare the results from two institutions, our institutional versions of the questionnaire had to be as close to identical as possible. Our questions varied only slightly to account for institutional differences (e.g., terminology differences like "1st year undergraduate student" vs. "freshman") and practices (e.g., Office of Research Ethics requirements). It was also necessary to coordinate the timing of the questionnaire to avoid the effects of a changing SM landscape.

While preparing to run the study, we recognized that it would have been simpler to conduct it independently at each of our two institutions. Anyone wishing to run a similar questionnaire at their own institution could do so without partnering with another institution, and still obtain valuable data. We do not think that our questionnaire was any less effective for having been run at two institutions.

1. Please checkmark the social media you use below (check all that apply).

- ❑ Facebook
- ❑ Twitter
- ❑ Snapchat
- ❑ LinkedIn
- ❑ Google + (Google Plus)
- ❑ Reddit
- ❑ Instagram
- ❑ Tumblr
- ❑ Pinterest
- ❑ YouTube
- ❑ Flickr
- ❑ Foursquare
- ❑ Other (please specify): ________________________

2. From the list above, which social media would you use to follow the library? (check all that apply).

- ❑ Facebook
- ❑ Twitter
- ❑ Snapchat
- ❑ LinkedIn
- ❑ Google + (Google Plus)
- ❑ Reddit
- ❑ Instagram
- ❑ Tumblr
- ❑ Pinterest
- ❑ YouTube
- ❑ Flickr
- ❑ Foursquare
- ❑ Other (please specify): ________________________

3. If you used social media for library updates, what kind of information would you want to see? (check all that apply)

- ❑ News
- ❑ Events
- ❑ New Resources
- ❑ New Services
- ❑ University news
- ❑ London, Ontario news
- ❑ Course related information
- ❑ Other (please specify): ________________________

4. Is there anything you think is *not* appropriate for the library to include on any social media sites?

5. What is your status at the university?

- ❑ 1st year undergraduate
- ❑ 2nd year undergraduate
- ❑ 3rd year undergraduate
- ❑ 4th year undergraduate
- ❑ Graduate student
- ❑ Other (please specify): ________________________

6. What is your gender?

Figure 1.1 UWO survey.

1.5 ETHICS APPROVAL

Because of our intent to publish our research, we both sought and obtained approval from our institutions' offices of human research ethics (Office of Research Ethics at UWO, the Human Research Protection Program at CSI). Libraries wanting to conduct a similar study without publishing likely need not seek such approval. Obtaining this approval can required anywhere from four-six weeks (CSI) to three-four months (UWO) or more. As such we recommend that the reader give themselves adequate time for this important step.

1.6 TIMELINE AND RESPONSE

We ran the study at both institutions for four months, from September 1 to December 31, 2016. This timing was ideal given the amount of Information Literacy instruction which occurs in the Fall term. Four months turned out to be adequate for obtaining enough responses ($N = 602$ at UWO, $N = 637$ at CSI). The reader might want to expand this time frame to two terms in order to obtain more responses, if they use our approach (see later).

1.7 SAMPLING AND DISTRIBUTION

We initially both thought it would be easiest to obtain data by distributing the questionnaire to students via email. However, there are issues with such an approach. For instance, survey emails are easy to ignore, lose, or forget. In addition, the email approach proved impossible at both UWO and CSI; the 'all students' email aliases are unavailable to researchers due to concerns of 'spamming' students. Distributing a paper questionnaire was effective because students completed it on the spot, as opposed to completing it online.

The questionnaire was delivered at the end of Information Literacy instruction sessions at both institutions. This sampling method (convenience sampling) garnered plenty of responses. At CSI we received a large proportion of our responses from first-year students. While many first-year sessions exist at UWO, the questionnaire was not delivered at any of these. We acknowledge that this may have skewed the results. At the same time, while the sample was not random, each institution collected over 600 responses over one academic semester, and the results were obtained immediately. To broaden the diversity of the sample, the reader may wish to distribute paper questionnaires throughout the library or make questionnaires available at the reference or circulation desks.

At UWO, ethics approval required that an 'invitation to participate' script be read to potential participants. This would not have been necessary if we had not intended to publish our research. Students received a print copy of the Letter of Information (to keep) and the questionnaire (to fill in and return before leaving).

At both institutions this approach proved to be very effective at gathering responses. Students seemed happy to fill in the questionnaire, even though it was optional with no incentives offered. This approach was also very easy to execute. At UWO, the print Letter of Information included a link to an online version of the questionnaire, but all respondents opted to use the print questionnaire. At CSI, the print questionnaire was distributed without a link to any online version. The only inconvenience of this approach was that we both had to manually enter the results into our chosen survey software (Qualtrics at UWO, SurveyMonkey at CSI). Both pieces of software are user-friendly and support data analysis (cross tabulations, creation of charts and graphs). Qualtrics is the software supported by UWO's IT department, and SurveyMonkey is affordable.

We recommend that the reader consider the following:

- *Recruiting colleagues to help with the delivery of the questionnaire.* At UWO this worked quite well in helping to reach more students.
- *Trying to reach a reasonable number of students from each year of study.* At UWO, unfortunately, no first-year undergraduate students were reached via this method of sampling. This was not deliberate, but rather the result of chance; no library instructors for 1st year undergraduate courses stepped forward.
- *Making the questionnaire anonymous and voluntary,* and making it mandatory that respondents are 18 years old or older, if ethics approval is required at the institution.
- *Excluding Information Literacy instruction sessions if there is an associated graded assignment,* to help avoid any possible perception of persuasion.
- *Have a student employee distribute the questionnaire* to avoid potential student perception of an expectation that they are using the library's SM tools.
- *Not disseminating the survey via SM* (e.g., via the library's Facebook or Twitter accounts). This recruitment strategy may be tempting, but may skew results as it would likely attract respondents who are already using SM to view library posts.

1.8 QUESTIONNAIRE RESULTS

We analyzed our data according to institution, gender, and year of study. While this analysis provided some interesting results, we will not cover our detailed findings in this chapter. This may be presented in a later publication. Instead, below we provide some highlights of our results.

We received more female than male respondents. Almost half of the CSI respondents were Freshmen, while two-thirds of the UWO respondents were third or fourth year undergraduate students. We did note some differences based on gender and year of study.

When is a difference large enough to merit attention? For our own purposes, differences of 10% or higher were worth investigating. While this number is somewhat arbitrary, it was chosen because it highlighted a reasonable number of differences for us to consider.

In terms of SM tool preferences, YouTube, Facebook, Snapchat, and Instagram were the SM tools most used by students at both institutions. Students were most likely to follow the library on Facebook. The library was less likely to gain followers on Twitter, Instagram, or YouTube. It seems unlikely that we will gain many followers via Snapchat.

At both of our institutions, "Events" was the most popular kind of information that students wanted to learn about via the library's SM accounts. News, new resources, new services, university or college news, and course related information were also popular choices. Local news was the least popular.

In terms of what types of content should not be shared via library SM accounts, those most frequently mentioned were personal information (contact information, photos of people), 'inappropriate' content (e.g., racist, sexist, or homophobic language), and advertisements.

1.9 RECOMMENDATIONS AND LIMITATIONS

We recommend that a reader planning to conduct such a study consider making a few changes to our questionnaire.

List fewer (five to six) SM tools. For questions one and two, including a long list of SM tools for students is tempting, but should be avoided. With a long list of SM tools, there is the risk that students will just check-off everything, or nothing at all, to save time. In retrospect, we could have listed five or six SM tools (Facebook, Twitter, Snapchat, Instagram, YouTube, and perhaps Google+) and still obtained just as much useful data. In other words, keep it simple. We recommend selecting SM tools based on current library use and the most up-to-date 'best SM tools' type lists available. Include a "none" option to differentiate between no response and "none."

Avoid the use of the word "follow." For question two, rather than asking "...which social media would you use to follow the library?," we recommend asking "Which social media tools would you use to look for information or content related to the library?" There are a number of reasons for this. Users do not need to 'follow' the library on any of these platforms in order to view the library's content. For example, many people watch YouTube videos for entertainment purposes but may not think of subscribing to their library, or even look for library assistance, therein. Anyone can view any of our YouTube videos without subscribing to us. They can also find library tweets by searching Twitter, without needing to follow us. In the end, it is 'views' or people reached rather than 'followers' or subscribers that is the primary analytic in YouTube and other SM tools. 'Followers' or subscribers are just one means to the end of increasing the size of our audience. There is also an issue with this "would you...?" sort of question in general. Students' reporting that they would hypothetically 'follow' the library via various SM tools may not translate into their actually 'following' their library via these tools.

Furthermore, even if students are 'following' their library via SM, they may not be interested in the content of their library's SM posts. Counting 'followers' is but one, superficial measure of the success of a library's SM strategy, and does not mean that students are 'engaging with' the library via SM.

Be explicit in labeling of library news, events, resources, and new services as library related. For question three, "News," "Events," "New Resources," and "New Services" should likely have been labeled "Library News," "Library Events," "New Library Resources," and "New Library Services," respectively. We had assumed that students would have understood that "library" was implied, but this may not have been a safe assumption. We speculate that the popularity of the "Events" option might decrease if it were labeled "Library Events." In addition, the reader should choose 'kinds of information' options based on their own categorization of the types of content their library has shared via SM.

Ask "What type of information should not be included in the library's social media accounts?" rather than asking "Is there anything you think is not appropriate for the library to include on any social media sites?" Many respondents may have misinterpreted the wording of our question, taking "not appropriate" to mean "inappropriate," and "inappropriate" in turn to mean sexually explicit, racist, sexist, homophobic, hate speech, etc. While it is obvious that such content should never be considered for inclusion in library SM posts, students seem to have taken the question out of that context.

Ask additional questions, but know what will be done with the findings before opting to include them. For example, students could be asked about their engagement with their library's SM accounts. Have they commented on, liked or shared posts to their library's SM account? Brookbank (2015) asked students which SM tools they use, to rank these in terms of where they most want to hear from their library, how often they use each tool, and for what activities. Respondents could be asked how often they would want the library to post content via various tools. Again, it is important to know how these findings will be used before including such questions.

1.10 SUGGESTIONS FOR FUTURE RESEARCH

While our questionnaire provided us with the information that we were after, there is further research that could be done in the area of student preferences for various SM tools vis-a-vis their academic library. It would be interesting in the future to examine our true number of Facebook and Twitter followers by going through the lists to examine followers' profiles (if public). This would be useful for obtaining a demographic profile of these followers. We may discover that the bulk of our libraries' SM followers may comprise community members and local nonprofits.

Further research could be conducted by contacting 'followers' of the library's SM accounts and asking them for their reasons for following the library's SM, including whether or not there is anything unique about the library's SM presence. This might also provide more reliable information regarding what students want to hear from their library via SM. Such an analysis may accompany a future iteration of our study.

1.11 WHAT TO DO WITH THE RESULTS

This questionnaire was a worthwhile venture at both institutions. It was easy to run and we were able to gather a large number of responses over the course of one term. Data analysis was simple to conduct. It would be simple to run this study on an annual basis, with slight changes from year to year. At both UWO and CSI, we obtained valuable data regarding which SM tools our students would use (and would not use) to seek information from our libraries. In the future, we could ask more questions about the types of activities students engage in on our libraries' SM channels.

1.11.1 The University of Western Ontario

At UWO this research will be used to inform our evolving SM strategy. We are currently considering consolidating some of our numerous Facebook and Twitter accounts. Our Facebook presence seems to be worth some time and effort, and may continue to attract followers. In terms of assessing our Twitter presence, we need to measure our success not in terms of followers, but in number terms of likes, comments, and retweets. The same could be said for Facebook. We recognize the low number of Snapchat and Instagram users interested in following Western Libraries. A solution to this problem has been identified, as described in see Maddock, Tanner and Fazekas's case study on Snapchat later in this book (see Chapter 10c1: Snapchat in Academic Libraries: We Ain't Afraid of No Ghost). Western Libraries may explore this solution for Instagram as well. A library should consider its SM strategy carefully before investing much time and effort on Snapchat, Instagram, or any other SM tool. Libraries should assess the type of content that students are seeking via a SM tool before investing much time and resources in establishing a presence on that specific tool. Finally, it may also be necessary to identify other strategies (e.g., contests) for increasing our number of SM followers or viewers.

1.11.2 The College of Staten Island

At CSI, many students reported that they would follow the library on Facebook, Twitter, or YouTube. The Library's active Facebook account has had very little engagement with students. Outside of this study, one author (Polger) has observed more student engagement (likes, followers, comments, retweets, shares) with the CSI Library on Twitter than on Facebook, following the Web Librarian's efforts to build community on Twitter. Most of the shares of, likes of, or comments on library Facebook posts in 2017 were by faculty members or student library employees. The Library's Google+ page had no engagement with its followers, leading to a decision in Fall 2017 close the Google+ SM account and to focus more of the library's SM efforts on Twitter.

We have also observed that students learn about the library through other competing communication channels including the University's event calendar, the library website, and printed promotions. Students may feel they are adequately informed by just one of these channels, and may not peruse or visit library SM accounts except to fulfill particular tasks. They may feel that SM is more for leisure than for academics. The library may need to do more to promote these accounts to students through official college communication channels. It may also be worth providing incentives for viewing the library's SM accounts. First-year students are required to obtain a College Life Unit Experience 'CLUE' credit, and may seek Library CLUE credit workshops on the CLUE calendar, not on the library website or SM accounts. Currently there may be few other incentives for students to use the library's SM tools. At present, most of the library's Facebook and Twitter followers are faculty and community members, not students.

Young and Rossmann (2015) suggest thinking in terms of using SM tools for community-building rather than marketing, arguing that an increased sense of community leads to student success. They managed to increase the percentage of their SM followers who were students, and the interaction rate (comments, favorites, likes, retweets). They placed importance on 'personality' and 'intentionality' (strategy) in tweeting, and on interaction with students. Their greatest successes were in posting information in the categories 'local community' and 'student life.' By switching our emphasis from marketing to students to engaging them with content and "personality" that appeal to them, we can hope to increase our percentage of student followers and increase our interaction rate.

Wan (2011) looked at Association of Research Libraries (ARL) member libraries' Facebook pages and analyzed how they communicated with users. 'Success' was measured by the number of followers or 'fans' these pages had. He assigned 'content categories' to posts; most of these are related to promotion/marketing. The four most successful of the 159 'active' ARL library Facebook pages posted more about 'events' than the others, suggesting one means of obtaining more followers. Wan (2011) also suggests "posting more topics of interest to users" (p. 318).

Hagman and Carleton's (2014) SM strategy includes collaborating with student library employees, who are more familiar with campus event and pop culture trends than library staff. A SM guidelines document ensures that student library employees communicate in a professional manner.

1.12 CONCLUSION

In our study, we examined the SM preferences among students at two academic libraries; one in Canada and one in the United States. To our knowledge, this type of study has never before been conducted. Importantly, we asked students what SM tools they would use to follow the library, and what kinds of information they wanted from the library via SM.

We determined what SM tools they use, what SM tools they would use to follow the library, and the type of information they did and did not want from the library on SM. We compared responses across institutions, genders, and years of study. Our data revealed much about gender and year of study at the university or college, thus our SM postings need to be curated appropriately. It is essential to understand one's target audience before investing time and resources in using SM tools.

Dan Sich wishes to thank his colleagues at Western Libraries for their assistance in running the questionnaire.

REFERENCES

Brookbank, E. (2015). So much social media, so little time: Using student feedback to guide academic library social media strategy. *Journal of Electronic Resources Librarianship, 27*(4), 232–247. Available from https://doi.org/dx.doi.org/10.1080/1941126X.2015.1092344.

Gerolimos, M. (2011). Academic libraries on Facebook: An analysis of users' comments. *D-Lib Magazine, 17*(11/12). Available from https://doi.org/10.1045/november2011-gerolimos.

Hagman, J., & Carleton, J. (2014). Better together: Collaborating with students on library social media. *Public Services Quarterly, 10*(3), 238–244. Available from https://doi.org/10.1080/15228959.2014.931207.

Office of Institutional Planning & Budgeting—Western University. (n.d.). *Western facts.* (2017) <https://www.ipb.uwo.ca/facts.php> Accessed 26.09.17.

Wan, G. (2011). How academic libraries reach users on Facebook. *College & Undergraduate Libraries, 18*(4), 307–318. Available from https://doi.org/10.1080/10691316.2011.624944.

Young, S. W. H., & Rossmann, D. (2015). Building library community through social media. *Information Technology and Libraries, 34*(1), 20–37.

CHAPTER 2

Social Media Committees: Sharing the Library's Voice

Alejandra Nann[1] and Nina Verishagen[2]
[1]Copley Library at the University of San Diego, San Diego, CA, United States
[2]Saskatchewan Polytechnic Library, Saskatchewan Polytechnic, Saskatoon, SK, Canada

2.1 INTRODUCTION

Social media has great potential in the academic library environment to boost connections with the academic community and connect with students who may never have walked through the door. With increased demand for access to and awareness of digital resources, social media promotion just makes sense. Although a social media presence is "free" in monetary terms (excluding post-boosts and other directed advertising), time and energy are required to effectively manage social media in an academic environment. Libraries must consider their audience, evaluate and select platforms, and develop the library's voice. A social media committee (SMC) can accomplish all of this.

This chapter provides two examples of academic library SMCs. The first is at Copley Library at the University of San Diego, which serves 8900 students at the undergraduate and graduate levels. The second is at Saskatchewan Polytechnic, which serves more than 27,000 students across four geographically distinct campuses and five library sites. This chapter presents what it took to develop, operate, and sustain these teams. We provide tips to effectively administer SMCs while emphasizing the committee's importance in harnessing and sharing the library's voice.

2.2 UNIVERSITY OF SAN DIEGO'S COPLEY LIBRARY SOCIAL MEDIA COMMITTEE

2.2.1 Background

At the University of San Diego (USD), Copley Library was one of the first university entities to establish a social media presence. In 2006, we launched a pilot project to verify whether investing energy in social

Social Media
DOI: https://doi.org/10.1016/B978-0-08-102409-6.00002-X

media would be worthwhile. An unofficial Facebook group was created to test interest and shortly after, a more official Facebook group was developed. The page's focus was to promote library events and services and to actively engage with those community members who had joined the group. In the early days of Facebook, once a group hit a certain number of members, they were invited to switch over to a Fan Page (what is now a business page). When our Facebook group was invited to become a Fan Page, it was an obvious move in the right direction.

The immediate success on Facebook opened our eyes to the potential of social media. We quickly understood we had not embarked upon a trend, but rather the beginning of an interactive 2.0 revolution. Additionally, our library did not (and still does not) have a dedicated social media librarian, so we needed a way to continue to evolve. In 2012, the Dean of the Library, who was receptive to the growing role of social media in academia, granted us permission to officially create a Social Media Committee (SMC). The committee's purpose has remained steadfast since its inception, that is, to promote library services and events, and ensure a positive presence on the Internet through a variety of ever-evolving social media tools.

2.2.2 The Committee

The librarian who spearheaded the original Facebook pages was the SMC's original chair and held the position from 2012 to 2018. I was an original member and took the role of chair in early 2018. In our earliest days, we understood that in order for the SMC to represent the library accurately, it must be a collaborative effort with members from each library department. We currently have five members from the Collections, Access, and Discovery Department; one from Archives, Special Collections, and Digital Initiatives; and two from Reference. We have always found eight members to be a manageable number because it is big enough to invite a variety of perspectives, yet small enough to work efficiently. We try to recruit staff and faculty who are knowledgeable and interested in social media management, and we recommend that each member of the team has a personal smartphone and be willing to use it for committee work. Although some social media tools can be managed via desktop applications, others cannot (e.g., Instagram). In addition to providing members the opportunity to learn about and develop their social media skills, membership has the added benefit of developing connections with staff members from other library departments.

As chair, I work with each member at the beginning of their term to assess their comfort level with each platform, establish their individual interests, and manage the workflow. For example, some members only post on Instagram and Facebook; others write blog posts and tweet. Members on any library committee serve two years and may renew for another two-year term. Oftentimes, members choose to stay on the committee beyond the two years, while others rotate with colleagues in the same department. This turnover provides fresh perspective.

2.2.3 Engaged Flexibility

Remaining flexible is crucial in social media management. Although the committee's membership numbers have remained constant, the composition has shifted at times due to retirements, sabbaticals, job reassignments, or members wishing to work on something else because they can no longer keep to the schedule. In addition, there are members who enjoy posting only on certain platforms over others. The majority of the SMC is scheduled to post on all four platforms, but two specific members focus their posting on two or three platforms. One member in particular loves posting on Facebook, Twitter, and Instagram, but does not enjoy writing blog posts. This member does not write blog posts, but in return, he posts more on Facebook. This type of flexibility works and ensures that posting is equitably distributed every semester.

2.2.4 Monthly Meetings

Since its inception, the SMC has met monthly. In the early days, the discussions mainly surrounded our success at connecting with the community and assessments of progress. Once the committee developed better processes, we switched from meeting monthly to meeting in-person nine months out of the year. We do not meet in March, July, or October since students are on break, and post assignments have already been assigned at an earlier meeting. Once the foundational work is complete, meetings held during the semester are used to discuss platform updates, contests or event participation, scheduling changes, and unfinished business.

2.2.5 Setting the Schedule

At the first meeting of each semester, we discuss the successes and challenges from the past academic year, possible themes, ideas for posts for the upcoming year, and the current state of our platforms. We also set a posting schedule for a minimum of four months to accommodate each member's busy schedule. Members come into this meeting with an idea of when they can and cannot post due to scheduling conflicts (conferences, vacation, busy time of year, etc.). However, there is an understanding that whomever becomes aware of a situation that requires immediate communication, such as a power outage or a minor flood (both of which have happened in the past), posts to Twitter or asks another member to post. Once the SMC is aware of such an event, the chair assigns individuals to provide updates until the situation resolves.

2.2.6 Kick-Off Meeting Topics

2.2.6.1 Platform Selection

From the start, the committee has sought to integrate the social media platforms that best suit our library. We therefore created subcommittees to investigate different platforms. The two to three member teams examined the following for each platform:

1. How were other libraries using the platform?
2. Which features would benefit our library?
3. Are the benefits of the platform equal to the effort required to administer it?

Following this evaluation, our social media presence extended beyond Facebook to include Twitter, Pinterest, Flickr, Instagram, and a WordPress Blog. Overtime our assessment techniques have become more user-oriented. Our presence on Facebook, Twitter, and WordPress were well received based on anecdotal feedback and increased number of likes and followers, but our efforts on Pinterest were not. We learned that we could have a more meaningful visual presence on Instagram and Flickr, which is used primarily as an image archive.

2.2.6.2 Using Our Budget

The SMC has a modest budget of $100 per semester. So far, we have used it to boost Unicorn Posts and purchase contest prizes.

Unicorn Posts

In the past six years, we have had our share of unicorn posts. Unicorn posts are those that unexpectedly go viral. Also known as marketing unicorns, these posts are so popular and infrequent, "they end up delivering almost half of the value of your overall marketing efforts" (Kim, 2017). On August 21, 2017, an SMC member posted a picture of two staff members viewing the solar eclipse. It reached 1184 people, which surpassed most posts during the academic year. At the June 2017 committee meeting, it was unanimously voted to use part of the SMC budget to boost these types of posts in order to engage more users. According to Kim (2017), finding ways to replicate unicorn posts benefits a social media presence. The committee has tried to replicate this first success by creating and boosting picture and video posts of students at events. It can go either way, really. Students are either really excited to be included in one of our posts, or they get embarrassed by it. During Banned Books Week in September 2017, a post that included a theater class doing a performance in front of the library had 530 views. It may not have been as high as our last unicorn post, but it was above our average reach. So in our opinion, it was effort and money well spent.

Contests

Contests are a great way to engage with the collegial community and build follow-ship. Therefore, we try to host one each semester. The budget goes toward contest prizes—incentives to increase the response rate—and we usually purchase university paraphernalia from the bookstore such as water bottles, coffee mugs, and school supplies. Creating contests is a committee effort. Each member is asked to research contest ideas from various organizations with a social media presence. During meetings, we discuss contest ideas that have the potential to engage our users, but which require little effort (from the user perspective). Contest ideas that seem to be the most successful include library-related riddles or little games, for example, we once asked our followers to use three words to describe their library experience. The member in charge of the contest is required to pin the post on Facebook and promote it on our various platforms.

2.2.7 Creating Efficient Workflows

2.2.7.1 Content Pillars

As mentioned earlier, posting responsibility was originally assigned by the Chair based on member's interests, and the work was mainly autonomous. After a time, members began to feel overwhelmed with this system of self-management. We therefore established a posting schedule to provide clear assignments and a rotation of post responsibilities for different platforms. Creation of content was still left to the individual poster. As this work evolved, we realized that content creation was an issue for many members who feel reluctant to post their ideas for fear that they might be repetitive, boring, unengaging, or all of the above. To add to this, we often discussed the issue of how to post during less active times at the library. What do you post when there is nothing to post about?

Around the same time we learned the University Communications department was using our WordPress blog to stay up-to-date on library news and events. This brought forth another realization—that having specific standards for all our social media was becoming essential and that content creation could no longer remain autonomous. If our content was going to be reused, we needed to ensure quality. We had to find a way to establish a uniform voice and tone, yet retain the unique qualities and perspectives of our various SMC members.

The committee chair began attending Institutional Marketing Meetings to learn how marketing can make an impact in the success of an organization and the future of the university. At a June 2016 meeting, USD's School of Business presented their social media strategy and discussed the importance of Content Pillars; this was the solution we were looking for! We adapted The School of Business presentation to identify the core topic of our platforms and create specific content pillars (see Table 2.1).

2.2.8 So How Do Content Pillars Work?

According to *The Ultimate Guide to Pillar Content for your Website*, a content pillar is described as "a long, exhaustive article or web page focused on one specific topic or theme that you can turn into many smaller pieces of content to fuel all those channels you may be struggling to fill (Whittemore, 2017)." Pillars are developed in advance and provide a roadmap from which committee members develop posts based on such themes as time (week, month, semester), subject (news, promotions, library resources), and platform. Since we do not use a third-party scheduling system, our content pillar documentation has become a critical piece in our workflow. We have developed a pillar for each platform and our posting schedule reflects this.

Table 2.1 Copley Library's social media platform purpose, content, and audience

Platform	Purpose	Content	Audience
Facebook	Promote library events, contests, and resources	Fun and engaging	Current students, faculty, staff, alumni, parents
Twitter	Send alerts, news, and announcements	Immediate news and relevant news in Academic Librarianship	Current users of the physical space, current affiliates, surrounding community, academic librarians
Instagram	Keep followers up-to-date on what is happening inside and outside of the library	Library events, behind-the-scenes images (e.g., book donation processing)	Current students, faculty, other departments on campus
WordPress Blog	Update library patrons	Past events, current news, and updates on the upcoming year	University community, alumni, university publications

Facebook posts are on Mondays, Wednesday, and Fridays of every week. Mondays are dedicated to promotional material including workshop reminders, library contests, and other library and relevant campus events. Wednesdays are dedicated to highlight an important library resource or service or offer research tips. Friday posts are more light-hearted and can range from fun facts or a reminder about the following week.

Tweets are sent out Tuesdays and Thursdays every week. As mentioned previously, Twitter remains the spot to post alerts and announcements of last-minute issues occurring at the library or on campus. Other content pillars include academic and library topics that are trending, recent news from the library, and retweets from academic and credible Twitter accounts such as Library of Congress, American Library Association, and the Scholarly Kitchen. To simplify tweeting for our members, two retweets are equal to one original tweet.

Similar to Twitter, the SMC posts on Instagram on Tuesdays and Thursdays every week. Content pillars for Tuesday usually pertain to "Daily life at Copley" that can include workshops, events, or programs happening at the library or a process happening behind the scenes. Hashtags such as #dailylifeatcopleylibrary and #uofsandiego are always used on Tuesdays. Thursday's content pillars include "Throwback Thursday" posts. We request images from Special Collections that include photographs of students or events at Copley Library. Hashtags including #tbt #toreropride are required as they are popular hashtags among the student demographic and USD alumni.

2.2.9 Future Considerations

The SMC has taken great strides to improve Copley Library's presence on our platforms, but social media is not a static entity. Each platform requires constant attention to changes in features and functionality. Consequently, our future plans involve an investigation of features that have been released in the last year, for example, Instagram and Facebook Stories.

We plan to continue attending university-wide marketing team meetings to learn how other departments on campus are managing their social media platforms. Attending these meetings will help our committee get a better grasp of where the university is heading and how we can help expand the vision. We understand that our work is ever evolving and that our purpose may change overtime and we are excited to see what the future has in store.

2.3 SASKATCHEWAN POLYTECHNIC LIBRARY'S SOCIAL MEDIA COMMITTEE

2.3.1 Background

In 2014, as the newly minted Marketing Librarian, I was given control of the library's social media platforms: Facebook and Twitter. When I discovered more than 10 library employees had administrator rights on our Facebook page, I thought, *this cannot be good.* However, it was not until a staff member responded to a patron's Facebook comment with a sassy remark that I started pulling permissions and changing passwords. I became power hungry and controlling. And after a short time, I started to get lonely.

I spent a lot of time figuring out how to gain followers, creating posts, and asking the entire library staff (via emails) to just *give me something* to post. And all the time I wondered: Who will manage the platforms when I am away? How do I find out what's going on at the other campuses, which are located in different cities, and with whom I rarely have face-to-face contact? And then I had an 'aha!' moment. I realized our library's social media voice couldn't be just my voice, it had to be made up of the library's most valuable resource—its people. So I began efforts to develop a Social Media Commitee composed of interested employees with a desire to administer social media platforms, as well as work together to create workflows and documentation. Permissions would be granted, and social media work would become more efficient and effective.

2.3.2 The Committee

Staff members interested in learning more about social media responded to the original call for members. Their interest and enthusiasm created a sense of excitement in the small group. However, our library system covers an entire province and it was therefore critical to have representation from each campus. To achieve geographic representation, supervisors "voluntold" some members to join the committee. Although not an ideal approach to recruitment, this was an opportunity to define roles that ensured everyone—including those skeptical of social media—would participate. In response, the Campus Representative role was created to provide representation from each location, but the representative is not required to perform administrative duties. Since its inception, the SMC has had four distinct roles:

Committee Chair

- Chairs social media meetings;
- Main administrator to social media platforms;
- Reviews posts on Hootsuite;
- Posting responsibilities as required.

Administrators

- Has administrative access to social media platforms;
- Has posting responsibilities, as assigned.

Resource Person(s)

- Has administrative access to social media platforms;
- Selects resources to be featured in posts;
- Provides a monthly list of library resources (to post) to Administrators;
- Posting responsibilities as assigned.

Campus Contact

- Provides insight about activities at their campus, does not have to attend meetings but is invited. If unable to attend monthly meetings, Campus Contacts have informal meetings with the committee chair as needed.

The Committee is currently made up of six members. All positions are filled, and there is at least one representative from each campus.

2.3.2.1 Purpose

Our first task as a Committee was to develop a Terms of Reference that included the committee's Purpose, as well as information and guidelines related to Membership and Roles, Meetings, and Workflow (see Appendix B for key excerpts from the Committee's terms of reference).

Our original purpose was (and remains) to use our social media presence to engage with the academic community at all four campuses. The SMC serves as a forum to consider best practices for online communication, to brainstorm new ideas and to create social media content. The committee also aligns its work to the library's Social Media Goals (see Appendix A) to ensure all committee activities fulfill our mandate of making connections with library patrons (staff, faculty and students).

2.3.2.2 The Library Voice

We also worked to develop a Social Media Guidelines document, which defines the library's "voice". To quote from that guideline:

> *The library voice is your voice! Be professional, but also be authentic "the unique way we think and how we say things helps us come across as authentic, which makes us seem "more human" online" (King, 2012, p. 6). Don't turn your online interactions into Institutional speak, leave in the quirks and personality.*

These guidelines also cover: The Anatomy of a Good Post, and Tips for Creating Posts (see Appendix C). This is a reference document that is also used in the training of new members. It is evaluated each year and updated when required.

2.3.3 Creating Efficient Workflows

The committee meets monthly for 45 minutes during the year (September–June) and once during the summer (July–August) via Skype for Business. The standing agenda includes four items:

1. Successes and loose ends from the previous month;
2. Post ideas for the following month;

3. Post Assignments;
4. Additional Miscellaneous Items, which can include discussion about updates to each platform and changes to our account management software (Hootsuite).

The committee's workflow allows for one month of preparation. So, for example, when we meet in early January, posts for that month have already been planned and scheduled so we focus on content and assign responsibilities for February.

2.3.4 Scheduling Posts

Saskatchewan Polytechnic Library subscribes to Hootsuite to manage our social media posts. Although we currently use only three social media platforms (Facebook, Twitter, and Instagram), we decided to invest in this tool to schedule and release posts during busy times of the year; to schedule and release posts during off times: evenings, weekends, and holidays; to easily view and curate other social accounts, such as our institution's account; and to access analytic information.

Using this software is similar to using social media platforms because they all require training and a commitment to remain up-to-date with constantly changing features and functionality. For example, about a month before writing this chapter, Hootsuite began to enable users to push posts straight to Instagram instead of requiring approval before posts went public.

2.3.5 Training

As stated previously, there has been an occasional and ongoing need to engage in training for technological updates. There is also, at times, a need to train new committee members. In these cases I assign a current member to train the new member on our regularly used tools: Facebook, Twitter, Instagram, Hootsuite, and Canva.com.

We use Canva.com to create visual posts. It is an easy-to-use program and the free version includes thousands of templates. All team members feel comfortable using it, and in many cases the tool has extended into other aspects of their work, for example, print poster design.

2.3.6 Data Collection

At the end of each academic year, each Librarian Service Coordinator must provide their manager with a detailed report of that service area, including metrics.

As the Marketing Librarian, I am tasked with preparing a Marketing Report which includes social media metrics. Every month I pull the monthly social media statistics for each platform. Our Hootsuite subscriptions allows us to download a Profile for Twitter and Facebook (see Fig. 2.1).

I also pull more detailed data directly from Facebook and Instagram to identify which posts had the most impact. Here's how:

- Facebook—from your profile page click on Insights > Export Data > Select a date range and Export Data.
- Twitter—from your profile page click View Your Top Tweets > Last 28 Days (option here to change the date range) then click Export Data.

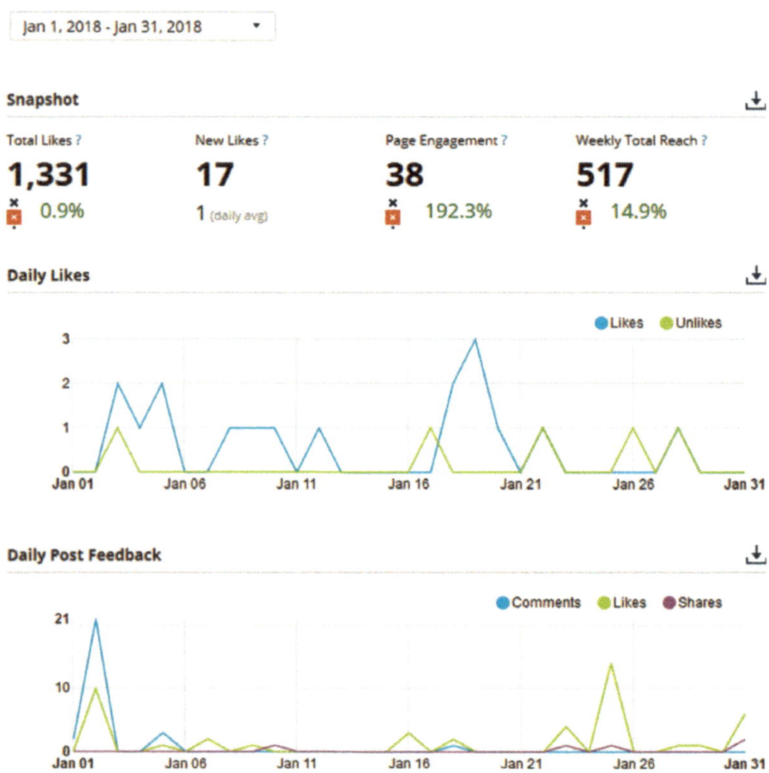

Figure 2.1 Saskatchewan Polytechnic Library Facebook page overview Hootsuite analytics.

Instagram Analytics are not as sophisticated. For these, I use the Analytics tool to view the information, take a screenshot for the past 7 days, and save the screenshots in a folder.

2.3.7 Relationship With the Organization or Buy-In

We have always maintained a close relationship with our institution's Communications and Marketing Department and as a standard operating procedure I liaise with this department for all library promotional activities. As part of this relationship, they design our profile pictures and cover photos—usually professional stock photos of current students designed to align with the library's overall visual identity. This has been an excellent relationship. When we request a new profile picture, they provide it. When we ask them for a repost or retweet (to their 33,000 Facebook for 8000 Twitter followers), they do it. When they ask us to hold back from something, for instance, they did not want us to develop a Snapchat account until they had a chance to consider an institution-wide approach, we respect their requests.

2.3.8 Future Considerations

Social media platforms and practices change year by year—even day by day. To keep up with changes, ensure we are using appropriate platforms, and evaluate our work, we hold a Social Media Refresh meeting each spring. Past meetings have revolved around major plans for the upcoming year. For instance, in spring of 2016 we laid the foundations for our successful monthly Facebook Contest (see Chapter 8).

In the Spring of 2018 our meeting will largely revolve around the separation of post content on Twitter (where our identifiable follow-ship is mostly faculty and staff) and Facebook (mostly students). We will need to plan different types of posts for the different segments of our populations and adjust our workflow accordingly. This meeting will also provide the opportunity to discuss the potential impact of the Facebook privacy scandal. These changes, however, are simply the latest examples of the social media challenges and opportunities we face each academic year.

2.4 TIPS FOR ANY SOCIAL MEDIA COMMITTEE

2.4.1 Harness and Share Your Library's Voice

- Remember that although the committee's functions include many technical and workflow aspects, ultimately, its main reason for existence is to develop and share your library's voice.
- Ensure membership is representative of your library's workforce.

2.4.2 Not All Platforms Are Worth Your Time

- Assess your followers and engagement through analytics at regular intervals and gather feedback from your community (see Chapter 1).
- Continually explore and evaluate your social media options.

2.4.3 Remain Up-to-Date on Specific Platforms

- Keep track of new features and functionality.
- Discuss changes with your SMC and make plans to deal with changes.
- Ensure someone on the committee keeps abreast of social media trends by reading news stories, blog posts, and news releases.

2.4.4 Use Analytics

- Analytics provide invaluable information about your followers such as when they are viewing or engaging with your posts. Use this information to inform your plans and schedules.

2.4.5 Meet Regularly

- Schedule regular meetings with your committee members to keep up-to-date with different departments, or different library locations. Regular meetings also ensure forum for discussion and brainstorming. Even when you don't think they are necessary, you might be surprised by the ideas that emerge!
- A standard meeting agenda is a good way to sustain the committee.

2.4.6 Maintain Flexibility

- In a large institution with a collaborative culture, it is crucial to be mindful that every member has a full-time job aside from their committee responsibilities, and therefore the chair must be flexible with work assignments. Assigned tasks may also take longer than estimated if regular duties have to take precedence over committee work.

- It is also important that members feel comfortable telling the chair when they are unable to fulfill their duties at certain busy times of the year. Include an agenda item to discuss successes and loose ends from the past month as a jumping off point for problems members may be experiencing.

2.5 FINAL WORDS

As is the case with most trends in the library, social media platforms and users are constantly evolving. In order to maintain a successful social media presence, libraries must have a set of dedicated staff who can remain current and respond to changes promptly. Our respective libraries are staffed by a diverse group of individuals. They are our most valuable resource for social media management. Their collective perspective creates the library voice we share on social media.

REFERENCES

Kim, L. (2017, January 4). *The 10 best online marketing strategies to make you a unicorn [blog post]*. Available from https://medium.com/marketing-and-entrepreneurship/the-10-best-online-marketing-strategies-to-make-you-a-unicorn-5c2fff3c99ae

King, D. L. (2012). *face2face: Using Facebook, Twitter and other social media tools to create great customer connections*. Medford, NJ: CyberAge Books.

Whittemore, C. (2017, September 19). *The ultimate guide to pillar content for your website [blog post]*. Available from https://www.simplemarketingnow.com/content-talks-business-blog/pillar-content

APPENDIX A: SASKATCHEWAN POLYTECHNIC LIBRARY SOCIAL MEDIA PLAN 2015–20

Social Media Goals

In Alignment with the Library Services Vision of:

- Building an intuitive digital presence and;
- Creating a Dynamic Community Environment

Saskatchewan Polytechnic's social media platforms will fulfill the following goals.

Make Connections with Library Patrons (Staff, Faculty, Students)

- To inform and streamline (some posts appear in multiple places).
- To learn about our users based on their platforms, preferences, participation and posts.
- Ultimately we would like to engage our users in this way, in order of importance a-c:
  - **a.** Students actively throughout their academic careers - anywhere from 10 weeks to 4 years (most users are on Facebook, also many on Instagram).
  - **b.** Faculty throughout their entire career (Facebook and Twitter).
  - **c.** Staff throughout their entire career (Facebook and Twitter).

  Measurement: Engagement on platforms (likes, shares, comments).

Facilitate Interactions with Library Patrons (Staff, Faculty, Students)

- Meet patrons where they are.
- Ask questions and start conversations.

Measurement: engagement on platforms (likes, shares, comments).

Actively Promote Resources

- Targeted (Academic calendar, specific program needs) posts.
- Promotion of all types of resources.

Measurement: interest via bitly clicks.

Promote Library Events and Programming

- Invitations and participation in events (live tweeting, mentions of performers, patron participation, and photographs).

Measurement: mini survey at event (how did you hear about this event?), engagement on platforms (likes, shares, comments).

APPENDIX B: SASKATCHEWAN POLYTECHNIC LIBRARY SOCIAL MEDIA COMMITTEE TERMS OF REFERENCE—KEY EXCERPTS

Purpose

The purpose of the Social Media Committee is to engage the Saskatchewan Polytechnic Community at all four campuses, through our social media channels. It is a forum to consider best practices for communication from the library to the community, to brainstorm new ideas, and create social media content.

Membership and Roles

All members will participate in round-table discussions, the creation of social media content and the development of important documents. Each member is considered a contact for their respective campus, meaning, they will keep the committee informed of scheduled events, "library moments," and the general going's-on at their location. Additionally, each member will be assigned one of the following distinctive roles:

- Chair
- Administrator
- Resource Person
- Campus Contact

Workflow

On the first week of each month, committee will have a quick meeting to discuss postings for the next month. For instance, January 1st meeting will discuss February posts. After the meeting, duties will happen as follows:

Resource Persons(s) will find and send content (as agreed upon in the monthly meeting) to *Administrators* **by the end of the 3rd week of each month.**
Administrators will develop and add posts to Hootesuite **by the end of the 4th week of each month.**

The *Committee Chair* will review Hootesuite **on the first week of the following month**, and pull and save statistics from the previous month. Each person on the committee is expected to either post or notify an administrator of a needed post on an ad hoc basis (when something unexpected comes up).

APPENDIX C: SOCIAL MEDIA COMMITTEE GUIDELINES DOCUMENT

The Library "Voice"

The library voice is your voice! Be professional, but also be authentic "the unique way we think and how we say things helps us come across as authentic, which makes us seem "more human" online" (King, 2012, p. 6). Don't turn your online interactions into institutional speak, include your quirks and personality.

Avoid library jargon – for example use ***library website*** instead of ***library catalogue***

The Anatomy of a Good Post

Every post must be connected to either a library service, event or resource.

Facebook:

- An image or video,
- text (no more than required to communicate the message),
- a shortened link,
- mention@Saskatchewan Polytechnic when appropriate.

*Note this post would have been stronger had it included a mention of Saskatchewan Polytechnic's Facebook page.

Twitter:

A good post will include

- Hashtags (no more than 3, no less than 1),
- text,
- an image,
- a shortened link,
- a mention or popular hashtag.

Tips for Creating Posts

If you are having a difficult time developing posts outside of scheduled events and the committee's discussion, here are some tips.

How to get started with a post:

- Scan digital resources
  - Go into digital resources and check out the features, you might find something that you didn't know about.
- Stuff happening around campus
  - Check the Sask Polytech social feeds.
  - What are they posting? Can we connect to it?
- Scan through paper resources
- Go out into the stacks and find a book that might make an interesting post. Scan through online images

   - Search for words of interest in *ImageQuest* – in May 2016 I wanted to create a post about Spring, when I conducted a search in ImageQuest I came across pictures of lakes, so I decided to look up the Great Lakes, which made me wonder if we had a book about Great Lakes. It led to a post linking to this book: *Great Lakes Water Waters* - http://bit.ly/1N9aj0d
- Ask your colleagues what's going on in their work area. Perhaps you can develop a post about Interlibrary Loans, for example.
- Check out what other libraries are posting.

CHAPTER 3

The Right Social Media Platform for Your Library

Morgan Swan
Rauner Special Collections Library, Dartmouth College, Hanover, NH, United States

Deciding to create a social media account for your library can be intimidating. For one, there are so many options out there. How do you know if you have chosen the right one, or if you have unwittingly chained yourself to an aging platform that your audience is in the midst of abandoning?

Also, creating an account brings with it a certain level of professional obligation and engagement: if you initiate a social media presence for your institution, you'd better populate it with content for the long haul. The road to social media success is littered with the burned-out shells of over-zealous curators of digital content who ran out of gas mere months into the life of their account.

However, despite all of the cautionary tales, being engaged with your students, faculty, and staff via social media (as well as with the world outside the university) is an important way to promote your collections, provide essential services, and connect in a meaningful way with the academic community. Mon (2015) underscores the value of libraries being on social media in her book *Social Media and Library Services*:

> *Improving outreach and connecting with new audiences has been a major reason for libraries launching social sites. In July 2012, Nielsen (2012) reported that there were 171.8 million United States users of social media sites. By 2013, Pew Internet estimated that 73% of all online adults in the United States were social media users (Duggan and Smith, 2013), while Nielsen (2014) found that 64% of users visited social media sites at least once each day. In 2012, Pew Internet (2014b) found that 81% of teens were using social media. (p. 25)*

The question, then, is how to employ social media as an asset to your institution without it becoming a liability. This chapter seeks to help you answer that question by providing advice about how to evaluate the wide array of social media platforms available to you and how to select one that is best suited for your needs, both in terms of desired outcomes and practicality.

Social Media
DOI: https://doi.org/10.1016/B978-0-08-102409-6.00003-1

The following advice is meant to scale with regard to size and type of institution as well as the mission of the library. Although this advice is nested within the context of a special collections library at a small liberal arts college, I believe that the larger lessons that can be gleaned from our experience are applicable regardless of institution.

3.1 CONSIDER YOUR INSTITUTIONAL CONTEXT

Although it may seem obvious, it is important that you think carefully about your library's place within the larger institution. Understanding the mission of your institution and being clear about the library's role in that mission can help serve as a criterion to refine your social media options.

For example, I am employed by Dartmouth College, a four-year private liberal arts college located in Hanover, New Hampshire. With just over 4000 undergraduates and about 2000 graduate students (mostly in the sciences and professional schools), Dartmouth is the smallest member of the Ivy League in terms of student population and sees undergraduate education as its primary mission.

The college is in a fairly remote area, which means that maintaining strong communication and fostering goodwill with alumni is often a challenge. The college's Office of Communications employs an assistant director for digital engagement whose primary duty is to create content for the numerous institutional social media accounts, including Twitter, Facebook, and Instagram. Also, Dartmouth College Library, the parent institution to my library, has an outreach program with a staff member assigned to manage the Library's various social media accounts, which include a WordPress blog, a Flickr page, and accounts on Twitter, Facebook, YouTube, and Instagram.

Rauner Special Collections Library, where I work, is one of nine small libraries that operate under the larger auspices of the Dartmouth College Library (DCL). Our core mission mirrors that of the college and the DCL, which is to provide immersive and transformative learning experiences by engaging in all aspects of the educational continuum, thereby preparing students for a lifetime of learning and responsible leadership as informed global citizens. Moreover, the Library proactively supports undergraduate, graduate, and professional student academic success through innovative educational programs. Rauner is a significant contributor to those strategic objectives.

It is important to know exactly where your own library or department falls in the overall institutional hierarchy and to understand the lay of the land for a number of reasons.

First, you do not want to duplicate efforts or step on somebody's toes. We determined early on that a focused social media presence would make more sense. We did not want to duplicate the multiplatform social media efforts of the larger Library. Ultimately, we did select a social media option where the DCL had previously established an account. However, we felt comfortable moving forward because we had already discussed the possibility of opening an account with the DCL's Education and Outreach Librarian, and because we first determined that our goals would not be in competition with those of the larger library. Moreover, we agreed to supply the library's social media manager with original content for their Facebook page, which would help them by providing library-related content and help us by using their account to promote our collections.

Second, you can identify potential roadblocks or possible allies well before you take the plunge and commit to a specific platform. In our case, we identified a potential ally, the social media manager at Dartmouth's Office of Communications. We were lucky enough to form a partnership. The social media manager was able to share her expertise as far as institutional social media regulations and advice for managing a fledgling account. We were able to make her job easier by creating original, and most importantly, re-usable social media content.

Third, understanding your institutional context can provide clarity about who your intended audience should be for your social media outreach efforts. Knowing who your audience is will help you determine which social media platform makes the most sense for your institution. For example, if you are a small liberal arts college whose primary mission is undergraduate education (like Dartmouth College), then it does not make sense for you to select a platform whose users are not undergraduates. Conversely, if you are a large research institution whose mission is reaching a global scholarly community, you should consider platforms that have the ability to impact a wide variety of demographics.

3.2 IDENTIFY YOUR INTENDED OUTCOMES OR GOALS

With all of the social media platforms that appear in a flash and then disappear almost as quickly, it can be nerve-wracking to know whether or not you are constantly missing the boat. There can be a temptation to create as many accounts as there are platforms or, when faced with analysis paralysis, to decide to reject social media participation altogether. While both of these responses are completely understandable, I personally believe that they are too reactionary. You compromise your ability to promote your collections and your library when you either try to be all things to all people on social media or, conversely, you decide to flee the realm of social media entirely.

Instead, objectively considering what you hope to gain from social media can be a very freeing exercise that helpfully reduces your options and refines your social media strategy before you even choose a specific platform. Once again, this is where understanding your library's institutional context can help you. Also, it does not hurt to be clear about your own departmental mission; the better you understand your own purpose, the more precise you can be about your intended social media outcomes.

As I mentioned earlier, Rauner Library's primary mission is undergraduate education. Over the last 12 years, the number of classes held at Rauner using primary sources has grown exponentially with an increased awareness of our services. Still, although Rauner has experienced a high level of success with classroom engagement, we would like to see more students use our materials for their own independent research. We typically have a few undergraduates each year who conduct research in our reading room, but we believe that it should be possible to inspire more students to utilize our resources for their projects.

One of the reasons we feel that students are not visiting us more often is because special collections libraries and archives have a reputation for being standoffish and intimidating. From past conversations I have had with students, I have noticed two underlying trends. One, students seem surprised at the ease of accessing "something cool." Two, our enthusiasm to share these materials with our students is not being readily conveyed outside of the classroom. Clearly, although special collections librarians might have been excelling in a classroom environment, we were not doing as well as we liked with student researchers who were seeking to use our collections for their individual assignments and projects.

With this in mind, we decided that we wanted to create a social media brand for the library that was fun, enthusiastic, and friendly. We also wanted to provide greater awareness of our collections in the hopes that exposure to underutilized collections would spark some interest and curiosity in students. Keep in mind, of course, that your goals for your library's social media presence may be very different depending upon your institutional context and your departmental priorities. Your intended outcomes may also be strongly influenced by the social media presence that you already have in place (and the baggage that comes with that preexisting brand, for better or for worse).

3.3 TAKE STOCK OF YOUR CURRENT SOCIAL MEDIA COMMITMENT

If your library or department does not have a social media footprint online as of yet, don't despair. In fact, this may be a positive starting point for you. It means that you haven't already created an expectation among your audience about what your brand should be. If, however, you are like most institutions, you probably have some sort of social media account connected with your library, be it Twitter, Facebook, WordPress, or perhaps even Myspace. Again, do not despair; however, you will need to take stock of what those platforms are and if they are helping your social media goals. If your current accounts are not working for you, then you will need to re-tool those accounts to bring them in line with your goals or eliminate them. If you feel that your current accounts are functioning well in the service of your institution, then the next logical step is to decide whether you really need another account or if enhancing or adapting your current presence will suffice. With social media, it is difficult to put the toothpaste back in the tube. In other words, it is relatively easy to delete a social media account if it does not work out, but it is harder to recoup the investment of time and resources. This does not mean you should not take risks; you just want to make sure that creating more accounts is the right answer.

At Rauner, we have a blog that posts twice a week and enjoys monthly visits and interactions from scholars all over the world. When we began the blog back in 2007, we wanted to harness the enthusiasm that we and others felt about our collections and share that excitement with the world. Our goal for the blog was to share discoveries of cool archival materials in an informal but intellectually responsible manner. Over the last 10 years, we have experienced a high level of success with our twice-a-week publication schedule and have leveraged our nearly 800 blog posts into a discovery tool for undergraduates. The blog also functions as an alternative library catalog that keeps track of useful teaching information. We decided to use Blogger as our platform instead of

WordPress because of the relative simplicity of managing and posting to a Blogger site and the fact that it was free. We also weren't seeking to turn our blog into a financial asset, so didn't really care about all the bells and whistles that WordPress provides. The downside is that we don't technically own the content, so Google could turn off our site at any minute.

Our blog has been an important component of our strategy to promote the Rauner brand and our collections to the scholarly community over the past decade. Therefore, when we considered expanding our library's social media presence, we did not need to think about whether we should keep the blog or not: it was clearly an asset. However, we did need to think about how our new social media platform would complement our preexisting outreach tools. We also needed to consider how much time and effort would be required to sustain a reliable posting regimen. Given that blog posts are primarily text-based, we knew that we wanted our second social media platform to be primarily image-based. Also, because our blog had a wide appeal to numerous demographics, we wanted our second site to focus specifically on undergraduates. While one of our goals was highlighting collections at Rauner, our main focus was having a social media platform that could foster positive connections with Dartmouth undergraduates who wanted to discover something cool in our stacks.

3.4 UNDERSTAND THE PROS AND CONS OF EACH PLATFORM OF INTEREST

With our institutional context, outreach goals, and existing social media presence in mind, we began to explore specific social media platforms that might be suitable for our needs. Although there are numerous options out there, we decided to consider four of the most well-known social media platforms at the time: Facebook, Twitter, Instagram, and Tumblr. We wanted to maximize our impact by selecting established and popular platforms while also keeping in mind the need to keep maintenance as simple as possible and focusing on image-based content.

3.4.1 Facebook

Facebook, arguably the most widespread social media platform of all time, has seeped into every crevice of our society. It is hard to find someone in the undergraduate demographic who does not have a personal account, and the platform is initially free to join.

Pros:

- Your odds of connecting with your desired audience are very high, regardless of demographic.
- Facebook has a high level of flexibility with regard to content and outreach.
- You can post photos and videos as well as traditional text-based posts.
- You can create affinity groups and post upcoming events.

Cons:

- Facebook makes you pay for advertising. If you want the platform to reach its full potential and reach as many people as possible, you will have to pay to "boost" your post.
- Your financial investment can quickly mushroom if you are trying to consistently and frequently reach out to your constituents.

3.4.2 Twitter

Although Twitter is not primarily an image-oriented platform, it is one that is very popular with the 29-and-under crowd, and it does have the capability for posting images. We found that Twitter's strengths were ultimately also its weaknesses.

Pros:

- Twitter is very easy to use and allows one to develop a strongly interactive relationship with your constituents.
- Twitter is relatively low stakes because each post is relatively ephemeral compared to those on other platforms, where you can build a library of images or be prompted to repost content from years ago. Locating past tweets is possible, but can be difficult because of the search capability (or lack thereof) of the platform.

Cons:

- Although pictures are possible, it is still an undeniably textual environment. This was not ideal for our goals.
- In order to develop and maintain relationships via Twitter, you may need to invest a significant amount of time engaging directly with your constituency, which means that you may end up spending more of your work day than you would like developing content.
- Twitter's posts are highly ephemeral, which means that if you are seeking to create stable, easily accessible content, Twitter is not really a good fit. It can be difficult to locate past content efficiently and productively.

3.4.3 Tumblr

Tumblr was a platform recommended to us for consideration by a recent undergrad at the college. Although Tumblr might not be considered social media by some, it is still a great way to provide access to images and content.

Pros:
- It's really simple to set up a page, or even multiple pages, within a few minutes.
- Tumblr allows you to schedule posts directly. You can line up multiple posts to go live on specific dates, which will let you front-load content to be posted automatically during those times in the academic term when other responsibilities demand priority.

Cons:
- The downside to Tumblr for some is that it can be overly simplistic and that it relies primarily on image-driven content but still feels like (and is often referred to as) a blog.
- At the time we considered this, Tumblr did not allow you to link to images on external sites. Tumblr now offers this functionality.

3.4.4 Instagram

Instagram is a social media platform that has skyrocketed in popularity over the last several years and boasts a very high level of user engagement relative to other platforms like Facebook or Twitter. The online tech news publisher Tech Crunch has reported that Instagram more than doubled its user base between 2015 and 2017, going from 300 to 700 million users in that amount of time (Constine, 2017). Instagram is an image-based platform that uses hashtags as a way of creating connections and community by tagging images with keywords that will appeal to niche demographics.

Pros:
- Posting images to Instagram from a mobile device is extremely easy.
- There are numerous tools that will allow you to edit and enhance your photographs or videos before you post them.
- Instagram is heavily utilized by more than half of all 18–29-year-old internet users.

Cons:

- You have to post frequently and regularly, and you have to post images that are visually engaging, in order to get people to stop and look at your feed.
- Development of community on Instagram really lives or dies by the use of hashtags and the participation in various themed events and challenges, so it's important to keep up to date on what's happening in the larger Instagram world.
- An iPhone or Android device is necessary if you want to use the full functionality, including posting. There is some limited desktop functionality. This makes it less than ideal for scheduling and posting content if your staff don't own smartphones or don't want to use them for work.
- Instagram does not allow followers to download your images, which means that it's not a great platform for distributing content to your users that is intended for re-use.

3.5 DETERMINE WHICH PLATFORM BEST MATCHES YOUR LIBRARY

Once you've evaluated each of the platforms that are of potential interest to you and your institution, you then must make the tough decision about which platform is best for your purposes.

In the end, we decided not to use Facebook primarily because the larger Library already had a robust presence on Facebook and we also didn't like the idea of paying money to reach our audience. We decided not to use Twitter because the DCL had a preexisting account. Also, we decided that Twitter was unrealistic for us because of its text-based format and the transitory nature of its content. Although we considered Tumblr as a viable option for a while, we worried about the ability to form community quickly as well as its similarity to our blog post format. We wanted a different feel to our second social media platform and did not like the idea of having two blog-like accounts.

Ultimately, we decided to choose Instagram as our new social media platform and created an account named @raunerlibrary. The reasons for selecting Instagram were because it was primarily visual-based (which provided a pleasing contrast to our text-based blog), because 71% of 18–29-year-old internet users (and therefore by undergraduates, our primary demographic) use Instagram (Smith and Anderson, 2018), and because it allowed for development of relationships with followers (something we wanted to emphasize as a part of creating our brand).

By the time you read this book, it is very possible that the zeitgeist will have moved on to other social media platforms besides the ones that we considered during our exploration. Ultimately, however, what is important is that you evaluate each possible social media application as it comes down the technological turnpike through the lens of your institution's contextual situation, your own desired outcomes for social media, and what sorts of social media commitments you already have in place (as well as how much time you can give to a new account). With that information in hand, it should be relatively easy to sort through the various platforms and find one that works best, if not perfectly, for the needs of your library.

REFERENCES

Constine, J. (2017, April 26). *Instagram's growth speeds up as it hits 700 million users*. TechCrunch. Available from https://techcrunch.com/2017/04/26/instagram-700-million-users/.

Mon, L. (2015). *Social media and library services*. Morgan & Claypool Publishers Available from. Available from https://doi.org/10.2200/S00634ED1V01Y201503ICR040.

Smith, A., & Anderson M. (2018, March 1). *Social media use in 2018*. Pew Research Center: Internet and Technology. Available from http://www.pewinternet.org/2018/03/01/social-media-use-in-2018/.

CHAPTER 4

Social Media Best Practices: Implementing Guidelines for Disability and Copyright

Sarah Christensen and J.J. Pionke
University of Illinois Urbana-Champaign, Urbana and Champaign, Illinois, United States

4.1 INTRODUCTION

The University of Illinois at Urbana-Champaign (U of I) comprises over 20 subject libraries and units, with librarians and staff from each unit often managing multiple social media accounts. Including only Twitter, Facebook, and Instagram platforms, there are over 50 social media accounts for the U of I Library system. While individual subject libraries and units need to maintain content and a tone appropriate for their audience, the Library system as a whole has recently attempted to implement a set of best practices related to the management of social media accounts. While there are many points to address in a set of best practices, such as crisis management, patron privacy, and customer service, we chose to focus on accessibility and copyright for this chapter as they span disciplinary audiences and are critical for libraries to address as we aim to be inclusive, accessible, and model ethical scholarship. Accessibility and copyright are disparate topics, though both are critical to address in a communications plan that many people at various stages of their careers will be using. Both topics are also somewhat of a minority in the social media world, where many account managers focus their time on content strategy and engagement. As an academic library, it is important to take the time to make sure our communications are both legal and accessible to everyone.

In early 2016, a Social Media Working Group (SMWG) was organized, in part to develop best practices related to managerial topics such as accessibility and copyright, but also to help content managers keep abreast of new social media trends, streamline communication within the Library system, and communicate and engage with patrons. The SMWG

Social Media
DOI: https://doi.org/10.1016/B978-0-08-102409-6.00004-3

is an informal group of content owners and content managers that meets once per month during the academic year. Content owners are typically librarians or full-time staff members who are responsible for the overall account, while content managers perform day-to-day posting responsibilities. Content management is typically delegated to graduate students from the School of Information Sciences (iSchool) who have assistantships in the library. During these monthly meetings, the group hosts speakers and panel discussions on topics such as content strategy, assessment, diversity, scheduler tools, crisis communication, handling negative feedback, and politically or culturally sensitive posts. The SMWG supports the U of I Library's *Framework for Strategic Action, 2015–2018*, which ensures an integrated and coherent user experience and to develop a consistent and integrated library-wide outreach, engagement, and marketing strategy (University of Illinois Library at Urbana-Champaign, 2015).

Using the infrastructure of the SMWG and the related expertise on campus, the U of I Library system has implemented a set of best practices that include accessibility and copyright. In doing so, potential issues are addressed prior to social media managers posting content, rather than after. Best practices make it easier for new content managers and graduate students to learn to manage social media accounts, as there is regular turnover within the student population. These best practices make our accounts more inclusive to those with disabilities, and provide clear guidance in dealing with intellectual property rights in an interactive online environment.

4.2 LITERATURE REVIEW

Much of the literature on social media in libraries focuses on why libraries should use social media, with numerous case studies detailing different ways libraries have implemented various platforms. However, several authors have focused on the importance of strategic planning when adopting social media tools (Choi, 2012; Maisiri, Mupaaikwa, & Ngwenya, 2015; Midyette, Youngkin, & Snow-Croft, 2014; Steiner, 2012). In particular, Maisiri et al. (2015) write that strategic planning:

> *...helps a library answer questions on the why and how of the processes in a library and looks at the whole organization or a large part... It differs from a policy which is a guideline, principle, rule, regulation or law that is used as a reference point in decision making or choosing the appropriate behavior to follow. A policy can act as a code of conduct. The aim of policies is to foster consistency and a common understanding. (p. 251)*

Swanson (2012) discusses procedural practices, noting that these should be differentiated from policies and strategic plans as the long-term impact of procedural documents is to prevent change. Due to the large, decentralized nature of the U of I Library system, the SMWG focused on developing a set of best practices, which falls somewhere between a policy and a procedural document. While not official, the SMWG document is a set of guidelines discussing management issues such as copyright and accessibility.

Several authors have explored copyright as it pertains to social media, focusing on topics such as user-generated versus user-found content, terms of use (TOU) for social media platforms, fair use, and the Digital Millennium Copyright Act (DMCA) safe harbor provision. Gutierrez Alm (2014) provides an overview of these topics and how they intertwine, focusing on the copyright implications of user-generated content. While Gutierrez Alm details the ways that copyright law does not work well with social media, due to broad licensing agreements and promoting infringement, Halbert (2009) offers an argument for broader protection for user-generated work. Carpenter (2012) offers an analysis of a fair use defense for user-found content on Pinterest, a platform considered to be second-generation social media as it is distinguished by relying on user-found content. First-generation social media, such as Facebook, Instagram, and Twitter, was designed for users to post their own content. Levinson (2017) is more specific about fair use on social media platforms, writing that for the first factor of fair use, courts should broaden their conceptualization of transformative use in a digital environment. In addition, she encourages courts to weigh attribution when analyzing market harm to copyright holders, the fourth factor of fair use. It is clear from copyright and social media literature that courts have not yet caught up with technology, as each author calls for updating copyright code through the legislative process.

In terms of social media and accessibility, library literature is silent. While various toolkits and guides, especially at the federal government level and most notably the digital.gov website, discuss how to make social media posts more accessible to people with disabilities, there is no discussion of accessibility, libraries, and social media within library literature. The library literature does, however, go in depth about website accessibility and to a lesser extent finding aid accessibility. For instance, Southwell and Slater (2013) examined special collection finding aids to determine how accessible they were for people who used screen readers. They discovered that while finding aids were marginally accessible, they clearly had not been made with accessibility in mind (Southwell and Slater, 2013). The most popular finding aid software, LibGuides by Springshare, is constantly changing, and the most recent investigation of accessibility of LibGuides is a blog post from 2015 by Magnuson where she highlights the many problems of LibGuides 2.0. Many of the problems have either been addressed by SpringShare or acknowledged as being problematic due to the coding of the software and integration of other coding elements. The single largest reason that there have been no follow-up posts or articles about accessibility and SpringShare is that the company has vigorously taken on accessibility. Every monthly patch that goes out contains accessibility upgrades, which are discussed on the SpringShare website. LibGuides' nearly constant rate of change is a good example of how large systems with lots of users, like social media in general, are also in a constant state of change. Therefore, examining literature that focuses on the discussion of accessibility of the various platforms is basically out of date the moment it is printed.

4.3 SOCIAL MEDIA AND COPYRIGHT

The way people communicate and share information has changed dramatically with the advent of social media. The openness of social media is seemingly at odds with copyright law, even though the primary function of the law is "to promote the progress of science and the useful arts" (U.S. Const. art. I. § 8 cl. 8). The instantaneous sharing environment of social media has produced complex problems that copyright law has not yet caught up with, and has produced a mass of social media users that completely disregard copyright.

Social media platforms ask users to agree to their terms of use (TOU) when registering for an account, which require users to license the rights to their content. While the TOU for Facebook, Twitter, and Instagram each state that the user maintains the rights to any user-generated content, each platform asks the user to agree to a broad nonexclusive license. In the end, these licenses are so broad that they allow the platform to do nearly anything with the content (Gutierrez Alm, 2014). These social media platforms then claim protection for themselves through indemnity terms as well as the DMCA safe harbor provision, which protects internet service providers who do not have knowledge of infringing acts from legal action (Gutierrez Alm, 2014). To comply with the safe harbor provision, platforms must provide a means to comply with takedown notices. With safe harbor provisions in place for social media platforms, a copyright holder's only recourse for infringement would be to sue the individual or organization who shared the copyrighted content.

Often, social media users re-post information of interest shared by other users or found on an external website and share it with their friends or followers. In some instances, this practice may be infringing on the exclusive rights of distribution and reproduction. According to Gutierrez Alm (2014), there is also the possibility of third-party infringement, whereby a user shares content that already constitutes an infringement.

If libraries are organizations in the business of sharing information, how can we successfully navigate our social media accounts, while also being mindful of doing so ethically? In developing these best practices, the SMWG met to discuss common questions that arose in relation to copyright, and what solutions exist. Often, content managers were unsure if they could post a certain image, or had trouble finding the copyright status of something that they wanted to re-post. Below are our recommendations:

4.4 PRACTICAL GUIDELINES ON SOCIAL MEDIA AND COPYRIGHT

Create your own content

- Generating original content that is targeted to your campus audience is likely to be more engaging, as opposed to posting content designed for a general audience. This could include library events, news, search tips, and features for specific databases, or highlighting items in the collection (especially items in the public domain). In creating content, you own it and therefore do not have to worry about infringing on the copyright of a third party.
- There is flexibility in instances where you might be reposting news of interest from other organizations, especially on platforms that explicitly encourage this behavior in their terms of agreement.

Determine if fair use is applicable

- Section 107 of the US Copyright Act provides a framework for allowing the unlicensed use of copyright-protected works in certain circumstances. Factors that are considered when determining if a use of a work is considered fair include the purpose and character of a use,

nature of a copyrighted work, amount and substantiality of the work used, and effect on the potential market value for the copyright holder. Fair use is an essential part of copyright law that should be promoted and used.
- When sharing a copyright-protected work on social media, ask yourself if your use might be considered a fair use. Are you adding to the conversation by adding commentary? Are you sharing more of the work than you need to?

Research the original source of content you want to share
- Taking the time to research sources is a good example for libraries to set for their users. Find out if something is in copyright or not before posting, and include proper attribution to avoid perpetuating plagiarism.

Ask permission
- You must ask permission from the copyright holder if there is something you would like to share that is protected.

4.5 SOCIAL MEDIA AND ACCESSIBILITY

The Americans With Disabilities Act of 1990 (ADA) stipulates that public buildings and services need to be accessible to people with physical, mental, cognitive, or sensory disabilities. Web accessibility is not mentioned in the ADA. However, Section 508 of the Rehabilitation Act of 1973 and as amended in 1998 states that all federal websites and documents must be accessible for people with disabilities. Publicly accessible institutions use both the ADA and Section 508 to guide them in how to make themselves more accessible physically and electronically for all people regardless of ability.

Making social media accessible is relatively easy, and more importantly, it helps your message reach more people. According to the World Health Organization (2014), 15% of the global population has a disability that impacts their daily living. That is not an insubstantial percentage of people and as the "Baby Boomer" generation in the United States continues to age, the number of people with some kind of disability is going to increase. Developing good accessibility habits for creating content so that everyone, from cradle to grave, can receive and understand your message is a good habit to form.

The SMWG invites staff from the Disability Resources & Educational Services unit at the University of Illinois Urbana-Champaign each academic year to discuss making our social media accounts more accessible. During this meeting, we learn more about different types of disabilities and what needs each group may have, including technological aids such as screen readers and captioning systems. The following guidelines are the results of those meetings:

4.6 PRACTICAL GUIDELINES ON SOCIAL MEDIA AND ACCESSIBILITY

Use plain language

- Avoid using acronyms, jargon, or abbreviations.
- Keep posts, videos, and audio short and to the point.
- Your posts, on whatever platform you are using, are reaching a wide audience that runs the gamut of ability. Stick to somewhere around a fourth to sixth grade reading level.

Use CamelCase

- CamelCase is the term for using capitalization in hashtags(#) in order to more easily distinguish the words, such as #EventName rather than #eventname (Digitalgov, 2017). This is particularly important for people with dyslexia and visual impairments.
- As hashtags are an important way to track events and the conversation around them, making the hashtags more accessible will go a long way in helping people be more involved and engaged in your events.

Provide image descriptions

- Using image descriptions with any photos, memes, or other visual media on social media will help people using screen readers to understand what the image is. If there is an "alt text" box before posting, put the image description there. When there is not an "alt text" box, many people will add a short image description in the text post. Look at the support section for individual platforms for instructions about how to do this.
- Image descriptions should be concise and provide context and may not necessarily be a direct description. For instance, if you have an image of your library with an acrobat team forming a human pyramid in the lobby as part of a tweet about your circus themed week, the image description might read "Five acrobats form a human pyramid

in the lobby of HomeTown Library." Notice that there is not a literal description of how the pyramid is formed or what the acrobats are wearing, only that they are there and forming a pyramid in the lobby of the library (WebAim, 2017).

- Descriptions should be clear, free of jargon, and relay the most important information in the image. Descriptions are particularly useful for people with visual impairments and for people who might need more explanation for what they are looking at.

Caption your video

- Whether you are using YouTube or Vimeo or some other video platform, caption your videos. Many of the platforms now make it easy to caption and captioning allows people to follow your video more clearly and easily. This is especially true for people who have hearing impairments or for whom English is a second language. Always ensure what the computer believes is being said is what is actually being said.
- Do make sure that the captions are easy to read on the screen. If the background of the video is dark, choose white captions and vice versa if the background is white. Also make sure that the captions are large enough to read easily (Leisinger, Moring, & Rubin, 2014).

Include link shorteners

- Providing links to sources of information is an accepted practice on social media platforms. Make sure, however, that the link is short and meaningful. Links that are along the lines of bit.ly/xYz24DC do not mean anything to anyone. Instead, change that shortened link to something that is easy to remember: bit.ly/CircusWeek. Notice the use of CamelCase in the shortener in order to make it easier to read.
- Link shorteners help people make sense of what they are seeing and contextualize the shortened link so they can follow more easily where the link goes. This cuts down on confusion, especially for people with dyslexia, dysgraphia, or dyscalculia. Link shorteners also help reduce the amount of time that a person using a screen reader will have to use in order to hear where the link is going (Chronister, 2013).

Use multiple platforms

- What is accessible for some people on one platform might not be accessible to others. It pays to use different types of social media platforms to get your message out. For example, while a visual-based platform might be perfect for discussing art and design, people with visual impairments are going to be more focused on text-based platforms.

Incorporating a text-based social media platform will go a long way toward including people with visual impairments in your discussion (Digitalgov, 2017).

Provide contact information

- If there is a problem with the accessibility of your content, give people a way to let you know and do not bury that contact information several layers deep. Put the contact information front and center in your profile. Make it easy for people to get in touch with you. In general, people want to know what their library is up to, the services that are provided, and the resources that are available. Providing contact information and putting a person in charge of accessibility says that the library has a serious commitment to being accessible for everyone (Digitalgov, 2017).

While these are basic guidelines for accessibility, individual social media platforms may have their own built in accessibility features. It pays to explore the help documentation to take advantage of what each platform provides. If the social media platform does not provide accessibility features, plan accordingly to disseminate information or hold conversations on that platform in an accessible manner.

4.7 CONCLUSION

Making your social media messages accessible and within copyright does not have to be hard or overwhelming, though it does require a little forethought and modification to existing workflows. Soon, these considerations will become second nature. Improving accessibility and copyright adherence is not only the right thing to do, but also helps people understand and connect to the library more easily.

While we often think of social media as part of our public relations and marketing strategies, for many people, especially people with disabilities, social media is a key component in their daily lives. Social media allows many people with disabilities to reach beyond their disability into a broader world of human interaction and relationships. Good social media accessibility and copyright habits encourage discussions and the forming of connections. Engaging the community in conversations via social media can help users overcome isolation, which has always been a goal of libraries. Nestled in the centers of communities, whether academic or public, libraries have always been places of learning, gathering, and discussing. Our social media accounts should reflect this role by being inclusive, accessible, and ethical in how we share information.

REFERENCES

Carpenter, C. (2012). Copyright infringement and the second generation of social media websites: Why Pinterest users should be protected from copyright infringement by the fair use defense. *Journal of Internet Law, 16*. Available from https://papers.ssrn.com/sol3/papers.cfm?abstract_id=2131483/.

Choi, C. (2012). *Is your library ready for a social media librarian?* Available from http://docplayer.net/14000702-Is-your-library-ready-for-a-social-media-librarian.html.

Chronister, M. (2013). *Gov URL shorteners and how to use them*. Digitalgov. Available from https://www.digitalgov.gov/2013/12/20/gov-url-shorteners-and-how-to-use-them/.

Digitalgov. (2017). *Federal social media accessibility toolkit hackpad*. Available from https://www.digitalgov.gov/resources/federal-social-media-accessibility-toolkit-hackpad/.

Gutierrez Alm, J. (2014). "Sharing" copyrights: The copyright implications of user content in social media. *Journal of Public Law & Policy, 35*, 104–130.

Halbert, D. (2009). Mass culture and the culture of the masses: a manifesto for user-generated rights. *Vanderbilt Journal of Entertainment & Technology Law, 11*(4), 921–961.

Leisinger, R., Moring, G., & Rubin, J. (2014). *508 Accessible videos—How to caption videos*. Digitalgov. Available from https://www.digitalgov.gov/2014/06/30/508-accessible-videos-how-to-caption-videos/.

Levinson, L. (2017). Adapting fair use to reflect social media norms: A joint proposal. *UCLA Law Review, 64*, 1038–1078.

Maisiri, E., Mupaaikwa, E., & Ngwenya, S. (2015). Strategic planning for social media in libraries: The case of Zimbabwe. In A. Tella (Ed.), *Social media strategies for dynamic library service development* (pp. 250–262). Hershey: Information Science Reference.

Midyette, D., Youngkin, A., & Snow-Croft, S. (2014). Social media and communications: Developing a policy to guide the flow of information. *Medical Reference Services Quarterly, 33*, 39–50.

Southwell, K. L., & Slater, J. (2013). An evaluation of finding aid accessibility for screen readers. *Information Technology and Libraries, 32*, 34–46.

Steiner, Sarah K. (2012). *Strategic planning for social media in libraries*. Chicago: ALA TechSource.

Swanson, T. (2012). *Managing social media in libraries*. Oxford: Chandos Publishing.

University Library. (2015). Framework for strategic action. Available from https://www.library.illinois.edu/geninfo/libraryinit/framework_for_strategic_action/.

WebAim. (2017). *Alternative text*. Available from https://webaim.org/techniques/alttext/.

World Health Organization. (2014). *Disability and health (fact sheet no. 352)*. Available from http://www.who.int/mediacentre/factsheets/fs352/en/.

FURTHER READING

Boudreaux, C. (2009). *Social media policy database. Social media governance: Empowerment with accountability*. Available from http://socialmediagovernance.com/policies/.

Harmon, C., & Messina, M. (Eds.), (2013). *Using social media in libraries: best practices*. Lanham: The Scarecrow Press.

Johnston, J. (2015). "Loose tweets sink fleets" and other sage advice: Social media governance, policies and guidelines. *Journal of Public Affairs, 15*, 175–187.

Magnuson, L. 2015. "Accessibility testing LibGuides 2.0." *ACRL TechConnect*. Available from http://acrl.ala.org/techconnect/post/accessibility-testing-libguides-2-0.

Mon, L. M. (2015). *Social media and library services*. San Rafael: Morgan & Claypool Publishers.

Pomerantz, J., Hank, C., & Sugimoto, C. R. (2015). The state of social media policies in higher education. *PLoS One, 10*(5). Available from https://doi.org/10.1371/journal.pone.0127485.

U.S. Copyright Office. (2017). *U.S. Copyright Office fair use index*. Available from https://www.copyright.gov/fair-use/index.html.

University Library. (2017). *Library blogs and other social media*. Available from http://www.library.illinois.edu/blog/index.html.

CHAPTER 5

Using Scheduling Apps to Streamline a Social Media Workflow

Samantha Paul and Michael Holt
Valdosta State University, Valdosta, GA, United States

5.1 INTRODUCTION

There has been a lot of research done on the use of social media in academic libraries. Social media is designed to be easy to use and, from a personal standpoint, it can be easy to create content. However, when managing social media for a business, institution, or academic library, it can be a little more challenging especially while maintaining a brand and projecting a personality that is both professional and personable. While one has the flexibility to play fast and loose with content on personal social media accounts, for an academic library, content needs to be more carefully crafted and curated. Combined with a need to post regular content, the academic library social media workflow needs a strategic plan. Implementing an editorial calendar can be one way to create content appropriate for an institutional platform (Solomon, 2016, p. 46; see also Lawrimore, 2017). Editorial calendars can help you create a detailed "planning document" that is visual and strategic (Solomon, 2016, p. 46).

Once the content is created, the next step is posting it. With a personal social media account, this can be easy as there is only one cook in the kitchen and you have the ability to post content directly from your smartphone or computer to your own social media account in real time. Depending on your academic library and your workflow, this is not always an option for an academic librarian or an academic library social media team. As suggested by Peacemaker, Robinson, and Hurst (2016), "it is important to develop management practices that facilitate collaboration and flexibility to support all of the voices in an academic library. This requires a coordinated approach that includes content strategies, writing style guidelines, an editor or team for each platform, and editors

Social Media
DOI: https://doi.org/10.1016/B978-0-08-102409-6.00005-5

managing platforms on a day-to-day basis" (p. 105). This is where a scheduling app can come into play.

Scheduling apps or more broadly, social media management tools, can be a useful addition to any social media strategic plan. Most social media platforms can easily be managed with a third-party application (Twitter) or within the social media platform itself (Facebook), but some popular social media platforms (Instagram) have limitations as far as integrating third-party applications. Instagram's terms of use (ToU) and design limits the functionality of third-party applications to post to your Instagram. This can have its benefits from a security standpoint. But when managing a social media platform like Instagram for an academic library, especially when working in a team or implementing an editorial calendar, this can have its drawbacks and requires a few extra steps. However, there are applications that can make managing an academic library's Instagram easier, even with these extra steps. In this chapter, we will share our impressions of some of the more popular third-party scheduling apps on the market, as well as how we used a project management application, Trello, at Odum Library to reproduce some of the functionality of social media management applications.

5.1.1 Summary

- Strategic plans are essential for any social media platform.
- Editorial calendars and social media management tools can help individuals or teams create, visualize, and schedule posts consistent with the academic library or institution's brand or image.

5.2 HOW WE PICKED THE APPS TO REVIEW

We researched online to see what social media management tools were cited as the best or appeared to be the most prevalent in libraries or the public relations field (Clutch, 2017; Maurya, 2015; Zeevi, 2015). Some factors that informed selecting an app to review were:

- Popularity
- Price
- Instagram integration.

We thought Instagram integration was an important factor when selecting a social media management tool because while the social media platforms frequently used by libraries are Facebook and Twitter (Peacemaker et al., 2016, p. 103), Instagram is another important platform that can reach users with different kinds of content. We think finding an app that can handle both these common social media platforms and Instagram is very helpful in the long run. When we had a short list, we selected nine applications to examine in more detail. You will note that we only review six apps in the following section. Three apps were eliminated from the running. One app boasted Instagram functionality, but we could not find evidence of it in the app itself. Complications with requesting demos eliminated two other apps from consideration, which, in addition, were cost prohibitive for an academic library. For one week, we used the various apps to post to our personal Instagram accounts. Odum Library already uses a social media management tool to schedule Twitter and Facebook posts, so we were interested in testing the Instagram functionality.

5.3 COMMON THEMES AND TRENDS

Of the nine apps that we selected to test Instagram scheduling, most of them had a mobile app presence. We think that the presence of a mobile app is critically important for a social media management tool, especially when it comes to Instagram functionality. Since Instagram does not offer a way to post content outside of its mobile app, working entirely within a mobile ecosystem for creating and posting content is convenient.

Generally, the first step was to download the app. One application, Autogrammer, had no mobile app available and required you to use a browser to schedule posts.

Next up was using the application right out of the gate or creating a login/password, then the application must be authorized to access your library's Instagram account. We found this to be the most disconcerting part from a security point of view. With relatively low stakes of using our personal Instagram accounts, one application, Autogrammer, triggered a rash of suspicious activities alerts that could only be solved by juggling between the Instagram app and desktop version, and eventually revoking that product's access (and changing the password for the Instagram account).

Once you authorize the account to access your Instagram, you can expect the ability to create your post, attach your picture, and schedule your time for publishing within the social media management tool. Most of the apps will then notify you when it is time to post to Instagram. When you get that notification, you open the app and start the publishing process. This publishing process, when done right will include a reminder to check that you are currently logged in to the intended Instagram account. Most apps indicate that they are copying the text from your scheduled post, then all you have to do is paste it into Instagram. Sometimes the picture also migrates over, or you may have to select it from the album created by the social media management tool. Some of the apps that we tested have introduced direct publishing to Instagram; however, these features are available only with an Instagram Business account.

Many of the apps that we examined included basic metrics and many had expanded analytics only available at higher pricing tiers. This feature can be especially important for academic libraries that want to assess their social media efforts.

All pricing provided in the next section is from September 2017.

5.4 APP REVIEWS

5.4.1 *Name of App*: AgoraPulse

5.4.1.1 Price/Subscription Model

Price varies based on number of users and social media profiles: $49 a month (three profiles, one user, and limited data storage); $299 a month (40 profiles, 12 users, expanded data storage).

Pricing plans can be found at: https://www.agorapulse.com/pricing

5.4.1.2 Supported Platforms

Facebook, Twitter, Instagram, LinkedIn, Google+

5.4.1.3 Features/Benefits

- Excellent analytics data.
- Mobile app that integrates well with Instagram.
- Ability to track and respond to comments.

5.4.1.4 Why We Tested It

Frequently mentioned in literature as being a powerful tool that supports a number of social media platforms, including Instagram.

5.4.1.5 Our Impressions

- Somewhat expensive, especially as you add social media profiles or users.
- Mobile app does not check to make sure your posts are going to the right profile.
- Comment responding and tracking can be slow to push through to the app.
- Some analytics features not available at lower price points.

5.4.2 *Name of App:* Buffer

5.4.2.1 Price/Subscription Model

Price varies based on social media platform, user, analytics, and post limits: Free (one platform, one user with no analytics, and a limit of 10 scheduled posts) to $399 a month (25 users, up to 150 platforms, a limit of 2000 scheduled posts, and analytics).

Pricing plans can be found at: https://buffer.com/

5.4.2.2 Supported Platforms

Facebook, Twitter, Instagram, LinkedIn, Google+ , Pinterest (not offered at free tier)

5.4.2.3 Features/Benefits

- Excellent mobile app for working with Instagram.
- Multiple pricing tiers (including a forever free) that allows for cost-effective right-sizing.
- Reminds users with multiple Instagram accounts to make sure they are posting to the correct account.
- Offers direct publishing with Instagram Business account.

5.4.2.4 Why We Tested It

It was popular, had a forever free pricing plan, and supported posting to Instagram.

5.4.2.5 Our Impressions

- Notifications inconsistent at times.
- User-friendly design.
- Posting to Instagram was easy via the mobile app.
- A favorite among the applications we reviewed.

5.4.3 *Name of App*: Hootsuite

5.4.3.1 Price/Subscription Model

Price varies based on user, social media profiles, analytics, and other features. Free basic plan available. Professional-level pricing starts at $19 a month (1 user, 10 profiles, and analytics); $99 a month (3 users, 20 profiles, team workflows, and one-on-one training). Expanded plans available for business, $499, and enterprise, price unlisted.

Pricing plans can be found at: https://hootsuite.com/plans

5.4.3.2 Supported Platforms

Facebook, Twitter, Instagram, LinkedIn, Google+

5.4.3.3 Features/Benefits

- Widely adopted by social media marketers.
- Powerful analytics.
- Ability to run social sweepstakes.
- Offers direct publishing with Instagram Business account.

5.4.3.4 Why We Tested It

It is the most widely used social media manager in use today.

5.4.3.5 Our Impressions

- App user interface was not intuitive.
- Posting to Instagram was clunky.
- Better platform for managing Facebook and Twitter.

5.4.4 *Name of App*: Sendible

5.4.4.1 Price/Subscription Model

Price varies based on users and services. Three plans: $49 a month for 1 user and up to 20 services; $199 a month for 4 users and 100 services; $499 a month for 10 users and 300 services.

Pricing plans can be found at: https://sendible.com/pricing

5.4.4.2 Features/Benefits

- Easy-to-use app that works well with Instagram.
- Excellent monitoring and analytics features.
- Priority inbox for responding to comments.

5.4.4.3 Supported Platforms

Facebook, Twitter, Instagram, LinkedIn, Google+

5.4.4.4 Why We Tested It

It was listed in an article on social media management tools (Clutch, 2017) and it supported Instagram.

5.4.4.5 Our Impressions

- Notifications were consistent and came to e-mail as well.
- Two-hour refresh rate hinders ability to respond to comments.

- Features and pricing not as competitive with comparable social media management platforms.

5.4.5 *Name of App:* Autogrammer

5.4.5.1 *Price/Subscription Model*

Price varies based on social media profiles. Five tiers from $19 a month for one Instagram profile, five Facebook profiles, and five Twitter profiles to $179 a month for 25 Twitter profiles, 25 Facebook profiles, and 20 Instagram profiles.

Pricing plans can be found at: http://autogrammer.com/

5.4.5.2 *Supported Platforms*

Facebook, Twitter, Instagram

5.4.5.3 *Features/Benefits*

- Affordable.
- All pricing tiers offer unlimited post scheduling.
- Bulk photo uploading is available for managing multiple Instagram accounts.

5.4.5.4 *Why We Tested It*

We wanted to try an app that emphasized Instagram.

5.4.5.5 *Our Impressions*

- Instagram is a very mobile-centric platform, yet Autogrammer has no app.
- The web user interface was clunky and made scheduling posts difficult.
- Signing up for the trial triggered security warnings on Instagram accounts.
- If you are managing an Instagram account, we recommend that Autogrammer be avoided.

5.4.6 *Name of App*: Schedugram

5.4.6.1 *Price/Subscription Model*

Price varies by account and followers. Starts at $20 a month per account for up to 10,000 followers; $100 a month per account for 1–2 million followers.

Pricing plans can be found at: https://schedugr.am/pricing/

5.4.6.2 Supported Platforms

Instagram

5.4.6.3 Features/Benefits

- It directly posts to Instagram via a bank of mobile phones.
- The app is easy to use.
- All tiers are designed for teams.
- Photo editing is part of the app.

5.4.6.4 Why We Tested It

We wanted to include the one app on the market that actually schedules Instagram posts and will then post them automatically without having an Instagram business account.

5.4.6.5 Our Impressions

- Platform worked exactly as advertised and posts went up on time with no problems.
- Powerful scheduling tools, but no analytics.
- May be a violation of Instagram's ToU.
- Affordable if scheduling and auto-posting to Instagram is a priority.

5.4.7 Summary

- It is important to right-size social media management tools to your team and workflow, but the price will likely increase.
- Trialing a social media management program is important. Popularity is not a reliable indicator of fit with your academic library's social media plan.
- Overall, we were impressed with Buffer. We were not impressed with Autogrammer.

5.5 TRELLO CASE STUDY

We originally adopted Trello, a project management app, to help with a LibGuides overhaul. We appreciated its flexibility and determined that we could try adding this product to our social media workflow. Trello works with a board, list, and card system (Fig. 5.1).

Boards can be created to organize to-do items or projects. Each board is eligible for one free "power-up." Power-ups allow you to integrate additional features or other applications like Google Hangouts, Evernote,

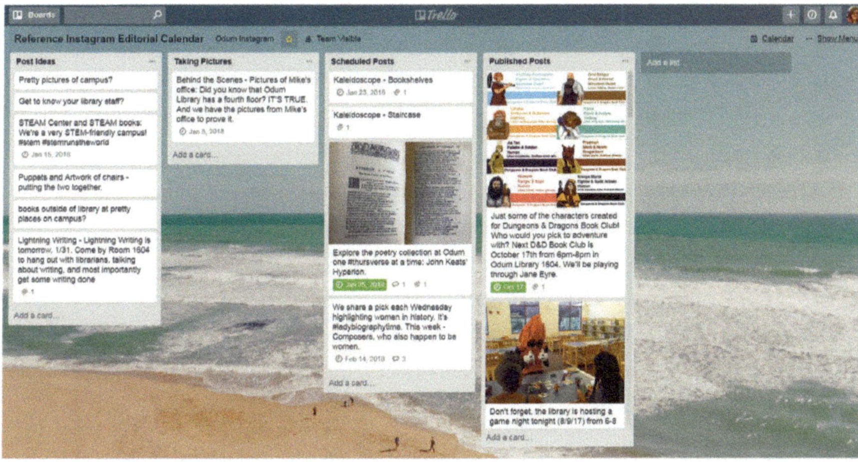

Figure 5.1 Odum Library Reference Instagram Editorial Calendar in Trello.

or Dropbox (Power-ups, n.d.). On each board, you can create several lists that can have descriptive titles. You then add cards to each list. Cards can be created in batches by pasting text or individually. If members of a board are enabled as an admin, they are able to drag cards between lists. This can be a great way to illustrate progress on tasks. Cards can be assigned to members. Cards can be a great way to coordinate efforts. Members of the board can communicate via comments. They can assign due dates. You can even create checklists. After using the service and appreciating its ease of use for our LibGuides project, we decided that it could help us manage our Instagram. Our social media team has been able to cobble together a content creation plan for our Twitter and Facebook using a Google Docs file and an expensive social media tool, Oracle Social Relationship Management (SRM). However, even with this expensive product, we still did not have a good way to manage our Instagram, a social media platform that we would like to promote more. As stated earlier in this chapter, Instagram poses its own challenges as far as its current design and ToU that limits content creation in advance. With Trello, our social media team was able to use our same Google document to identify tweets that we could transform to appropriate Instagram posts. We created several lists on our Odum Library Instagram board, *Reference Instagram Editorial Calendar*.

- Post Ideas. This list is used to brainstorm ideas for Instagram posts, including the captions and hashtags.

- Taking Pictures. Cards from post ideas are transferred to this list to indicate this process. Pictures, short videos, and GIFs can be attached to the card.
- Scheduled Posts. Cards from Taking Pictures are transferred to this list. A due date is assigned. Trello allows one free power-up to be enabled. We always enable the Calendar. Due dates are reflected on the calendar, which allows for easy visualization of content.
- Published Posts. Once a member of our social media team has saved the attachment to their phone and copied the caption, they visit Instagram and post. Cards are moved from Scheduled Posts to Published Posts and marked as complete.

Trello offers a lot of flexibility. The ability to access Trello via their website and their app allows for easier content creation especially for brainstorming sessions accomplished via Google Docs. The Trello app allows us to replicate, albeit crudely, the functionality of the third-party scheduling or social media management apps explored earlier in the chapter. Trello can mimic the content creation and scheduling found in many social media management tools, but falls short in the areas of assessment and social media monitoring. We find it easier to monitor Instagram through the app or Instagram website. However, larger academic libraries with more active followers might struggle with this limitation.

5.5.1 Assessment

Social media management apps are created to allow users to track posts, see metrics, etc. Waddell, Barnes, and Khan-Kernahan (2012) state that "libraries that lack systematic metrics for measuring success can find themselves pouring precious resources into social media upkeep without knowing if they are promoting their strategic vision" (p. 1). Trello was not designed with this functionality and therefore lacks these features, but the ease of use and flexibility of it may be a worthwhile tradeoff. At Odum Library, we are able to access our Instagram statistics via Oracle SRM, an expensive social media tool provided by the university's public relations department. For institutions who are looking for both scheduling and assessment as part of their social media management solution, Trello might not be a workable alternative without a separate analytics product. Several of the third-party scheduling apps we reviewed incorporate analytics and might be a better option for institutions needing both.

5.5.2 Pricing

Currently, Trello is a cost-friendly option. The functionality described in this case study is provided in the basic, free version. Trello does offer multiple tiers that have corresponding upgrades, benefits, and cost. For example, Trello Gold allows for 250 MB-sized attachments as well as additional power-ups. For the purposes of creating social media posts for an academic library, we do not believe upgrades are necessary. However, if your institution already provides access to an upgraded version of Trello, embrace it. The basic version of Trello provides a lot of great features. Upgrading to Trello Gold might be beneficial for the increased attachment size limit, but Odum Library has been able to successfully post videos to Instagram with the current basic version.

5.5.3 Why Trello Works for Us

Overall, using Trello at Odum Library has helped us organize both our LibGuides updates and Instagram efforts. The shared nature of the platform as well as the cards system has been helpful in allowing our social media team to visualize the entire workflow in order to create a post for Instagram. Since we started using the product to schedule posts, we have been posting more regularly. Although, it is not a traditional app for social media management, Trello has met our needs both as an editorial calendar and workflow manager for our Instagram account. Our use of Trello emphasizes the importance of choosing a social media management tool that fits with the goals and objectives of your academic library's social media platform. Sometimes, you do not need all the bells and whistles to get the job done.

5.5.4 Summary

- Odum Library's social media team uses Trello, a project management tool, to brainstorm ideas, organize the workflow, and create an editorial calendar for Instagram.
- Although it lacks metrics and social media monitoring, Trello can be a good way to mimic social media management tools at a fraction of the cost.
- Do not feel pressured to commit to a pricey social media management tool since low-cost and no-cost alternatives do exist.
- Connect with your institution's public relations department and inquire about their social media management tools and potential to share.

5.6 CONCLUSIONS

A social media management tool or scheduling app can be a useful addition to an academic library's social media toolbox. However, adopting tools marketed toward public relations and corporate customers can be difficult, especially on a higher education budget. This should not deter you from incorporating a scheduling app into your social media plan. In addition, many of the scheduling apps we reviewed offer tiered pricing plans, including free or basic plans, that can accommodate almost all academic library social media budgets.

Of the apps that we reviewed, we were the most impressed with Buffer. With its user friendliness and reasonable price tag, it may be a good option for academic libraries that are new to the social media management arena. Its free plan, albeit with a limited post allowance, could be an option for smaller academic libraries and smaller budgets. In addition, Buffer's pricing is pretty generous compared to other apps examined. Their "Awesome" plan, at $10 per month, is definitely affordable and comes with nearly all of the features Buffer offers, with the exception of analytics tools.

Alternatively, with the limited efficiency of the majority of social media management tools and Instagram, there is some room for creativity. At Odum Library, we have incorporated Trello into our social media plan to help us with Instagram. So even if incorporating a dedicated social media management tool is not the right fit for your social media workflow or budget, there are some creative ways to mimic the functionality.

REFERENCES

Clutch. (2017). *Top social media management software*. Available from https://clutch.co/social-media#leaders-matrix.

Lawrimore, E. (2017). Shoestring social media: Building a social media presence for UNCG's special collections and university archives. *North Carolina Libraries, 75*(1), 10–16.

Maurya, R. K. (2015, December 8). 15 free social media marketing tools. PC Quest. Retrieved from http://www.pcquest.com/15-free-social-media-marketing-tools/.

Peacemaker, B., Robinson, S., & Hurst, E. J. (2016). Connecting best practices in public relations to social media strategies for academic libraries. *College & Undergraduate Libraries, 23*(1), 101–108.

Power-ups. (n.d.). *Power-ups*. Available from https://trello.com/power-ups.

Solomon, L. (2016). *The librarian's nitty-gritty guide to content marketing*. Chicago, IL: ALA Editions.

Waddell, D. C., Barnes, M., & Khan-Kernahan, S. (2012). Tapping into the power of Twitter: A look at its potential in Canadian health libraries. *Partnership: The Canadian Journal of Library and Information Practice and Research*, 7(2), 1–12.
Zeevi, D. (2015, July 1). *12 best social media management tools* [web blog post]. Retrieved from https://blog.dashburst.com/best-social-media-management-tools/.

FURTHER READING

Fitzpatrick, P. https://pegfitzpatrick.com/blog/.
Kawasaki, G., & Fitzpatrick, P. (2014). *The art of social media: Power tips for power users.* New York: Portfolio/Penguin.
Zimmerman, S. B. https://suebzimmerman.com.

PART II

Tried and Tested by Librarians: Social Media Case Studies

CHAPTER 6

Instagram

6.1 CASE STUDY 1

Using Instagram to Engage Students During Library Orientation

Katie Hutchison[1] **and Stephanie Henderson**[2]
[1]Student Engagement & Archival Services Librarian, Walsh University, North Canton, Ohio, United States
[2]Reference Librarian, Northeast Ohio Medical University, Rootstown, Ohio, United States

Institution: Walsh University, Brother Edmond Drouin Library; 2890 students (Fall 2015) including undergraduate and graduate students. Private, liberal arts college located in North Canton, Ohio.

Campaign Purpose: Bring all freshmen and transfer students into the Brother Edmond Drouin Library for an orientation during a themed "Library Week" and let them explore the library and meet their Personal Librarian via a structured "InstaHunt" using Instagram.

Target Demographic: Approximately 438 freshmen and first semester transfer students.

Measure of Success: Student engagement with Instagram during library week. Before Library Week, the Walsh Library Instagram account (@walshulibrary) had about 15 followers. By the end of the week, we had approximately 70, an increase of 466%. We were able to maintain this follow-ship throughout the semester. Our Instagram account currently has 113 followers (as of October 2017).

Team: Four librarians (Instruction Librarian, Student Engagement Librarian, Public Services Librarian, and Library Director); support from library staff and General Education 100/110 facilitators and instructors.

Social Media
DOI: https://doi.org/10.1016/B978-0-08-102409-6.00006-7

6.1.1 BACKGROUND

All incoming Walsh University freshmen and transfer students are placed into a General Education (GE) 100 (First Year Institute) or GE 110 (Study Skills) class. Since the 2014–15 school year, the same group of students, incoming freshmen and transfers, were partnered with their own Personal Librarian (PL) as a part of the Walsh University Personal Librarian Program. This program connects these student to the subject specialist librarian for their major who contacts them throughout the year via emails and newsletters promoting library services, tutorials, and resources.

Before the 2016–17 school year, librarians would occasionally be invited into GE 100/110 classrooms for a typical one-shot instruction session where we would be asked to cover a considerable amount of information, including the PL Program, in an hour or less. In an effort to try something new, the librarians created Library Week as a substitute for our previous involvement with the GE classes.

The objectives of Library Week were twofold: to provide an orientation for incoming freshmen and to welcome back returning students. For the new students we sought to establish a summer reading text that all students read, identify starting points for pursuing a research topic, and connect students to their personal librarian. We offered a welcoming atmosphere for our returning students by collaborating with campus partners to provide workshops and activities.

Working with the coordinators for the First Year Institute, which oversees the GE 100/110 classes, it was decided that having the students physically come to the library would be beneficial to them in their first year of college. This group of faculty and staff also wanted the library portion of GE 100/110 to be tied to the common text, *Dead Man Walking* by Helen Prejean, C.S.J.

6.1.2 LIBRARY WEEK

Our first Library Week was held during the fifth week of Walsh's fall semester from September 26–30, 2016. We chose these dates for two reasons: it worked best with our GE instructors; and we had held informal welcome events for freshmen in previous years, but had small turnouts due to competition with other departments and campus players vying for student attention during those first two weeks of classes. The 2016 Library Week was deemed successful and another Library Week was planned for the same time frame—September 25–29, 2017.

The planning for Library Week began in Summer 2016. We chose to have an autumn theme and planned on decorating the interior of the Library with fall leaves, pumpkins, chrysanthemum flowers, and more. During the summer we had student workers decorate leaves and create signage for Library Week. One of signs read "Fall in Love with the #walshulibrary" and we encouraged InstaHunt users to use this to hashtag their images (Fig. 6.1.1).

We created much of the promotional materials ourselves using Canva and Adobe Photoshop Elements. Flyers went up in the Library and around campus with the Library Week lineup a week before the first event took place. Emails were also sent out with the flyer to announce Library Week to the campus.

The Library Week lineup included a jelly bean count contest that lasted the whole week and daily activities such as: a call number challenge; a Google power searching workshop; a collaborative program with the Career Center on finding jobs; a fun, ideal study space quiz; and more. The 2016 flyer can be seen in Fig. 6.1.2.

Figure 6.1.1 Our "Fall in Love with the #walshulibrary" sign promoted our hashtag and was hung from our second floor rail.

Figure 6.1.2 2016 Library Week flyer.

Anyone who participated in any aspect of Library Week was entered into a raffle drawing for a grand prize of a reserved study room for Finals Week. Additional prizes were donated and given away, including a Walsh University scarf and a Library Week mug filled with school supplies.

Of note, 438 freshmen or transfer students were scheduled to come to Library Week. We had 385 students come for a participation rate of 88%. A very short survey was included with the prize entry for participating in any Library Week event and 98% of students who completed the survey indicated they felt comfortable using the Library after participating.

6.1.3 THE INSTAHUNT

We chose to use Instagram over our other social media platform, Facebook. We chose Instagram because that was what our student workers said they were using and preferred. In addition, it seemed as if our Facebook account, though well established with over 250 followers, had a large alumni presence and less current undergraduates, our target group for Library Week and the InstaHunt. Over the summer the library had been doing some cosmetic upgrades including new chairs and lighting. Instagram was ideal because it let us take more photographs of the library's new upgrades. We also took into consideration that a new building on campus would be attached to the library via a walkway, and Instagram was a good choice for documenting the construction progress.

The InstaHunt was designed to be a mobile photographic scavenger hunt where the students explored the library by taking pictures on their smartphones using the Instagram app. The GE students were assigned a worksheet to complete and the InstaHunt section asked students to find:

- something confusing,
- the best study spot,
- your group with a someone that works in the library (ask who they are and what they do!), and
- the strangest book in the library.

In addition to the InstaHunt, the worksheet asked students to use a library database, create a citation, and contribute to an interactive display. Students were required to turn this worksheet into their GE instructor for class credit.

The rest of the Walsh community, those outside of the GE classes, were able to voluntarily participate in their own InstaHunt on the Thursday of Library Week. Their scavenger hunt asked for five photos since this was the only activity asked of them (vs the GE students who had other tasks) and

Figure 6.1.3 2016 InstaHunt Library card. The dates were the only thing updated for 2017.

reflected our hope that they were at least minimally familiar with the library. It asked them to find:

- the best study spot,
- something confusing,
- reference desk,
- DVD you want to watch, and
- strangest book in the library (Fig. 6.1.3).

The students spent about 15–25 minutes exploring the library and taking pictures. Anyone who participated in the InstaHunt was asked to show the images or posts to a librarian or circulation desk student worker to receive a coupon for 10 free color prints to be used at any time during the semester and their entry form for the Library Week prizes. Because library staff did not have to check or ask about each photograph, the process of giving out coupons was not too time-consuming for staff.

During the InstaHunts, librarians observed students enjoying the activity and making comments such as, "oh, I would totally study here!". The students also found some pretty strangely titled books, such as *Crying: The Natural and Cultural History of Tears* and *Bring Me a Unicorn* (not a children's book), and one audio-visual item that ended up being weeded called *Sports Sex-Ed Video.* In addition, it was also nice for the librarians and staff to be able to meet some of the students and say hello. Although we always encourage students to reach out and visit their personal librarians or stop in for one-on-one consultations, they do not always do this. Plus, the directive for the GE students to find "someone that works in the library (ask who they are and what they do!)" allowed students to meet more than just their personal librarians, such as some of our technical services staff which have offices away from the main library area.

6.1.4 WHAT WORKED

- Having the InstaHunt be a part of something larger: Framing the InstaHunt as both part of Library Week and part of the freshmen GE 100/110 orientation really encouraged participation that we would not have seen if it was a standalone event.
- Letting the students explore on their own: The students seemed to really like that we encouraged them to go through the Library on their own. Rather than just listening to someone who represented the

Library, they truly were able to immerse themselves and find all the fun spaces within our two floors.
- Letting the students work in groups: Students enjoyed working together (though they sometimes argued over what was the best study spot) and this fostered camaraderie within the GE classes. Working together in pairs or groups also helps with issues if one student does not have a working phone with them during class time.
- Encouraging the students to meet faculty and staff who work in the Library: The faculty and staff were eager to welcome the students and expose them to the friendly and helpful atmosphere of the library. Students also were able to meet their Personal Librarian during the InstaHunt.

6.1.5 WHAT DIDN'T WORK

- Some students did not want to post on their Instagram accounts: One student told a librarian that there was a "rule" of "one [photo] a day is OK" meaning she did not want to post the four images that were part of the InstaHunt. For students without Instagram accounts or for those who did not want to post on their own accounts, we suggested they direct message to the Library's Instagram account or email us.
- The preplanned hashtags: On the InstaHunt directions we suggested using the hashtags #walshulibrary and #libraryweek2016. A few students used these, but the majority did not. Some students made their own hashtags. During the marketing process for Library Week, we heavily marketed the Instagram account, but perhaps we should have marketed these hashtags as well.

6.1.6 RECOMMENDATIONS

- Make sure you already have an Instagram account ready to go before launching a project like this. You may need permission from your Marketing department before creating a new social media account and you would not want to be delayed by this step. Having a few followers in place will also let you spread the word through the app itself.
- Marketing! Whether you are doing an Instagram-based scavenger hunt as a standalone event or as part of something larger, you will definitely want to market both the program and your Instagram account.
- Have a plan in place for students who do not have Instagram or do not want to put images on their own account.

- Track the numbers: If your goal is to gain more followers, make sure you write down how many you started with so you can track your growth.
- Do a practice run: We had a student worker do the InstaHunt in the weeks leading up to Library Week so we knew approximately how long it would take the students to complete and so we could ascertain if anything in the directions was confusing and needed to be reworded.
- Have a hashtag and promote it: Even though many students did not use the hashtags we suggested, it is still a good idea to promote one. Having a hashtag will make it easier to find images if your account is not directly linked to what is being posted.
- Make sure you have the support of your entire Library staff: We are very grateful to our library staff for their assistance during Library Week. The circulation supervisor provided student workers for decorating, handing out directions for Library Week events, and making sure students who participated in the InstaHunt received their prize entry and color prints coupon.
- Have a plan in place for responding to students' posts: We responded to the posts about confusing things by clarifying what they were (see next section).

6.1.7 USING INSTAGRAM AFTER LIBRARY WEEK

There were a number of confusing things (either tagged with #confusingthings or labeled as confusing in emails or on their Instagram captions) in the library, so much so, that we decided to turn those pictures into a wall exhibit. Near the end of the semester we posted the images that had been tagged as being confusing to students and described what they were. For example, a mobile that hangs from the ceiling of the library was considered by many confusing. We provided the history of the artwork that was made by a former student (Fig. 6.1.4).

Our Instagram account has continued to grow. We also gained a considerable number of followers once we started posting weekly construction updates related to a new building, the Walsh University Global Learning Center, that is set to open on campus in April, 2018. We created the hashtag #viewfromtheredchair and we took the photographs from the same comfortable red chair overlooking the construction zone. Once construction expanded and the red chairs had to be moved, the

Figure 6.1.4 Archival boxes were one of the many #confusingthings that students took photographs of in both 2016 and 2017. Often students simply used the hashtag or labeled their image as "confusing." We replicated their images and used them to create our Confusing Things exhibit in 2016.

shooting location moved about 10 feet to the left and the hashtag changed to #viewfromtheglobe.

6.1.8 FINAL WORDS

Instagram continues to be a popular social media outlook for Generation Z undergraduate students. An Instagram-based scavenger hunt, or an InstaHunt, is a fun and imaginative way for freshmen and new students to experience and explore the library on their own in a structured, self-paced manner. In addition, having a hashtag specific to your library can encourage repeated posts even after your event.

6.2 CASE STUDY 2

Enhancing Your Instagram Following Through Interdepartmental Collaboration

Jen Park and Steve Fowler
Assistant Librarian for Access and Outreach Services, Mount Saint Mary College, Newburgh, NY, United States

Institution: Mount Saint Mary College, 2700 (2014–15) students on one campus, one library location.

Campaign Purpose: Instagram Contest: Interdepartmental effort to increase student following on Instagram accounts and boost online traffic through incentive-driven contest.

Target Demographic: Students.

Measure of Success: Increased student engagement with the page (liking, sharing, followers, commenting on posts).

Team: One librarian, support from departments across campus.

6.2.1 INTRODUCTION

Mount Saint Mary College is a liberal arts institution located in the Hudson Valley region of New York state. The college has a number of traditional undergraduate degree programs, most notably Business, Education, and Nursing. In addition to these programs, the college also offers graduate degrees in the aforementioned areas.

With a Full Time Equivalents of 2200, the student body at Mount Saint Mary College consists of traditional, nontraditional, and accelerated students. In order to best disseminate information, the Kaplan Family Library at the college recognized the need to increase engagement on social media platforms. After informally speaking with traditional students in regards to the platform used most widely among their age group, the library learned that Instagram was the most popular as it provided information quickly in a photograph format. Therefore the Library set up an Instagram (IG) account in order to provide students with a variety of information about library services, programming, and any operational changes (such as hours), which may occur.

After a number of unsuccessful attempts to gain followers, the Library was stumped as to where and how to proceed to increase the numbers. Through general conversations with the college's Writing Center, it was learned that they also had a low social media following. Curious as to whether other departments were experiencing the same issue, the two departments contacted other student support departments and found they had low numbers of Instagram followers as well. Through collaborations, brainstorming, crowdsourcing, and re-grouping, a number of departments worked together to successfully boost their IG followers.

6.2.2 THE DILEMMA

Impervious to the knowledge that other departments were struggling with gaining Instagram followers, the Library initially attempted to gain Instagram followers through one program-heavy week: MSMC Library Week. The Library heavily marketed its Instagram account through the weeklong programs and events. Even with the promotion and push of this new account, few followers were gained during that week. Not to be quelled by the low engagement, the Library continued to use the social media platform to update the few followers of upcoming programs as well as post live updates to the page during their programs. With still just 11 followers, the Library contacted the college's Marketing department.

Using IG as the platform to reach incoming, current, and recently matriculated students, Marketing assisted the Library in gaining followers by posting photos from programming events to the college's IG as well as used the Library's signature hashtag (#msmclibrary) to encourage their followers to follow the Library's page. However, it became apparent there was a disconnect between Marketing's followers and the Library's followers. In December 2016, the Library hosted the ever-popular therapy dogs event. Over the course of two hours, dogs were available for petting and hugging for stress relief before finals. While Marketing's photo and hashtags of the canines elicited close to 300 "likes" on the college's IG account, the Library's IG received only three-four likes per dog picture. It was surmised that the lack of activity on the Library's page was due to the library taking low-quality photos on a tablet and then uploaded to Instagram. Having used a professional camera, Marketing's photos were of better quality than the Library's. With Marketing tagging the Library's IG account, it was a shocking revelation that followers simply did not move on to the library's page from Marketing's page. In further conversations, the Library staff wondered if this was due to the student not being interested in the Library's photos, not finding them to be relevant to their daily life, or simply feeling that any information about the library is simply found on the Library's website. Either way, it was clear that a new initiative needed to be taken in order to gain followers. As it turned out, the Library was not the only department on campus with a lack of social media followers.

Concurrently, the Writing Center was experiencing trouble gaining followers for their social media accounts. Prior to the collaboration, the Writing Center's engagement on Facebook and Twitter had stagnated. Students who followed their Facebook and Twitter accounts rarely liked or retweeted any content the office posted. Their audience increasingly consisted of faculty and alumni, instead of the intended student audience. As a result, the Writing Center created an Instagram account. They quickly discovered that Instagram's culture among the student demographic permits far more engagement. Students do not hesitate to like, comment, tag friends, or even repost content on Instagram. This was a stark contrast to Facebook culture among students, which, in the departments' experience, has shifted to consuming content, not engaging with it.

6.2.3 PROPOSAL FOR COLLABORATION

Since they are located within the same building, the Library and the Writing Center have a strong relationship. Collaboration between these departments had occurred in the past, and the two offices continuously work together when assisting students with research and writing. When the Writing Center reached out to the Library to gauge whether the Library would be interested in collaborating on a social media initiative, the Library was happy to do so.

In addition to reaching out to the Library, the Writing Center also reached out to other departments on campus that had Instagram accounts. By the welcomed response, it was immediately apparent that social media engagement was an issue shared by departments across campus. An initial meeting date and time was set to begin brainstorming what would become a successful contest.

6.2.4 PLANNING

Although situated on a small campus, the attendees at the first meeting were unfamiliar with one another's roles. A general meet-and-greet session began the meeting among the participating departments: Library, Writing Center, Campus Ministry, and Career Center. (The representative from the Study Abroad office was unable to attend this meeting.) Discussions began as to which population the departments wanted to reach. While each population on campus is important, the participating departments wanted to focus on student engagement and interaction. Therefore, it was decided that Instagram would be the focus as it was the most widely used platform that could be accessed without needing specific technology (e.g., smartphones to access Snapchat). The ability to update Instagram from mobile devices was ideal for the departments across campus.

In addition to deciding on the population and social media platform, the first meeting's agenda also addressed the length of the contest, the incentives that would ensure contestant participation, the date of the contest, and the most budget-friendly methods of promoting the contest. With a further understanding of each person's departmental duties, the group was able to divide the work among this informally dubbed "social media contest committee."

6.2.5 SPEAK WITH TARGET DEMOGRAPHIC ABOUT CONTEST DESIGN

Wanting to showcase each department's services, the social media contest committee decided that each participant must visit each department one time throughout the week. The contestants would take a selfie of themselves at a designated area within the department (e.g., Information Desk within the library), post that selfie, tag the department within the post, and also follow the department. The end result would be that the person would need to visit the five participating departments, upload five different selfie photos, tag each photo with the department's IG handle, and follow each department. The agreed upon incentive for contestants was four Visa gift cards each in the amount of $50. Winners would be drawn at random on the Monday following the contest.

In order to stir up some excitement, the Library discussed this contest and the rules among the Student Library Advisory Group. This group, fondly referred to as the "Library Knights," meets once a month with the Outreach Librarian and Library Student Staff Coordinator in order to brainstorm ideas and provide input into library services and programming ideas. At this particular meeting, the librarian was merely relaying the contest rules and the opportunity for the students to win $50 gift cards when the students unanimously declared that they would not be participating in the contest. Stumped, the librarian asked the students what they disliked about the contest. After all, the Mount has a small campus and visiting each department to take a photo is not too daunting. The students provided insight into their social media lives; they did not want to flood their personal IG accounts with frivolous photos of departments across campus. They are selective with which photos are posted to their accounts and do not want to overload their accounts with dictionary selfies and other content that is as not meaningful to their lives (at least, on the surface) as people, food, and scenery. Accepting of this revelation, the librarian discussed what type of contest the students would participate in. The conversation centered mostly around the idea that the students enjoy having a social media presence, but do not want to be outwardly seen. Their accounts are private and they are selective. The Library representative took this information back to the Writing Center representative whom had received a similar reaction from the focus group he conducted. Thus, the second meeting of the social media contest committee centered around modifying the contest rules and procedures.

6.2.6 MARKETING

The Writing Center took on the task of creating a promotional flyer using Canva, an online graphic design tool with customizable templates. These flyers provided readers with the instructions on how to participate in the contest (see Fig. 6.2.1), and were then distributed across campus to be hung in common areas.

Additional marketing efforts included promotional Instagram posts prior to the actual event (seen in Fig. 6.2.2) and a slide on the digital signage in the Library as well as around campus. Furthermore, throughout the week, several of the participating offices directed students to the relevant department's account. For example, on Monday, the Writing Center created a post directing students to follow the Study Abroad office's Instagram account and "like" its contest photo. Most offices also mentioned the following day's department in their contest photo post so

Figure 6.2.1 Flyer promoting the contest.

students could more easily keep track of which department they needed to interact.

The designated day of the week for the library was Friday. The Library's corresponding Instagram post is depicted in Fig. 6.2.3.

6.2.7 WHAT WORKED

When the committee convened to finalize plans for the contest, they instead found themselves revamping the initial contest idea. The departments still wanted to showcase themselves as a resource for students, but needed to do so from a social media standpoint rather than the students physically visiting the departments. After some discussion, it was decided that each department would be assigned a day throughout the week to

Figure 6.2.2 Contest promotion post on Instagram.

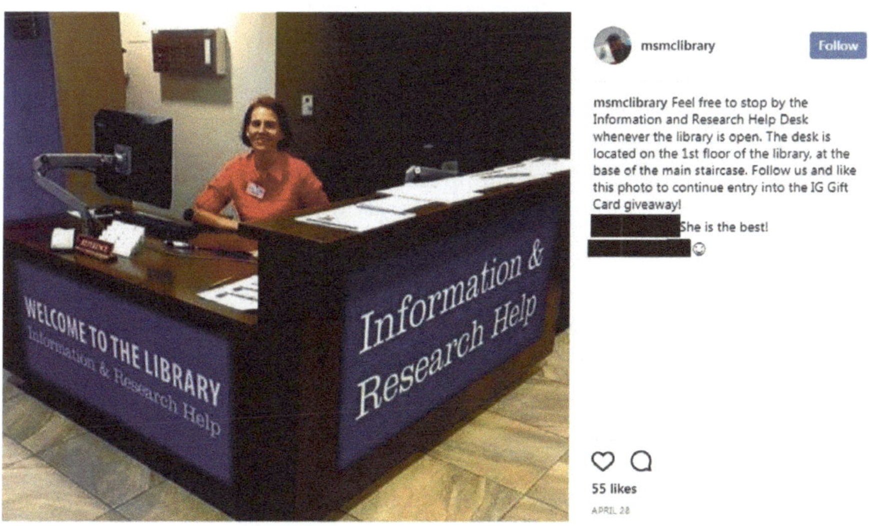

Figure 6.2.3 Library's Instagram post for contestants to "like."

promote their department. For example, if the Writing Center's day was Monday, the following would need to occur:

- Writing Center posts a photo to Instagram with a particular caption specific to that department.
- Student follows the Writing Center's Instagram page.
- Student "likes" the Writing Center's post.

After the event, following the announcement of the winners, each department suffered a slow decrease in followers, who were exclusively interested in entering the contest. This was both disappointing and encouraging because it revealed that even students who were not interested in the department's services considered the incentive, a $50 Amazon gift card, worth their time and effort to enter the contest. After about two weeks, the followings stabilized, and each department posted final gains of between 50 and 70 followers. For an event that required little work and virtually no financial cost, the return on investment was excellent.

While the contest was a success and each department increased its followers, it would be apropos to address the necessity of working with a cohesive group of colleagues. As stated earlier, this was the first time many members in the group met and worked with one another. The group was fortunate to have had hard-working members who understood the opportunity this would provide for their departments. In addition, complete transparency was a key factor in the success. Without the welcomed setting for comments and concerns, as well as the will to succeed, this contest may very well have flopped.

Another positive outcome of this contest was the positive relationships built among the departments. Professionals were able to learn each other's duties and gain an underlying respect for one another. Recognizing individuals on campus or at campus events has been a pleasant result of working on this project.

Collaboration was also crucial in generating student engagement. While it would have been easy for students to ignore one department's posts about a gift card giveaway, posts from five different departments were more likely to command students' attention.

Although the group has not formally addressed the possibility of holding another contest similar to this one, after such a positive experience it is likely the group will reconvene to persuade another class of students to follow their departments on social media.

6.2.8 WHAT DIDN'T WORK

Assuming that students would utilize their social media in a particular way for a contest would have failed us had we not spoken with the student body about this. It is important to discuss the contest with the target demographic. While the contest was successful in the sense that students began to follow the Instagram pages, we lost many followers once the contest was over.

6.2.9 RECOMMENDATIONS

Working with a variety of departments remarkably helped the marketing and promotional process of the contest. While a library would certainly be able to undertake and adapt this contest for itself, it is highly recommended that a number of departments work together in order to be more visible to the constituents in those areas. It is also important to consider your target audience. The committee decided not to include the Alumni Affairs department, as we specifically wanted to strengthen the relationship between the participating departments and the current students.

6.2.10 FINAL WORDS

After several months of planning and revision, the IG Contest left each department with 50–70 new followers. For many of these departments, such as the Writing Center, this increase doubled its Instagram following, resulting in a substantial boost in digital visibility among students. Furthermore, the collaboration provided a professional network which department representatives could access to initiate future collaborations and projects. Moving forward, a few aspects of the event could have been improved.

Since the contest underwent a lengthy transformation before the structure and rules were established, the committee needed to push the event back by one month to allow time for marketing and promotional efforts to reach the student population. While readers of this chapter now have a guide to follow if they want to replicate this event, starting the planning process early is highly recommended.

One of the ideas that became evident during focus groups is that minimal effort from students yields the greatest success. The first concept for our contest required students to post a selfie of themselves; in the final version, they could enter by tapping their touchscreens as little as two times per day. Those striving to increase student engagement online should lower their expectations of student participation. A student's social media presence is a carefully curated representation of the best parts of their lives; they are not willing to spoil the reputation they have constructed for themselves online, even if there is a worthwhile prize.

On a similar vein, rules for the contest should be as clear and simple as possible. Even in its current form, the IG contest's rules are clunky. They cannot be summarized in a single sentence, which makes communication and advertising more challenging.

The most vexing problem posed by the IG contest is its limited scale. As mentioned earlier, the simpler an event's concept, instructions, and outreach is, the more successful it will be. Building on the IG Contest with more complexity would only result in a more confusing event. Thus, to improve on this event would require stripping away excess elements; however, since the contest was created with the modest goals of boosting online traffic and increasing IG followings, eliminating either of those requirements would have greatly hindered the success of this event. In this way, the IG Gift Card Giveaway is fixed in its scope.

That being said, several more offices at the Mount Saint Mary College have opened Instagram accounts since the committee started to plan the IG contest. Expanding the event to include these departments will not complicate the rules any further and can only help increase engagement. The social media committee is satisfied with the outcome of this event and is currently considering additional improvements with advice from our student body.

6.3 CASE STUDY 3

Student Social Media Representatives and Instagram: Connecting With the Campus Community Through Library Student Workers

Laura Wilson and Heather Domenicis
Outreach Librarian and Heather Domenicis, Student Social Media Representative,
College of the Holy Cross, Worcester, MA, United States

Institution: College of the Holy Cross Libraries in Worcester, MA; an undergraduate liberal arts school with 2900 + students and three library branches.

Campaign Purpose: We hired a student worker to post to the libraries' Instagram account, in order to feature our branch Music Library, to gain followers to our page, and inspire interactions on our posts.

Target Demographic: Students.

Measure of Success: Statistics associated with our account show that we gained a significant increase in both followers to our Instagram page as well as activity on our posts since hiring a student social media representative.

Team: One librarian and one student social media representative.

6.3.1 THE SITUATION

As the outreach librarian for the College of the Holy Cross Libraries, I oversee all of our social media accounts, which include Facebook, Twitter, and Instagram. In the summer of 2015, I decided that I wanted more followers and post engagement on the libraries' Instagram account. I was struggling to consistently generate social media content that was interesting, engaging, and featured topics not just in the Main Library, where my office is located. Our Instagram account accumulated new followers at a snail's pace, and audience engagement with my posts was limited at best. I noticed that our campus Chaplain's Office had a popular Instagram account with over 1000 followers, and nearly 100 + likes or comments on each of their posts. I met with the social media administrator for this popular account, and learned that they had one student social media representative working eight hours per week to generate content for their Instagram and Snapchat accounts. I decided to copy this idea, and hired a student social media representative to give a student voice and perspective to our Instagram account. My co-author for this chapter is a student worker in the campus Music Library. She was the student social media representative during the 2016–17 academic year.

6.3.1.1 Here Are Some Things to Consider/Steps You Can Take When Hiring a Student Social Media Representative

- Create an online application for the position in Google Forms. The application I use includes a lengthy description of the position duties and requirements, as well as information regarding password security, appropriate language, and content for posts. Additionally, there are a series of questions that ask the students what social media platforms they personally use, why they want work in the position, and what ideas they have for the libraries' social media accounts.
- Advertise the student social media representative position to student workers already employed in the campus libraries. I asked my colleagues who supervise student workers to help promote this position to students they thought might be interested in this type of work. I also created flyers for my colleagues to pass out to the students, so they have written documentation about the position, as well as a link to the online application, and my contact information.
- Give the students ample time to apply for the position. I gave the students two weeks to apply for the position.

Training the student social media representative was easy and involved one face-to-face meeting at the beginning of the academic year. During this meeting, we discussed the libraries' social media policy that includes information on appropriate content and language of posts, as well as how to handle any negative feedback they find on our site. I also shared the account password, and discussed account security with the student. Initially I had been slightly worried about sharing our Instagram login information with a student worker, but my colleague from the Chaplain's Office assured me that he had not had any problems sharing login information with his student workers. To date, I have not had any problems either.

During our training meeting, we discussed the content that the social media representative would post to Instagram throughout the year. We decided that she would post to our social media sites every Monday, and focus on topics she found interesting in the Music Library for #musicmonday. In addition, she interviewed a library staff member to introduce them to the campus with basic information and a photo. She emailed me these staff interviews, and I posted them at other times during the week, when I had open space in my daily social media schedule. To make this shared social media schedule easy to follow, I generated a daily list of posts for the entire semester using Google Sheets. The balance between my and Heather's ideas provided direction for her to cover what I hoped she would advertise to her fellow students on campus, as well as generated content about topics that she believed would be interesting to our campus community, particularly her peers in the student body.

6.3.2 IN HEATHER'S WORDS: HER EXPERIENCE POSTING TO OUR LIBRARIES' INSTAGRAM

6.3.2.1 Music Mondays

Music Mondays is a hashtag we created when we realized many students at our college did not even know the Music Library existed. Many students who utilize the Music Library for study or research are music majors or enrolled in a music class. Contrary to popular belief though, our Music Library is open to all students. We hoped that Music Monday posts would advertise the Music Library as a space for any student while also showcasing the services the Music Library has to offer. To make our posts more organized and easier to find on Instagram, I always used the hashtags #musicmonday and #hclibs. Occasionally, I used other hashtags relevant to the post, that way if people searched more general hashtags on Instagram, our posts would show up too.

Typically, I try to post about something relevant to a campus event or a holiday. For example, when the Theatre department was about open *Little Shop of Horrors*, I found the score in the Music Library and posted about it in an effort to generate student interest in the show. The week of St. Patrick's Day, I posted about Celtic music housed in the Music Library. Between the number of likes and comments on these posts, it was obvious they were well-received by our followers. The most important thing is to post about something relevant or something students are interested in. The musical *Hamilton* is no longer new, but many students are still very interested in the show, and some classes at Holy Cross study it in their courses. When the Music Library acquired new *Hamilton* materials, I posted about them, and incorporated song titles in the caption.

Figure 6.3.1 Music Monday post.

I used multiple *Hamilton* hashtags because those were popular Instagram hashtags for people to search at the time (Fig. 6.3.1).

Generating posts based off previous student input is also a great idea. One time, Holy Cross' student government association posted their weekly "What's Wrong Wednesday" with a focus on the libraries. One student commented asking that the libraries make phone and laptop chargers available for checkout when students forget to bring their own. My supervisor (and co-author) replied to the comment, telling the student that the libraries already have phone chargers. That a student had no idea chargers were available at the libraries told us that we needed to advertise this service better. For Music Monday the next day, I photographed a friend using a library phone charger and used it to advertise this service on our Instagram.

6.3.2.2 Library Staff Interviews

I also conducted library staff interviews. Each interview lasted 10–30 minutes. Usually, I would ask the following questions:

- What is your position in Holy Cross Libraries?
- What are your responsibilities?
- How do you help students?
- What is your favorite thing about your job?
- What is your favorite thing about Holy Cross?

By keeping it limited to these few questions, I am able to better condense the interview into a readable Instagram caption that is short enough

Figure 6.3.2 Staff interview post.

that people want to read it but long enough to fit all the interview information I gather. I tried to keep the questions student-centered as students are our primary audience on our Instagram.

As for my advice to other student workers posting to a library Instagram account, the most important thing is making sure you are connecting to other students in a relatable way with your pictures and captions. As a Millennial, it is my observation that many Millennials care about their follower: following ratio; they want to be following the same amount of accounts (or less) than follow them. To protect the privacy of our students, we do not follow them back. This means we have to keep our students interested enough to keep following our account even though it may affect their follower: following ratio (Fig. 6.3.2).

6.3.3 ANALYZING SUCCESS

When I first hired a student social media representative in the Fall of 2015, our Instagram account had 224 followers, with an average of 5–10 likes or comments per post. Now, two years later, our account has 550 +

Figure 6.3.3 Post about the Music Library's vinyl record collection.

followers, and each post generally averages between 20 and 50 likes and comments per post. With over a 100% increase in followers and average post activity, I attribute a large amount of this success to having student-generated content on our page. Some of the student-developed posts have been our most popular, including an image of the Music Library's vinyl record collection. I was only vaguely aware of this collection, and I would not have thought to create a post about it. Nevertheless, Heather knew that this topic would be of interest to her peers, and her post received nearly seventy likes in 1 week (Fig. 6.3.3).

6.3.4 WHAT WORKED

- The in-person meeting at the beginning of the semester sets the stage for the entire year. This meeting allows the student social media representative and me to discuss ideas and goals for the social media account.
- The cloud-based schedule hosted in Google Drive allows us to easily update information in real-time, therefore clearing up any confusion about what Heather should work on each week, whether it is something I want her to promote, or something she creates entirely on her own.

- Giving the student social media representative freedom to post about topics she is interested in, not just what I want her to promote.

6.3.5 WHAT DIDN'T WORK

- Assuming organization and scheduling will just happen "organically." I had a student social media representative the year before. I did not create a schedule of posts for this student, and therefore, I never knew when he was going to post. Due to this lack of coordination, we often posted on the same day, within minutes of each other. This left me feeling like I had to scramble to create additional content.
- Not providing any topic suggestions to the student social media representative. Without a post schedule, the first student social media representative was often stumped for ideas. Instead of focusing on a single library, I told him that he could post anything at all about any of our campus libraries. The student ended up doing weekly interviews of other students studying in our main library, inspired by the popular "Humans of New York" photoblog. This created very interesting content that our followers did engage with, but these posts did not promote the libraries' services or collections.
- Assuming all students are interested in social media work. I have struggled to hire a social media representative from our branch Science Library. Student workers from that library have stated for the past two years that they do not have enough time to commit to the position, despite the fact that they would only need to work one hour per week to create one or two posts. I have had success recruiting a student social media representative from our Archives department thanks to the head archivist specifically recommending the position to one student they thought would be good for the position. I may try this strategy for the Science Library in the future.

6.3.6 RECOMMENDATIONS

The idea for student social media representatives was inspired by another campus office's popular Instagram account. We suggest that you follow as many campus departments, offices, sports teams, and club accounts as you can find. Monitor what they are doing with their accounts, and engage with the content they post. Note what works and what does not work for their accounts regarding content, language, style, etc. Keep in contact with the account administrators to share ideas, and possible collaborations. You never know when the opportunity to promote each other's resources or collaborate on a campaign may arise.

Give your student social media representative a loose schedule of posts to market the library and its services. Be sure to allow enough room in the schedule for the student to generate their own ideas. The content that is fully generated by your student social media representative may prove to be the most popular content on your site.

6.3.7 FINAL WORDS

By hiring a student social media representative, our followers and interactions on Instagram have increased by at least 100% in two years. Through the student-generated content on Instagram, the student body can relate to what their peers post on our site, and the librarians can learn what library topics interest the students on campus.

6.4 CASE STUDY 4

Are We Failing at Instagram?

Matthew Blaine and Jacalyn Kremer
Fairfield University, Fairfield, CT, United States

Institution: DiMenna-Nyselius Library, Fairfield University; 5137 students (2016–17).

Campaign Purpose: Instagram Assessment Study to determine effectiveness.

Target Demographic: Students.

Measure of Success: Increased engagement by undergraduates.

Team: One librarian, one social media coordinator, support from a library student worker.

6.4.1 INTRODUCTION

At the DiMenna-Nyselius Library at Fairfield University, Fairfield, CT, we maintain three social media accounts: Facebook, Twitter, and Instagram. Understanding who our followers are on the three accounts is key to generating targeted, engaging content for each platform. Over the past two years, approximately 60% of all our new followers chose to follow our Instagram account, 20% chose Facebook, and the remaining 20% chose Twitter. This large increase in Instagram followers compared to the other social media platforms is not surprising when you look at our student population. At Fairfield, our undergraduates are traditional college age students in the age range of 18–22 years old and comprise 80% of our total student population (Fairfield University, 2016). In addition, our undergraduate population is 61% female and 39% male (Fairfield University, 2016). This aligns with Instagram's demographics where 59% of Instagram users are ages 18–29 and the majority are women (PEW Research Center, 2017).

Since Fairfield University turns over its undergraduate population every four years, it is key we pay special attention to the social media platforms that are most popular with incoming classes. Although our three social media accounts have approximately an equal number of followers, the vast majority of the library's social media followers who are current students follow the library's Instagram account. This drove us to position our Instagram channel as the main channel for reaching current students and relegated Facebook and, to a lesser extent, Twitter into legacy channels for alumni, as well as outlets for maintaining faculty and staff connections. Consequently, we allocate more staff time to Instagram in order to create frequent and original photo and video postings targeted to our current students.

Our increased focus on Instagram led us to prioritize the evaluation of our Instagram postings and videos to determine what we are and, more importantly, what we are not doing well. How do we judge when we are successful or when we fail? Certainly, the increase in our number of followers is one indication of success. In July 2014 we had 356 Instagram followers, increasing 223% to 1149 as of July 2017. Consequently, based on the number of followers, we were achieving some success, especially since Instagram users see every post from the accounts they follow. One question is, though, are they just scrolling past our content without looking at it? We wondered if we could go beyond the number of followers and learn more about how our students are engaging with the content.

A review of our DiMenna-Nyselius social media policy shows our goals for our social media accounts go beyond the number of users. Our policy states "... our goals are to create awareness and to invite conversation on library and higher education matters. Maintenance of a social media account requires generating interesting, engaging, and useful content relevant to the library, posting this content regularly, and responding to questions and/or comments" (DiMenna-Nyselius Library, 2014). We wondered if these stated goals are quantifiable and assessable. Is it even possible to assess content as "interesting," "engaging," or "useful"?

6.4.2 ASSESSMENT STUDY

In the summer and fall of 2017, we carried out an assessment study of our Instagram account focusing on the concept of engagement in order to determine what we are doing well and where we could improve. We quantified "engagement" as follows:

Images: Likes + Comments
Videos: Likes + Comments + Views
Stories: Views only

We began by looking at the 140 image and video posts that we had created for the two-year period between July 2015 and July 2017. In addition, we analyzed 10 stories from the one-month period of October 2017. Due to the limited availability of analytics tools for Instagram at the time, we manually entered information pertaining to the posts' content, date/time of posting, number of likes, and number of comments into an Excel spreadsheet. For video posts, we also recorded the number of views the post received. For Stories, we only looked at views since that is the only data that Instagram records. It was time consuming to gather engagement data manually, so you can understand our relief when we discovered we could streamline the data-gathering process by changing our account to an Instagram Business account. In addition to providing all the engagement data we needed, Instagram Business also provides metrics on the average age, gender, and location of your followers, and time and day of week when they are most active. It is free to switch to Instagram Business and easy to comprehend with built in explanations of what the data means.

We analyzed the data to determine the engagement for each post. Since the number of followers of the Instagram account was not static but rather was increasing during the study's time period, we knew it was important to look at the engagement number in relationship to the number of users. For example, if two posts received the same amount of engagement but the total number of followers was less at the time of the first post, then the first post received higher engagement per number of followers than the other post. To take into account the changing number of followers over the time of the study, we divided the engagement number by the total number of users at the start of each academic year in order to weigh the engagement by the number of followers. We picked the start of the academic year since most of our increase in followers occurred at the first-year students' orientation at the beginning of the academic year. We then classified each post by category to see what categories had better engagement than other categories and, perhaps even more importantly, what categories had the least engagement. We note here it was possible for a single post to be classified under multiple categories.

We developed the following categories:

1. Building (interior and exterior),
2. campus life, such as orientation events,
3. collections,
4. events in society,
5. animals, includes our much loved therapy dogs at finals,
6. hours,
7. library events,
8. library services,
9. throwback/nostalgia, and
10. feel-good/humor.

We created these categories to encapsulate all of the content we posted on Instagram while making the categories as general as possible. Some of the categories are self-explanatory, like *building* that contains images of our library building, *hours* that includes posts about changes to our operating hours, or *collections* that contain posts highlighting library material. Some might not be immediately obvious though. *Throwback/nostalgia* relates primarily to content that comes from our Archives and Special Collections, which was featured heavily last year as Fairfield celebrated its 75th anniversary. *Events in society* covers national holidays, trending topics, or national news stories, while *campus life* describes content related to anything Fairfield. *Feel-good/humor* describes content developed with the primary function of getting our followers to smile, regardless of whether or not the content was meant to be informative. Now that we have established the categories, let us bring them to life with data.

As you can see from Fig. 6.4.1, the highest number of Instagram posts fell into the events in society, collections, and campus life categories. Our least used categories of posts are animals, hours, and throwback/nostalgia.

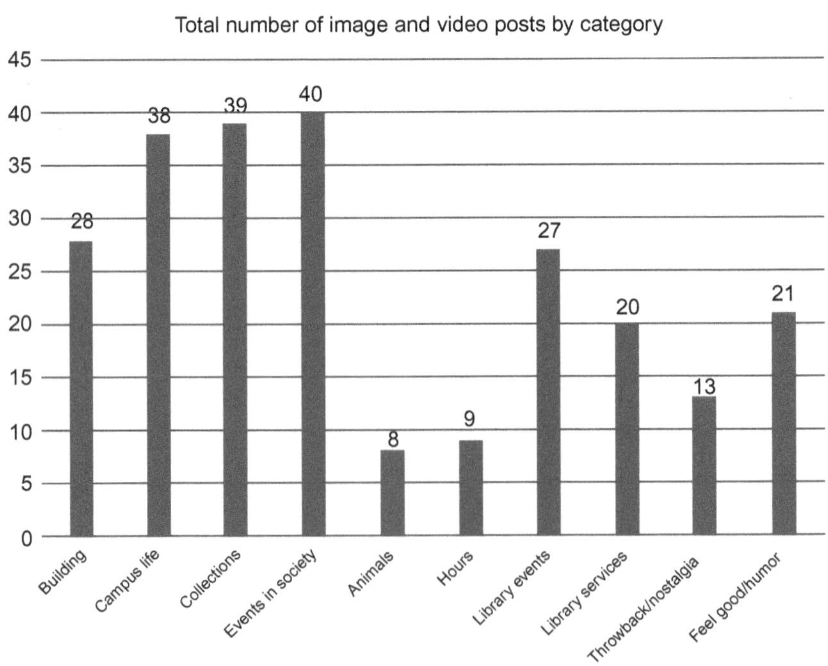

Figure 6.4.1 Total number of image and video posts by category.

6.4.2.1 Image Assessment

We analyzed the image posts independently from the videos and stories posts. We ranked the image posts by weighted engagement and then looked critically at the posts in the top 20% and also the bottom 20% of engagement. In other words, we isolated the 24 posts with the most engagement and 24 posts with the least engagement. We further examined these top and bottom posts by looking at what percentage of posts in a category fell into these 24 top or 24 bottom posts. See Figs. 6.4.2 and 6.4.3. For example, six animal posts were in the top 24 posts. In total, there were only eight posts

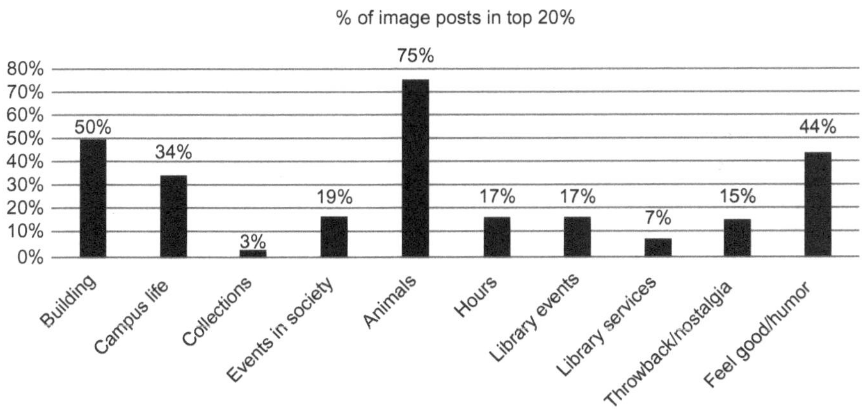

Figure 6.4.2 Percent of posts in top 20.

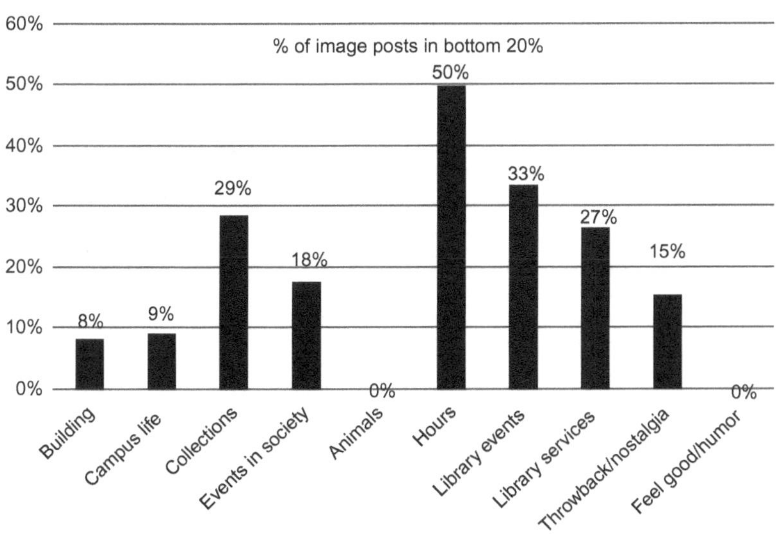

Figure 6.4.3 Percent of posts in bottom 20.

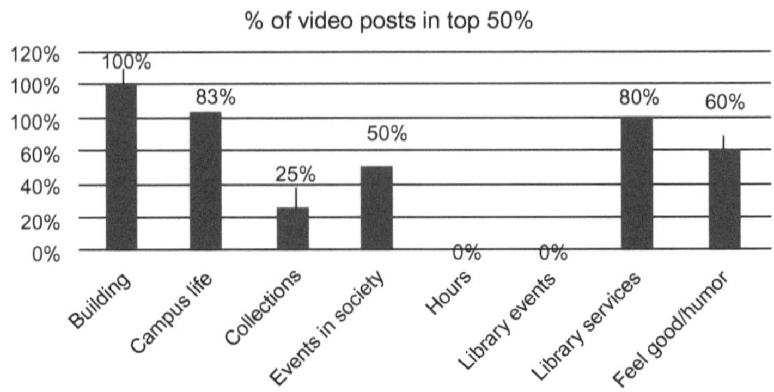

Figure 6.4.4 Percent of videos in top 50.

in the animal category so 75% (6/8) of the animal posts were in the top 24 engaged posts. What can we say? People love animals. Fig. 6.4.2 also shows strong engagement on building pictures as well as those posts in our feel-good/humor category. We see especially low engagement in the collections category where only 3% of the posts made it into the top engaged posts.

An examination of Fig. 6.4.3 shows the image posts associated with the categories of hours, library events, and collections received the lowest engagement.

6.4.2.2 Video Assessment

There were significantly fewer video postings than images during the study's time period. Since the total number was small (22 videos), we decided to examine the top 50% based on weighted engagement versus the bottom 50%. Fig. 6.4.4 shows the percentage of posts in a category that fell into the top 50% of engagement. Like our image posts, we see high engagement with videos in the building category. The next most engaged categories, campus life and library services, are surprisingly different from what we saw when we examined our top engaged categories for images. We did not have any videos that fell into the categories of animals or throwback.

A review of Fig. 6.4.5 shows the category with the least engagement is the same for videos as with images with the categories of hours, library events, and collections getting the lowest engagement.

6.4.2.3 Stories Assessment

Instagram Stories get deleted after 24 hours. We had only 10 stories to analyze because that is how many we were smart enough to save.

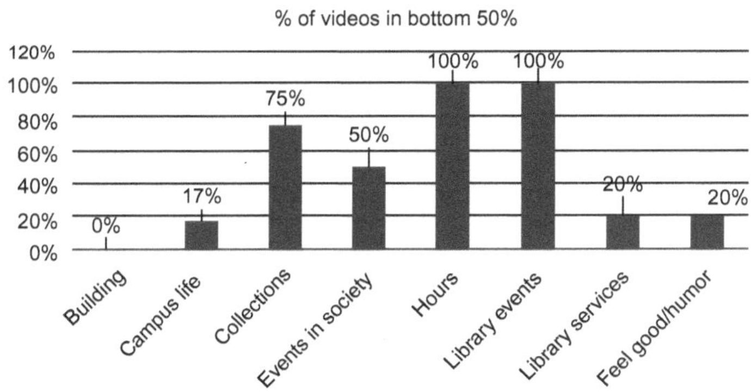

Figure 6.4.5 Percent of videos in bottom 50.

Therefore, our assessment data is limited, but our findings here align with our overall findings. Using the same categories that we used for our image and video assessment, we found that the stories fell into the following categories: library events five times, campus life four times, library services three times, collections two times, events in society two times, and feel-good/humor one time. We did not have any stories that fell into the categories of building, animals, hours, or throwback. Some stories fell into multiple categories. Since users cannot actively 'like' or comment on Stories, we could only look at views to quantify engagement. In general, the engagement numbers were on par with our video posts in that they averaged an engagement rate of 26% (the average engagement rate for video posts was 27% when just considering views). The difference in engagement numbers between the most engaging stories post and the least engaging stories post was much smaller than the difference between the highest and lowest image posts or video posts. This suggests Stories might have a steady engagement rate regardless of category.

6.4.3 DISCUSSION

Let us start the discussion of our study by addressing the question posed in the title of this chapter: *Are We Failing at Instagram*? The concept of whether or not we are *failing* at a social media platform can seem marginally abstract; however, it is indeed an important question to answer because we have to justify the expenditure of valuable, limited staff time. If these endeavors are not productive, there is no point doing them.

In looking at the charts depicting the top and bottom 20% of image posts, we see some noticeable trends in what is and what is not popular among our followers. Engagement is disappointing when we post content in the collections category (new additions, displays of materials), library services (research appointments, research prizes, or reference desk assistance), and hours (changes for holidays, vacations, etc.). Posts in the library events category, including finals events, also often fell into our bottom 20%. We quickly noticed these categories all contain information-heavy content that we feel duty-bound to share and promote to our followers. We observed similar results in examining the top and bottom 50% of video posts, in that posts related to our hours, library events, and collections had low engagement. This led us to ask ourselves the unsettling question: how do we respond to the evidence that our students are not engaging with our posts centered on the academic library's core functions?

It is discouraging to see our followers do not care enough about our collections, events, services, and hours to engage with it, especially when we had been following the best practices in literature that encourage us to share this type of content (Booker & Bandyopadhyay, 2013; Zohoorian-Fooladi & Abrizah, 2014). The academic library brand is built on excellent collections, research support services, and *library as place.* Our failing efforts on Instagram in the categories of collections, library services, and hours are, therefore, particularly disheartening. This leads us to wonder whether or not our presence on Instagram is valuable and worth maintaining.

Should we use social media to reach our students in the areas we care most about such as our excellent collections and valuable services, or should we reconsider the type of content we post in order to engage more with them? The majority of today's first-year college students were born in 1999 or 2000, so they were approximately five years old when Facebook was released in 2004 and 11 years old when Instagram came out in 2010. Their lives, specifically how they interact with each other and with information, have been profoundly influenced by these social media platforms and therefore, if we want to engage with our students, it makes perfect, logical sense to connect with them on these platforms. It is imperative though that we re-evaluate the content of our postings.

6.4.4 HOW CAN WE IMPROVE?

If we are, indeed, failing at Instagram by posting unengaging content, how can we correct this and use this communication tool effectively? To begin to answer this question, let us look at our successful posts, including both images and videos. It comes as no surprise to us that our most popular posts are the ones in the animals category that feature the therapy dogs we have visit during finals. That is common social media knowledge: dog and animal pictures are always going to be successful on Instagram (the common trope of the internet is that it is just a place for people to distract themselves with cat pictures). Beyond that category, however, we see that pictures of the building are popular, as are campus life related posts (these include pictures of students, campus-centric events, and anytime we have a visit from the school mascot). This makes sense, too, as it confirms to us that our student followers like seeing things related to their lives at Fairfield. Moreover, those posts that fell into the categories of building, campus life, and animals were always successful regardless of the format (images, videos, or stories).

What about the content that fell into the poorly performing categories though? After all, the main reason that we initially signed up for Instagram was to share information on our collections, services, events, and hours, and we dedicate a significant amount of time and energy (and therefore money) to these efforts. Through our analysis, we now recognize that certain content works better as an Instagram image or video or story, so choosing the right format is important.

6.4.4.1 When to Choose Videos

On video posts, Instagram displays the number of times the post was viewed rather than how many times the post was liked. Image posts display the number of likes. In order to have an Instagram page that outwardly displays a consistently high engagement rate, we decided to post content related to our poorly performing categories as videos. These videos were getting over 100 views and that looked significantly better than only a handful of likes. Although this might seem like a superficial experiment to make our page look more 'popular,' it did have measurable benefits in that more of the video posts related to library services were ranked in the top 50% and fewer were in the bottom 50%, unlike our image posts in that category, which were consistently in the bottom percentiles.

We recognize the higher engagement rate to be a reflection on how video posts can be more eye-catching than just a still image. For example, at the beginning of every fall semester, new students need to know where the IT office is in order to register their computers. Last year, instead of doing what we have done in the past and just post a photo of the door to the office, we made a time-lapse video of the route from outside the library building to where the IT office is located in the building. This video was among our most popular videos with over 350 views.

6.4.4.2 When to Choose Stories

The engagement that we were able to see on our stories is fairly on par with our permanent video posts, so we consider Stories to be another useful tool in pushing out promotional content or other material that might fall into one of the lesser engaging categories of posts (hours, library events, collections, library services). Since stories disappear after 24 hours, it is great for information that quickly loses its relevancy, like posts about operating hour changes due to inclement weather, giveaways, events, etc. Stories, in general, is a way for someone to share what they are doing in the moment while the main, permanent feed is a place to share what has already happened or something that is not necessarily tied to a moment in time.

6.4.4.3 When to Choose Images

Even with the new, flashier ways to use Instagram, there are still plenty of opportunities to use it as it was originally designed as a platform to post still images. Essentially, anything that fell into the most popular or most well-engaged-with categories is what you should still be posting as static images. Content that can be visibly appealing like photos of the building or the campus on a beautiful day should always be posted as static images. Photos of therapy dogs and animals and popular campus-related events like orientation are great candidates for image posts. These categories were among our most engaged with perhaps because they are already esthetically appealing and are not too heavy-handed with marketing and promotions.

Posts we categorized as having a feel-good/humor factor were often well received. These posts include humorous and fun topics, like when we posted about the summer fad of 2016, *Pokémon Go*. These posts did not always promote anything library related, but instead added to the overall campus conversation that happens daily on Instagram. This high engagement tells us a lot about the voice and tone that we should use on Instagram. This, we posit, is where we should be focusing more of our attention and why it is in fact important to be on Instagram. The objective might not be to use Instagram as a marketing tool for traditional library offerings, but rather use it as a communication tool to further establish our presence as part of the ongoing conversations on campus.

6.4.4.4 Other Ways to Improve Engagement

When thinking through what works, one of our best practices centers on our relationship with our university's social media coordinator. This relationship manifests itself in several different ways depending on the platform. On Twitter and Facebook, the university account will share content that we provide them or will directly retweet or repost our original posts. Typically, we will ask them to share information about our events and resources. On Instagram, it works a little differently because there is not a built-in reposting tool, so sharing other accounts' posts is not as easy. Instead, we will "takeover" the university's Instagram account for an event or other happening that we are hosting, meaning that the manager of the university account will give us a password to the account and we will post directly to their followers. In doing so, we are able to reach a much larger audience of their 10,000 followers, which dwarfs our respectable 1000+ following. This "takeover" is actually a fairly common practice for businesses on Instagram, so users are accustomed to it.

The results are measurable, as seen by looking at when we took over the university's Instagram account during first years' orientation this past summer. After a long day of orientation activities, the new students finish their day registering for classes at the library. After they finish, they exit the building full of relief and excitement, both of which are further agitated by a crowd of orientation leaders cheering them on and congratulating them on a successful orientation. The library staff is there as well to join in congratulating the students and to pass out some freebies such as buttons, travel mugs, and other swag. Fig. 6.4.6 shows two screenshots of similar posts that we shared on our own Instagram account (on the left) and on the university's Instagram account (on the right). The content of the posts was nearly identical, but we were able to reach roughly 10 times the amount of people when we used the university's account. The significance of this cannot be understated. In terms of maximizing our reach, this is a sure-fire way to go and we will undoubtedly utilize this outlet again in the future.

Figure 6.4.6 Instagram story on our account versus the university's account.

6.4.5 WHAT WORKED

- Animals and feel-good/humor-type posts, as well as images and video posts that related back to the university, are the most engaging.
- Posts associated with our university brand were popular, including those of easily recognized buildings, the mascot, and pictures of students.
- Creating videos and using Stories made the more mundane posts more visually appealing.
- Partnering with the university's social media accounts led to increased reach.

6.4.6 WHAT DIDN'T WORK

- Following what were some of the so-called best practices on Instagram by libraries was not productive, in that image and video posts related to hours, events, and collections received the least amount of measurable engagement.

- Image posts related to library services got little engagement.
- Video posts related to library events got less engagement than image posts about library events.
- As an outreach tool, using the Library's Instagram account alone does not get the message out.

6.4.7 RECOMMENDATIONS

- Switch your Instagram account to an Instagram Business account in order to effectively gather engagement data. Update an Excel doc or Google Sheet regularly (month over month, week over week, etc.) with statistics on your account, drawing from Instagram Business analytics.
- Post less-engaging content (hours, collections, and services-type posts) as videos or stories rather than as static images.
- Super important posts might best be done by the main college/ university account that has more followers. Take over your college/ university's Instagram account to reach more people.
- Post more feel-good content and animal photos and videos when you can.
- Use images and videos that align with and display your college/ university brand.
- Consider the mix of your content. Is it all about hours, services, and collections? Broaden your content to include animals that you might have around the building (our campus is full of wild turkeys and deer), feel-good/humorous topical posts, and beautiful campus life pictures including your library building.

6.4.8 FINAL WORDS

There is an inherent danger in using Instagram, in that we might seem like an uninvited guest to a party that nobody wants to talk to or worse, someone who barges in and ruins a fun conversation. The data supports this, as it shows that when we post about something relatable or fun/ light-hearted, the engagement is usually high. In contrast, when we post something that we are trying to promote or that is related to the core mission of the academic library, the engagement is disappointing. It is a harsh truth, but an important observation and one that we feel is necessary to understand how to be successful at using Instagram. Based on our data, if we continue to post content that falls into those high engagement categories and keep a tone that is friendly and fits within the campus conversation, then we will see better engagement and consider our efforts successful. Indeed, we are still using Instagram as a marketing and outreach tool, but instead of directly marketing our collections and services, we are marketing our presence as an integral part of campus life. This is akin to the approach we see in corporate marketing. Companies promote their brand and the lifestyle that they are selling through their products, rather than the actual products themselves. We can think like this too and consider what our "library brand" is and what lifestyle we are trying to communicate to our students.

As an academic library, we claim our identity as the intellectual heart of the university and we believe this applies to all academic libraries. Students see the library as the place they go to anchor themselves in order to focus and study, and we promote those lifestyle behaviors by posting visual reminders of how, if students come here, they will find a beautiful, calming space where they can work to achieve academic success. Everything we do, including our collections, services, and events, is built to support that lifestyle. By choosing more engaging content and adjusting the ways that we present content, like using more visually appealing videos or stories, we are promoting the totality of the library experience.

REFERENCES

Booker, L., & Bandyopadhyay, S. (2013). How academic libraries can leverage social networking to popularize their services: An empirical study. *Journal of the Indiana Academy of the Social Sciences*, *16*(2), 129–146.

DiMenna-Nyselius Library. (2014). Social media policy. Available from https://www.fairfield.edu/library/about/policies/socialmediapolicy/

Fairfield University. (2016). Fall enrollment quick facts. Available from https://www.fairfield.edu/about-fairfield/leadership-offices/departments/institutional-research/fall-enrollment/

PEW Research Center. (2017). Social media fact sheet. Available from http://www.pewinternet.org/fact-sheet/social-media/

Zohoorian-Fooladi, N., & Abrizah, A. (2014). Academic librarians and their social media presence. *Information Development*, *30*(2), 159–171. Available from https://doi.org/10.1177/0266666913481689.

CHAPTER 7
Twitter

7.1 CASE STUDY 1

Tweeting to Success: Managing an Academic Library's Twitter Campaign to Enhance User Engagement

Emy N. Decker
Georgia Institute of Technology Library, Atlanta, GA, United States

Institution: Atlanta University Center, Robert W. Woodruff Library (serves under 10,000 students at Clark-Atlanta University, Morehouse College, Interdenominational Theological Center, and Spelman College as a consortium library for these four Historically Black Colleges and Universities).

Campaign Purpose: Engage library student user groups via Twitter.

Target Demographic: Students.

Measure of Success: Increase in students participating in International Games Day 2015 compared to prior years.

Team: One tweeting librarian, and an additional five committee members on the Social Media Working Group.

7.1.1 BACKGROUND

Today's students, as contemporary users of the academic library, by and large engage with their surroundings digitally via social media. Recognizing that, the Atlanta University Center, Robert W. Woodruff Library (AUC Library) began social media campaigns on Facebook and Twitter in 2012, and later added an Instagram presence in 2015. In order to distribute the workload, a separate librarian managed each of the social

Social Media
DOI: https://doi.org/10.1016/B978-0-08-102409-6.00007-9

media campaigns, but a Social Media Working Group was established to keep the messaging coherent and cohesive for the library users. This case study provides an examination of the AUC's use of Twitter as a tool to promote the library and to get its services on the radar of the 21st century student users. The specific example of using Twitter to promote the ALA-sponsored International Games Day serves as the lens through which increased user engagement might be better understood.

7.1.2 INTERNATIONAL GAMES DAY

On November 23, 2015, our library hosted an ALA-sponsored International Games Day. ALA's National Gaming Day, first celebrated in 2008, focuses on the social and recreational side of gaming. Gaming at the library encourages patrons of all ages to interact with diverse peers, share their expertise, and develop new strategies for gaming and learning. At the library, patrons can socialize with their friends and play board and video games while surrounded by books, librarians, and a real world of knowledge. We had hosted this event for several years prior to 2015, but this year represented the first time that social media was employed to help promote the event. Previous years' Games Days had suffered from low attendance. Students who happened to be in the library were delighted to partake in the Games Day activities—everything from video games to board games, and other activities—but it seemed apparent that the message about Games Day had not really reached as many students as library staff would have hoped. Prior to 2015, library staff handed out small flyers advertising Games Day to students walking along the common quad from their campus toward the library. Once the Twitter account had been established, we used it to promote International Games Day 2015.

7.1.3 HOW TWITTER PROMOTED INTERNATIONAL GAMES DAY

After the back to school welcome messages had died down toward the beginning of September, the social media working group tweeted informational messages about library services, programs, and events. These tweets tended to be short in duration (meaning they were only tweeted once or twice) and were topical to the event. In these instances, Twitter was used as a messaging system. Tweets such as "Reserve a Study Room" with a link to the scheduling software alerted students to the availability of study spaces. Other messages such as "Visit the notebooks of Tupac Amaru Shakur in the Archives" also communicated to students the existence of rich resources in the library. When it came to Games Day, the Social Media Working Group decided to try an actual Twitter campaign to build awareness of the events.

While there was not an official tweeting schedule established by the Working Group, beginning in October, about six weeks prior to Games Day, the E-Learning Technologies Librarian tweeted the first mentions of the event for the year. A link to ALA's website included more detail, but the focus of each tweet was to share the date, time, location, and event itself. As the day drew nearer, we posted "catchier" more targeted tweets in order to capture student attention. Provocative, gaming-like tweets that inspired fun and friendly competition replaced plain, informational only tweets that only communicated event details.

7.1.3.1 Examples of Games Day Twitter Campaign tweets by Month

October

- International Games Day 11/23/15;
- Join us at the Library for IGD 11/23/15 @2 pm.

November

- Are you the next Michael Jackson? Just Dance IGD;
- Studying Economics? Try your hand at Monopoly 11/23/15;
- Can you beat your roommate at Jenga? Find out 11/23/15.

These tweets caught students' attention as evidenced by the fact that this was the first time any library tweets had been retweeted! Students seemed to enjoy the fun nature of these Tweets and we discovered, through their retweeting, that they were also inspired to strike up friendly competition with their friends, roommates, and classmates as Games Day approached. Following the retweets and the hashtags help us gather a sense of the efficacy of the Twitter campaign. The primary goal of using Twitter was to increase attendance but the secondary goal certainly included engaging students and causing them to think of the library as a place of recreation and respite, at least for this one day out of the school year.

7.1.4 USING TWITTER ON INTERNATIONAL GAMES DAY

The Social Media Working Group strategized the campaign leading up to International Games Day. However, live tweeting during the event further promoted the day's festivities. During the event, real-time updates about the game tournaments comprised the bulk of the tweets. These tweets functioned to attract further attention to the activities. For example, when the board games area was running a bit slow, tweets in real time brought some attention and pep to the event. Tweeting in real time also provided an opportunity to contrast the various games offerings. Tweets about the availability of snacks helped suggest an alternative activity to playing video games and announcing a Scrabble tournament allowed students an opportunity to use their minds in a fun, gaming atmosphere.

Perhaps not too surprisingly, most of the tweets that were retweeted during the event were those that mentioned the high scores and student's first names (with their permission—we had a short form for them to sign granting us permission to post their names) who achieved these scores. These tweets worked to incite a friendly competition between the Games Day attendees and allowed for participants to track high scores. Via Twitter, these game results were displayed in a fashion that was reminiscent of a score board—and the library's twitter site became the impromptu place to find this information. It also became a way to track high scores and provided students and the library staff score keepers a unified method for keeping tabs on the individuals who had won as well as the teams who were in the lead at any given moment.

7.1.4.1 Examples of "Day of" Games Day Twitter Campaign tweets

- "Devon outdanced us all in DDR" (Dance Dance Revolution)
- "Relax after dancing, Scrabble with us"
- "Beat team blue at Dominos"
- "Refuel your game with snacks by the café"

In order to keep the Twitter "conversation" active, students who engaged via Twitter during Games Day were rewarded with a mention or even an extra treat or soda in the snack room. Most of all, students who engaged in Games Day via Twitter could easily become "helpers" for getting students engaged in the festivities in subsequent years by sharing about the fun they had with their peers and the incoming freshman class.

We hoped that they would also be important allies to help spread the word about International Games Day in coming years.

7.1.5 ASSESSMENT

The Social Media Working Group understood the need to assess the success of the various social media platforms. Where "Likes" on Facebook can provide some clues and indicators about the library's Facebook page success, it can be more difficult to assess Twitter in a meaningful fashion. Given this reality, the Social Media Working Group designed a brief survey to give out to students who were participating in International Games Day. The one page survey probed student knowledge about the current library social media campaigns and delved a bit deeper to ascertain their interest in engaging with their library via Twitter.

7.1.5.1 Questions Asked on the Library's Social Media Survey

- Would you rather engage with your academic library on Facebook, Twitter, Instagram, or another platform?
- Would you consider engaging with your Library on all of the social media platforms that you use or only one or two?
- How often would you want to receive updates about your library on Facebook?
- What types of topics would you like to learn about via your library's social media presence?
- What would make you block the library on your social media feeds?
- What types of tweets from the Library would you be likely to retweet?
- Would you engage in a Twitter conversation with your academic library?
- How often would you engage your Library via Twitter?

The results of the survey indicated that the largest obstacle to student engagement via Twitter was likely their lack of knowledge that the library even had a Twitter site. Many survey respondents indicated their interest in engaging with the library about myriad topics provided that the library did not over use social media (as it would "get old" or "be annoying" eventually). It is certainly a fine line to walk. On the one hand, it is critical to use social media in the way that it was designed to interact with and engage others in the digital environment. However, some students reported that they consider their academic library as being somewhat like engaging a parent or older relative online, it can be a little "awkward" and "forced" according to qualitative data students provided. If the library uses Twitter just as a mode of communicating information, it loses its power as a mode of communicating in the digital sphere. On the other hand, if Twitter is overused or used in a way that seems too much like the library is trying to be the "buddy" of the students, they will become turned off and will begin to disengage.

7.1.5.2 Recommendations for an Academic Library Twitter Campaign

- Utilize Twitter to actively engage library users in the digital sphere.
- Keep the interest and "momentum" of Twitter up by responding directly to student tweets.
- Using the platform to communicate information is acceptable, but should be kept minimal in favor of students engaging as opposed to passively reading information about their library.
- Where appropriate, and with their permission, use student names to connect more actively with Twitter.
- Use a library event (such as International Games Day) to provoke interest in the library's Twitter site.
- Periodically, set up questions or conversations to pique interest in the library's Twitter site. By following certain events (such as Black History Month, the impending arrival of an author, etc.), students may be more likely to engage online.
- Allow students to lead Twitter conversations and allow the library to learn about student interests and needs via what they say online.

7.1.6 SUCCESSES

The main reason the AUC Library started a Twitter account was to ensure that the library had a way to engage students in the digital environment. Secondarily, it was to serve as a way to try to heighten awareness of the library's resources, programs, and services. The results of our social media survey indicated that most students would be willing to engage with the library via social media.

The AUC Library Twitter campaign worked well, overall, for International Games Day. Twitter, when used for specific events, tends to provide students with a way to communicate online and in real time, which then works to enhance student engagement. Part of the success of the Games Day Tweeting correlated to the work the Social Media Working Group ahead of the event to ensure a coherent and cohesive social media campaign. By strategizing to build a Twitter campaign, the library was able to gain more student interest in the library's Twitter account.

Following the International Games Day, the AUC archives had a series of guest scholar talks and used Twitter to tweet pictures and to quote the speakers. During the talks, the number of Twitter followers and retweets increased. As a result of the continued success, The Social Media Working Group developed a policy to allow for the Twitter account login and password to be shared with library staff. This allowed those who were hosting an event to make use of Twitter in order to engage library users in the online environment.

The 2015 International Games Day event enjoyed more student participation as determined by gate count numbers, but what precise role the use of Twitter may or may not have had is difficult to describe with any degree of certainty.

7.1.7 WHAT WORKED

- Using a committee to target communications via social media.
- Using Twitter to heighten excitement about events (in this case Games Day).
- Setting up a virtual forum wherein students could engage each other about the event in real time online.

7.1.8 FAILURES

Early on in the AUC Library's Twitter use, the site was used primarily to communicate information. As such, it functioned as a message board, but retweets were very rare and student tweets (if there ever were any) were largely ignored. Twitter was not being used as a social media platform, but rather as a one-way online announcement board. It was difficult to cultivate followers in the early days because Twitter was not being used in the way that it was intended. Once the committee started utilizing it to engage students more actively, it resulted in more followers and retweets. The AUC library discovered that using social media as it is intended—to have online conversations—is a lot more interesting and productive toward the goal of engaging library users than trying to use it as an online bulletin board.

7.1.9 WHAT DIDN'T WORK

- "Boring" information-only mass-messaging tweets.

7.1.10 FINAL THOUGHTS

An academic library using Twitter to promote an event might benefit from developing a specific and targeted campaign. Sometimes a committee is a viable option for managing a Twitter campaign as it can help in keeping the messaging coherent and consistent. It can also provide back-up support for the library staff member tasked with tweeting the event. When Twitter is used to publicize an upcoming event and then used to engage during the live event, retweets and the number of followers tend to increase. By using Twitter to engage users in the online environment, it works to complement and supplement the interactions that users have with the library in person.

7.2 CASE STUDY 2

Drop Everything and Tweet: Building Community on Your Campus

Joanna Ewing, Amber Wilson and Karen Pruneda
University of Central Arkansas, Conway, AR, United States

Institution: University of Central Arkansas (student population Fall 2016—11,487).

Campaign Purpose: We planned this outreach event as a community-building exercise that would highlight a variety of academic departments, student groups, and other nonacademic entities. The extended reach of Twitter afforded us the opportunity to share news and information about library services, as well as provide research tips and instruction.

Target Demographic: University of Central Arkansas community, including students, faculty, staff, and student athletes.

Measure of Success: During the Drop Everything and Read (DEAR) campaign month, 30 pictures were tweeted (10 tweeted by others, 20 by us), we gained 29 new followers (average new followers per month is 16.7), and we had significant DEAR-related engagement (82 likes, 33 retweets, and 4 replies).

Team: Social media committee, Library Technician for Education and Outreach, Interlibrary Loan Supervisor/Graphic Designer.

7.2.1 CAMPAIGN BACKGROUND

The University of Central Arkansas (UCA) Library decided to plan a Drop Everything and Read (DEAR) campaign as a fun way to encourage reading and increase campus engagement. We first came up with the idea of implementing a DEAR campaign after seeing pictures of faculty and staff reading on other university library social media pages. These images reminded library faculty and staff of our cherished childhood experiences with reading programs, and we hoped to capitalize on the UCA community's feelings of nostalgia to create a unique outreach opportunity. While our DEAR campaign was held on Twitter, Facebook, and Instagram, we decided to focus on Twitter for this chapter because its popularity and versatile sharing features made it an especially effective platform to spread this campaign.

Children's author Beverly Cleary coined the phrase "Drop Everything and Read" in her popular 1981 book *Ramona Quimby, Age 8* in response to reader letters mentioning sustained silent reading (SSR) activities in their schools (D.E.A.R. Day, 2018). DEAR programs are now held annually throughout the month of April to commemorate Cleary's birthday on April 16th. Although SSR has been practiced in elementary schools for at least 40 years, it is not as common in high schools and colleges (Moore, Jones, & Miller, 1980, p. 445). A review of school and public library websites reveals that these institutions frequently participate in DEAR-related activities, which typically promote children's exposure to books and reading. Academic libraries, on the other hand, mainly mention DEAR in reference to aspiring K-12 educators and reading to young children. Although it is not common to hold a DEAR event in an academic library, we knew that we could make this Twitter campaign a success due to the enthusiasm of the UCA community and our project management skills.

7.2.2 UCA LIBRARY TWITTER IMPLEMENTATION

The UCA Library's Twitter use has changed significantly since we first began using it in 2015. In the beginning, we primarily used Twitter as a way to tie existing library materials with historical events or national observations, such as Arkansas Women's Suffrage or Black History Month. We used various tools such as Hootsuite and TweetDeck to organize and facilitate the process.

Over time, we figured out other ways to use Twitter to engage with our campus community. The library's first major Twitter outreach campaign was for Banned Books Week in September 2015. We encouraged UCA students, faculty, and staff to "get caught reading a banned book" by taking a picture in front of our mug shot-themed library photo booth for a chance to win a campus bookstore gift card. We also used Twitter to share photos of library and campus events, such as speakers and therapy dog visits during final exams, as well as short videos with information about library services. We encouraged student engagement by sharing responses to questions we regularly posted on whiteboards (Fig. 7.2.1). We also promoted student creativity by tweeting pictures of art found on the whiteboard walls of the library's study rooms.

Figure 7.2.1 Example whiteboard question.

7.2.3 APPROACH/PLAN

For our DEAR campaign, we invited individuals across campus to share creative photos of themselves reading and post them on Twitter with the UCA Library's hashtag, #UCALibraryLife. Student photo submissions were entered into a draw to win an umbrella or study snacks. We announced our plans for DEAR in April 2016. Early in April we identified individuals within departments to contact via email. This strategic approach proved useful, as the contacts that we made helped spread the word within their departments. Next we planned out the posts that the library wanted to make, leaving space in the schedule for flexibility in case of overwhelming participation. These posts included information highlighting various UCA departments and student athletes who responded to our email communication. We strategically planned to incorporate suggestions of related library resources in our replies to tweets.

7.2.4 DEVELOPING ORGANIZATIONAL STRATEGIES

The UCA Library's External Marketing Committee is the primary group involved with social media activities. This committee initially met once a month, but met less frequently once we developed our social media ideas and philosophy. The committee uses Google Docs, Sheets, and Calendar to collaboratively plan and organize its social media campaigns. When we first started working as a committee, we created two Google Docs to plan possible posts and social media campaigns by month and by year. Previously used posts were changed to a different color for future reference. As the system became more fluid and we developed a common approach to content and implementation, we only referred to these Google Docs as needed.

For DEAR, we collaborated on a Google Doc to recommend and contact potential participants. We reasoned that individuals would be more likely to participate if they were contacted by someone they knew. After this initial communication, our Library Technician for Education and Outreach followed up to arrange times for individual photos in the library. The photos were taken with a high-resolution digital camera and the files were labeled with the name of the individual, the department, and the information to highlight about that department. This organization made it much easier for us to share and tag the departments' photos on Twitter. For example, we tweeted a photo of a History Department professor reading a book and tagged the post with @UCA_History. Departments then received a notification and could retweet the photos highlighting their students, faculty, and staff. We were careful to tweet and retweet pictures strategically to avoid overwhelming followers or running out of photos. Monitoring the library's hashtag daily allowed us to keep up with activity in the campaign.

7.2.5 IDENTIFYING COLLABORATORS

When identifying collaborators for the campaign, we targeted individuals whose participation would yield maximum exposure and encourage greater campus participation. In the spirit of building bridges across campus, we reached out to students, administrators, faculty, and staff throughout the university. We made a special effort to contact individuals who are not normally asked to participate in campus intellectual life such as custodial staff. Inclusion is an important value to UCA Library, and this is reflected by our social media activities. Moreover, we were fortunate that a librarian served on a committee with UCA's athletic director who could encourage the participation of student athletes. We also specifically targeted UCA's Division of Outreach and Community Engagement, since we knew that it actively uses Twitter and would be most likely to share our content. Our university's police department has a strong Twitter presence with conversational and humorous responses to students, so it was very important for us to make a connection with them. In exchange, the DEAR campaign provided the campus police with a new opportunity to connect with the community in a fun and positive way. We also targeted specific teaching faculty members in several departments, sometimes asking them to use specific props or backgrounds as appropriate (e.g., the observatory, laboratory equipment, etc.) (Fig. 7.2.2).

Figure 7.2.2 Example of faculty member reading in school setting.

7.2.6 MARKETING

We used email, print posters, and Twitter to market the DEAR campaign. We created an invitation email template for library faculty and staff to send out to a variety of departments across campus, both ones we knew well and others with whom we wanted to establish a relationship. Including example images of individuals reading with fun backgrounds related to their work, department, or a hobby in the emailed invitation inspired participation and set high expectations for creativity. The following text is an email that we sent out to an IT staff member:

> *Good afternoon _________,*
>
> *I enjoyed meeting you yesterday and talking about instruction, and I thought you might be interested in participating in the event below in order to raise awareness of IT instruction and/or offer a recommended resource.*
>
> *We're celebrating Drop Everything and Read Month at the library, and we wanted to feature photos of individuals from throughout the UCA community reading on our social media. We hope the photos will be a fun community-building event. Would you be interested in posing with a favorite book?*
>
> *You may submit your own photo with a background of your choice by tagging it with #UCALibraryLife on Facebook, Twitter, or Instagram. For Facebook, make sure to change the audience to "Public" before clicking the post button. You may include your name, department, title, the name of the book, and the author in the post if you would like, although it's not necessary. I included some example photos below for inspiration.*
>
> *Please email me if you would like to have your photo taken personally in the library or would like to submit your file as an email attachment. We would appreciate photo contributions before April 18, although we will accept them until the end of the month. If you know anyone else from UCA or IT who would be interested in participating, please pass along this email.*
>
> *Thanks for your help with this project!*

These emails were particularly effective because they reinforced or established relationships and offered to highlight that department's services. In this case, the IT staff member asked us to tweet about his department's Google Apps trainings. We were able to reach a larger audience by encouraging people to forward the email.

We also offered multiple ways to participate in order to accommodate varying comfort levels with technology or privacy. For example, some individuals wanted to maintain privacy of their personal Twitter accounts and felt more comfortable emailing the photo, coming into the library for a personal photo shoot, or asking their departments to tweet the

Figure 7.2.3 DEAR campaign marketing materials.

photo for them. However, we ideally wanted departments to tweet their own photos in order to engage a wider, more invested audience.

For print publicity, we asked our Interlibrary Loan Supervisor who has a graphic design degree to create a poster advertising the campaign and the contest. We provided the text and she designed the poster and a social media graphic with instructions to share a DEAR picture with the library's hashtag. The poster was displayed in the library and on a stand outside the door (Fig. 7.2.3).

We tweeted the contest graphic and information about the prizes several times. We then embedded participation instructions into the text of as many other DEAR photo tweets as possible. When individuals tweeted a DEAR picture, we replied "Thanks for posting your pic with #UCALibraryLife" in the hope that their followers would also participate. We sometimes included a shortened link to our Facebook post, which included contest rules, further details, or biographical information about the person featured in a photo. For example, we included a link to our Facebook page for additional information about the campus police officer in Fig. 7.2.4. Twitter has the option to include a link when posting, which is an advantage over other social media platforms like Instagram or Snapchat.

We also attempted to foster competition and increase participation through the text of posts. In the case of Fig. 7.2.5, we tagged a student group's Twitter page since the Biology Department does not have one.

Figure 7.2.4 Campus police officer tweet with link to additional information.

The student group did not ultimately retweet or like the post, which demonstrates that one cannot always anticipate results or know if someone is actively managing the Twitter account. The most popular posts were of student athletes and were liked and retweeted by a variety of groups, including students, athletic department staff, advising staff, and fans (Fig. 7.2.6).

Figure 7.2.5 Creative tweets foster competition.

Figure 7.2.6 Photos of student athletes received the most reaction during our DEAR campaign.

7.2.7 WHAT WORKED

There were several specific strategies that proved very successful for encouraging the campus community to participate:

Collaboration

- Getting buy-in at the department level.
- Determining mutual interests and highlighting these connections.
- Partnering with the Athletic Director increased student athlete participation and overall campaign engagement.

Communication

- Identifying and contacting the individuals responsible for campus accounts in an effort to foster greater participation.
- Emailing individual faculty and staff members to encourage participation.

Organization

- Creating an email template to save time when reaching out to departments or individuals.
- Using a Google Doc to track who had been contacted.

Fostering Creativity

- Posting example pictures and posts allowed others to understand the campaign, build upon our content, and brainstorm their own ideas.
- Suggesting that individuals include creative backgrounds related to departmental focus, hobbies, or interests.

Marketing

- Replying to departmental DEAR posts with discipline-related library resources.
- Encouraging departments to retweet library resource information.
- Personalizing responses to every shared post, tag, and reply encouraged more interaction but was time-consuming.
- Promoting our library hashtag made it easier to find and share posts related to the campaign.

Campaign Data

- 30 pictures were tweeted for campaign (10 tweeted by others, 20 by us).
- 82 likes, 33 retweets, and 4 replies related to DEAR campaign.

- 23.3 K impressions in the month of April, compared to the 2016 monthly average of 14.32 K, were the second highest of year (highest month was December due to the overwhelming popularity of therapy dogs and study snacks giveaways).
- 29 new followers gained in April (average new followers per month was 16.7).

7.2.8 WHAT DIDN'T WORK

Prizes

- Omitting prize information on Twitter images that advertised the DEAR campaign.
- Students did not seem enthusiastic or motivated by the prizes.

Twitter User Preferences

- Students' Twitter privacy settings may have prevented us from seeing DEAR-related tweets.
- Tweets that omitted the hashtag made it difficult to track the campaign participation.
- Lack of tweeting by students from personal accounts reduced the reach of the campaign.
- Not all campus departments have a Twitter account, so we were unable to tag them to generate enthusiasm, retweets, and additional DEAR posts.

Marketing

- Not advertising the post frequently enough.
- Failure to individually email students or clubs resulted in lower participation compared to faculty and staff members.

7.2.9 RECOMMENDATIONS

Our experiences using Twitter to host and promote our DEAR campaign allow us to provide several suggestions for other academic libraries interested in using the platform for outreach activities:

Marketing

- Publicize your campaign or event outside of Twitter (via email, campus listservs, or other means) to reach additional individuals/departments/programs.

- Use posts by departmental faculty as a springboard to share corresponding library services (e.g., link to subject LibGuides or other resources).

Communication

- Contact your university's student governance and other student organizations directly to encourage greater participation.
- Encourage competition among campaign participants by providing positive comments/feedback/aspirational examples.

Participation Guidelines

- For campaigns involving picture submissions, encourage faculty and staff to share their images via their departmental accounts if they would rather not use their personal accounts.
- If hosting a contest, provide rules using a graphic or an outside link (Facebook post, library website, etc.) to circumvent Twitter's character limit.
- Provide a variety of ways to enter contests, including liking, retweeting, or following, so as to increase the campaign reach and participation.
- Randomly select contest winners with an automatic number generator or by writing down names.
- Send both a private message and a reply to a contest winner's initial tweet with a location and deadline to pick up the prize after which it will be redrawn.

7.2.10 FINAL WORDS

Twitter is an engaging and interactive platform that appeals to students, faculty, and staff on different levels, allowing us to boost our outreach and community-building efforts across campus. The combination of Twitter and a campus-wide DEAR campaign ultimately proved very successful for our library. We gained 29 new followers and the campaign resulted in significant community engagement, including 30 tweeted pictures, 82 likes, and 33 retweets. Inviting a variety of individuals to participate in the campaign was beneficial in identifying potential future collaborators for other projects and building goodwill toward the library. We encouraged the community to share their love of reading books about a variety of different topics and genres. This helped our community to learn more about each other's interests, and to share their own vision of themselves or their department in turn. In the future, we hope to reach out more deliberately to student organizations to get them involved in DEAR and offer an additional prize for the most creative picture. DEAR allowed the campus as a whole to learn about each other and the resources we offer in a less academic way.

REFERENCES

D.E.A.R. Day, April 12th. (2018). In *Reading Rockets*. Available from http://www.readingrockets.org/calendar/dear#about

Moore, J., Jones, C., & Miller, D. (1980). What we know after a decade of sustained silent reading. *The Reading Teacher, 33*(4), 445–450, Retrieved from JSTOR.

7.3 CASE STUDY 3

What Do You Do When They Start Talking Back? Training Librarians for Next-Level Twitter Engagement Using Springshare's LibAnswers

Sheeji Kathuria[1] and Amanda Clay Powers[2]
[1]Mississippi State University, Starkville, MS, United States
[2]Mississippi University for Women, Columbus, MS, United States

Institution: Mississippi State University (MSU); 21,127 students as of Fall 2016.

Target Demographic: MSU affiliated accounts (faculty, staff, students, and campus offices) and surrounding Starkville, Mississippi community on Twitter.

Measure of Success: In implementing our new taxonomy for assessing and categorizing tweets, we were able to streamline the VR Librarian's workflow, develop an effective training plan, and improve the library's response time and quality.

Team: The Social Media Committee at MSU Libraries has a rotating membership of faculty and staff from all departments at MSU Libraries. The committee began sharing its Twitter responsibilities with the Research Services Department in August 2014. This Department includes 10 faculty librarians and one Coordinator who all help manage our "Ask a Librarian" virtual reference service.

7.3.1 THE SITUATION

The MSU Libraries Twitter account is managed by a Social Media Committee, which consists of a mixture of staff and faculty from all departments within the library. With the hard work this committee has put into social media engagement, the account now has more than 4500 followers and an extremely dynamic give and take with MSU and the surrounding community. This heavy engagement eventually began to include actual reference questions that many of the committee members were either unable to answer or were unavailable to answer if asked outside normal business hours. The committee needed a systematic way to assure that all the @msu_libraries Twitter comments and reference questions were being addressed in an accurate and timely manner.

Enter Research Services! In August 2014, MSU Libraries Research Services department adopted Springshare's virtual reference (VR) tool, LibAnswers/LibChat. With this system, we were able to check any tweets that were tagged with @msu_libraries. As our reference desk was staffed by a VR librarian until nine o'clock most evenings, it made sense that the work should be shared. This way there would be a structure in place for responding to tweets in a timely manner (e.g., immediate noise complaints). We were so excited about this feature that we began routing all of our tweets through this system without thinking of all the potential repercussions.

We soon saw the error of our ways. As soon as we turned this feature on, the VR librarians were overwhelmed with LibAnswers tickets that said things like, "@msu_libraries too turnt"(Fig. 7.3.1). Obviously, this was not

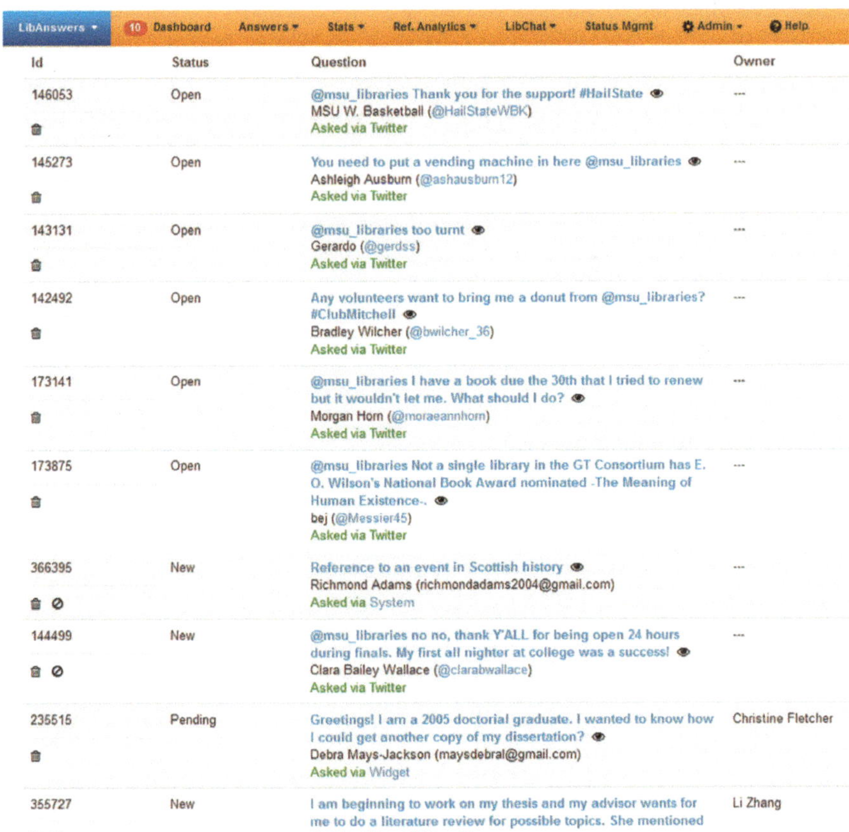

Figure 7.3.1 Tweets and traditional VR tickets in our LibAnswers dashboard.

a reference question. While a Social Media Committee member may have laughed and provided an immediate "like" and funny response to the tweet, our VR librarians were having the opposite reaction. Frozen by fear they responded stiffly at best, or not at all. This "turnt" business was not something "easy," like someone asking us to track down an obscure reference for a History thesis. The VR manager and Research Services coordinator soon decided that something needed to be done, and fast.

We tackled this situation in two ways:

7.3.1.1 Step 1: The Survey

We decided we needed to know more about what was panicking all the librarians. Twitter was easy right? Did not everyone know about how to get turnt? It had become clear that tweeting was not second nature to everyone, nor was it the same as doing a chat reference. For one, it was public. For another, fitting sensible responses into 140 characters (the limit at that point) was more of an art than a science. It was clear that we needed to get to know our colleagues better.

To get a feel for what was going on, we conducted a survey of the VR librarians. Did they use Twitter personally? Knowing this would give us crucial insight into how well they understood Twitter conventions and culture. For example, if a librarian did not know what a RT (shorthand for retweet) was, we were in for a very different sort of training program then if they were just nervous about their responses being public.

We developed and distributed a 14-question survey, assessing three different areas.

7.3.1.1.1 Survey Questions

Personal Twitter Usage

- Did you use Twitter before Fall 2014?
- Do you have a personal Twitter account?
- Do you follow the MSU Libraries' Twitter account?
- If you do use Twitter, check all the following Twitter abbreviations you have used: [check as many as apply]
  - RT
  - MT
  - HT
  - Via
- In what situation would you "Favorite" a tweet?
- In what situation would you "Retweet" a tweet?

- When is a reply visible to all your followers, versus only to the followers you and the account you are replying to have in common?

Twitter Experience With Virtual Reference Duties

- Did you respond to a Twitter question through LibAnswers in Fall 2014?
- If so, can you describe the procedure you used (i.e., did you consult the MSU Libraries Twitter page?)
- Do you feel confident speaking on behalf of the library when publicly posting on Twitter?
- Did you assign a Topic or Question Type from RefAnalytics to any Twitter question, mention, retweet, etc.?

Reflections on Twitter and Virtual Reference Program

- What was your comfort level with adding Twitter into the Libraries Virtual Reference program?
- Do you feel you need additional training on Twitter through LibAnswers?
- If yes, what kind of training would be helpful?

The survey was constructed in Google Forms, and distributed to nine VR Librarians in May 2015. We had a 100% response rate.

7.3.1.1.2 Survey Findings

We found:

- All nine VR Librarians had a personal Twitter account as of Fall 2014.
- Eight out of nine librarians used Twitter personally before Fall 2014.
- Seven out of nine have used the Twitter abbreviation RT, MT (Modified Tweet), HT (Heard Through or Hat Tip), or Via when tweeting.
- Six out of nine follow the @msu_libraries account (Fig. 7.3.2,7.3.3).

7.3.1.1.3 Open-Ended comments

Q: In what situation would you "Retweet" a tweet?

- "I have never done so. Not sure when I would."
- "When I find something very compelling, and I feel the way original author worded the tweet is the best way of saying it. . .."
- "If I want to share the opinion or news and feel it was worded by the original 'Tweeter' well. . .."

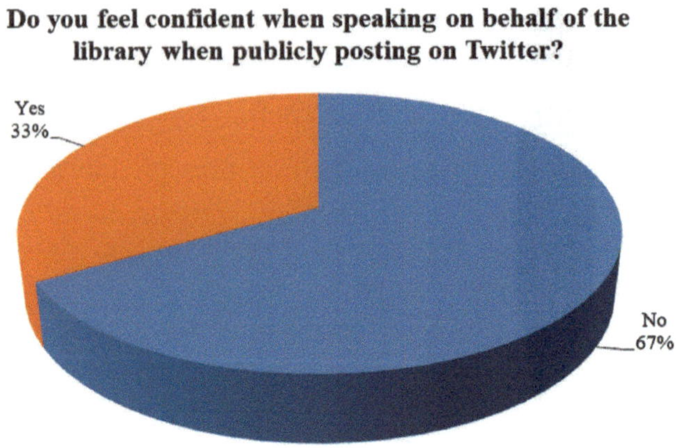

Figure 7.3.2 Survey responses to question, "Do you feel confident when speaking on behalf of the library when publicly posting on Twitter?" ($n = 9$).

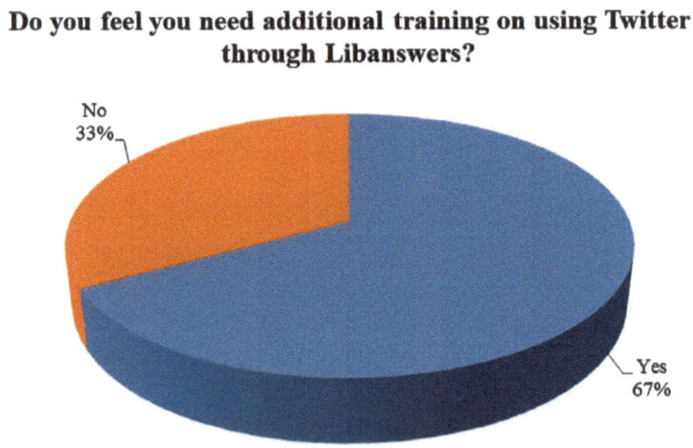

Figure 7.3.3 Survey responses to question, "Do you feel you need additional training on using Twitter through Libanswers?" ($n = 9$).

Q: What kind of additional training is needed?

- "Basically from scratch—I never use Twitter."
- "General best practices for Twitter."
- "I feel comfortable with Twitter itself, but I need to learn more about the workflow for closing tweets on the Dashboard; the workflow for answering tweets as they come in; and adding statistical information for both circumstances for different use cases."
- "General overview of best practices (i.e., what comments and questions should be responded to). And the use of tweet abbreviations like MT etc."

Our survey demonstrated that while all of the VR librarians had personal Twitter accounts, it was clear that the depth of experience varied widely from "start from scratch" to eloquent Twitter philosophies, and we needed to find a way cover it all in some sort of comprehensive training program.

7.3.1.2 Step 2: The Coding

The other piece that vexed us was with how to categorize the tweets to make them effective for assessment. We had been categorizing our chats for years, developing excellent tools to determine the types of communication we were having with patrons. We had no idea how to do this with Twitter, but we had a vague idea that training everyone to respond to tweets involved mainstreaming it into our existing service. In addition, we knew that not all of our tweets were reference questions. In fact, we were sure most were not. Was it even worth involving the Research Services department, if their expertise was only occasionally needed? Maybe not. We needed to start over from the beginning.

7.3.1.2.1 Traditional Codes for Virtual Reference Questions

- Online Catalog
- Topic Search
- Known Article Search
- Known Book Search
- ILL
- Theses & Dissertations
- Special Collections
- Library Employment
- Hours
- Compliments
- Complaints / Suggestions
- Access Services / Circulation Policies
- Website
- Instructional Media Center

We exported every tweet gathered by LibAnswers with the @msu_libraries tag from August 2014–July 2015 into Excel. We took inspiration from a qualitative research method and coding technique grounded theory, which typically entails multiple phases of coding where the researchers treat "data analytically and discover what they see in them" (Charmaz, 2004, p. 442).

We each took half of the dataset to come up with an initial set of independent categories. Coming back together, each set of categories was analyzed, and we discussed what commonalities existed. We went back and forth with this and further discussions until we felt we had a final list, complete with definitions and examples. It was necessary to standardize and simplify our definitions in order to make coding work easily for everyone, no matter who was coding. For example, anytime a "Thank you" was used it would automatically be coded as a Compliment.

Once the categories were finalized, we went back and recoded the dataset over again with the new codes. Our finalized set of codes, definitions, and examples are below:

7.3.1.2.2 Grounded Theory Coding Findings

Code	Definition	Example
Complaint / Suggestion	Negative comments, corrections, feedback	*We need more outlets! @msu_libraries*
Compliment	Positive comments, "thank yous"	*Dear new MSU students, I would highly suggest you start following @msu_libraries immediately. You will thank me later.*
Conversation	Library mentioned before the tweet text begins; public engaging the library in conversation	*@msu_libraries I will be there around 330 to make a sign*
Engagement	Mention of the library within a tweet	*Monday night study time at @msu_libraries*
External promotion	Promotion by the library or other account of outside entities, events, or campus- wide notifications	*Sunday night writing frenzy? Work out that idea with the writing center @msu_libraries in the IMC! #msuwrites* http://t.co/TO9SiVmzyK
Library promotion	Promotion by the library or other account of library "sponsored" events, entities, programs, or services	*Mark your calendars now for the #BannedBooksWeek activities next week @msu_libraries!* http://t.co/eN5CTamMwV

(*Continued*)

Code	Definition	Example
Library Tweet	Self-citation from the MSU Libraries' own Twitter account	*We are excited to see all the #GameDaySigns we printed in the @msu_libraries' IMC when @CollegeGameDay begins! #HailState #OurGameDay*
Question	Inquiry directed at library account in order to get an answer	*@msu_libraries I want to print off a poster for GameDay but idk what size to print. What size is best?*
Spam	Unsolicited click-bait	*yo @msu_libraries "Have you seen @Braddy478 "Money In The Air" viral video? #RT lemme know what you think* http://t.co/TyioLpnP9v"

Here is a breakdown of our Twitter transactions from 2014 to 2017 by type of code (Fig. 7.3.4).

Adding in Twitter codes to our VR backend revolutionized our work in many ways. It cleaned up our overwhelmed dashboard and made our work more concrete. With these codes, we were able to track the research department's work with Twitter and incorporate those statistics

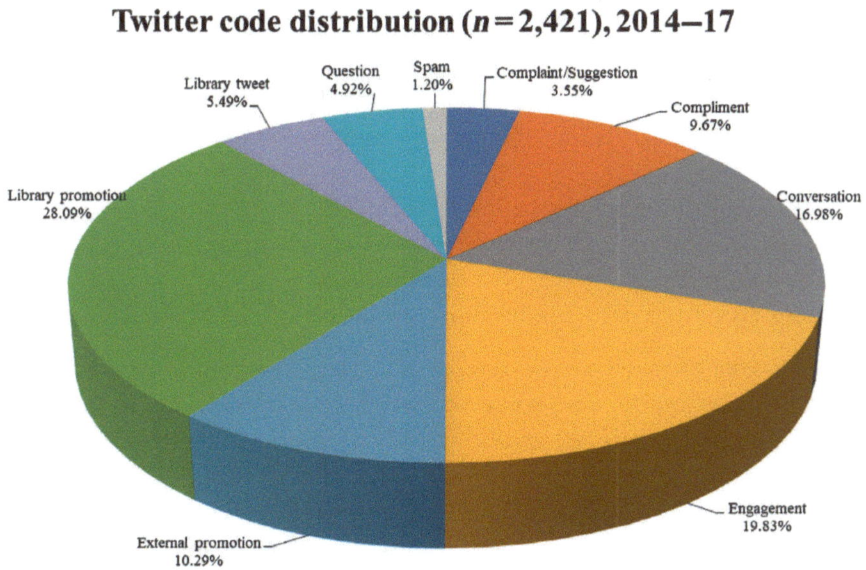

Figure 7.3.4 Twitter code distribution (*n* = 2421), 2014–17.

into our reports. We were also able to share the data with the Social Media Committee to incorporate into their own reports and marketing strategy. It was now possible to pull out all the tags labeled Compliments and Complaint/Suggestions and get those to the right departments within the library. It was also possible to see how much we were promoting others (External Promotion) and ourselves.

Full of data, good ideas, and new systems, we embarked on a plan to fully integrate Twitter into our VR services.

7.3.1.2.3 Training Plan

To create your own training plan that is specific to your library, consider asking the following questions:

Does your library Twitter account have a "voice?" In order to train your librarians on speaking as the library's voice, you may have to explore this explicitly yourself first. Are you funny? Serious? Do you use abbreviations or spell things out? Do you use slang, or do you keep it professional? Simple decisions like this will clarify expectation and help everyone feel comfortable responding to Twitter comments and questions accordingly.

Do your librarians regularly use Twitter? And if so, how are they using it? Even if they are using it all the time, not everyone uses Twitter in the same way. How do you want them to be able to use it for the library? Write it down and make your needs clear. Then check back in—do they have those competencies? If not, it can be taught:

- Focus on how to compose tweets effectively (character limit, tagging other accounts, using hashtags, replying to one account vs broadcasting).
- Start tweets with handles to limit the audience.
- Place a period or space in front of a handle to open the audience for the response.
- Assess comfort level with Twitter conventions (RT, HT, MT, via).

What kind of tweets are we getting? This is where the codes come in handy. Understanding the types of tweets that the library is likely to receive (not just questions!) and how to best respond to them will reassure any nervous VR librarian and provide a focus for training.

Twitter and VR systems change all the time! Think about how you will handle future staff training as the platform releases changes or updates. Face-to-face works better than email for updates.

7.3.2 WHAT WORKED

- Training our VR staff. Based on the survey results and coding system, we were able to move forward with a solid training plan with specific emphasis on where the Twitter "weak" spots were and how best to address them.
- Keeping the dashboard clean. With our coding system, we were able to close out our tweets that were not reference questions very easily.
- Using categories to organize tweets for analysis and training. With our new coding system, we were able to plan for training and Twitter feedback to our library administration.

7.3.3 WHAT DIDN'T WORK

- Tracking claims. From within LibAnswers, it is still difficult to tell if someone already answered a tweet, making for confusing and duplicate communication at times. Currently, it is critical for the "on duty" person to check Twitter directly before responding.
- Bringing everyone up to speed immediately. To accommodate comfort levels while training, we decided on a happy medium where VR librarians who serve on the Social Media Committee (think about the middle of a Venn diagram!) would be front-line on Twitter with the rest of the VR librarians as backup.
- Accounting for staff changes. With turnover in staffing, implementing an iterative assessment plan is critical.

7.3.4 RECOMMENDATIONS

- Leveraging tweets to gain administrative support. Our administration values the engagement and feedback we receive from our online community. Make sure your administration is on board with the time it takes to develop these workflows.
- Valuing opportunities to gain patron feedback. Given that the large majority of tweets are not actual reference questions, the VR librarians doing this work must value the comments and compliments and see them as providing important insight. Decide what your priorities are as a department before embarking on such a social media adventure.
- Investing in ongoing assessment. With staffing changes and LibAnswers updates, a microintervention training strategy, which

involves reviewing changes to the systems and determining if there is any need for additional training, is critical. Often this sort of training can be done briefly at regular department meetings.

7.3.5 FINAL WORDS

Our survey showed that VR librarians are coming to the table with a wide variety of skillsets and comfort levels with social media tools like Twitter. When introducing a new tool like Twitter into an established system, it is critical to assess both the technological capabilities and the human consequences. Everything that can be done should not be done just because it is possible. Assessing the system and then adapting the workflow and training based on that information has proven to be effective for us. Once the initial competency levels and tweet types are uncovered, any training needs can be assessed either as a group or one-on-one.

Our Twitter codes illustrate that patrons are engaging with Twitter beyond asking traditional questions. They are using Twitter to promote their own events, provide complaints, and give compliments about their engagement of library services. The "new" VR library program must be willing to listen to these and be able to engage in such behaviors publicly. This sort of feedback is actively solicited through tools like LibQual + , yet on Twitter the feedback is freely offered. Is not it worth taking the time to listen?

REFERENCE

Charmaz, K. (2004). *Grounded theory, . The SAGE encyclopedia of social science research methods* (Vol. 2, pp. 440–444). Thousand Oaks, CA: SAGE Publications, Inc.

7.4 CASE STUDY 4

Rising Above the Noise: Increasing Local Engagement Through a Global Hashtag Campaign

Emily Jack
University Libraries, University of North Carolina, Chapel Hill, United States

Institution: University Libraries at the University of North Carolina at Chapel Hill; roughly 29,500 students; 12 library locations.

Campaign purpose: Twitter #1lib1ref hashtag campaign: To increase engagement with the @UNCLibrary Twitter account; to establish a new identity and voice for our Twitter account; to show librarians as a useful resource for citation help and to model good information literacy practices in unexpected ways.

Target demographic: Students.

Measure of success: Increased engagement with #1lib1ref tweets compared to average Twitter engagement and compared to other tweets during that time. Our engagement rate for #1lib1ref tweets was 4.9%, compared to 1.6% for all tweets during that time, and 0.9% for the preceding comparable period.

Team: One librarian tweeting; 68 library staff members participating in #1lib1ref activities; 13 library staff members appearing in photos. Support from library administration and staff, especially the communications department.

7.4.1 BACKGROUND

In January and February of 2017, the UNC Library's communications department took advantage of a convergence of factors to launch a unique Twitter campaign.

Until this point, the communications department had consisted of just two full-time staff members, who handled internal and external communications for a large library system with 12 library locations and nearly 300 staff members serving nearly 30,000 students. Our limited staffing and the extensive demands on our time translated to a limited capacity for dedicated social media campaigns.

That changed in November 2016, when a new staff member joined the department with 20 hours a week to devote to social media. The staffing change gave us an opportunity to cultivate a more consistent identity and voice, and to plan and execute more elaborate social media campaigns than we had previously had the capacity for. The timing and scope of #1lib1ref suggested it might be a good fit for our library.

#1lib1ref is an annual Wikipedia hashtag campaign with the stated goal of getting every librarian to contribute one citation during the three-week-long project. The UNC Library had been involved in Wikipedia projects for several years but had not participated in #1lib1ref. The communications department saw in the campaign an opportunity to shape messages around one of its primary goals: emphasizing that the library's staff members are trusted experts and interesting people. The campaign would let us show off our librarians as a useful resource for citation help and model good information literacy practices in unexpected ways, all while introducing a new voice on our Twitter account.

By definition, participating in a hashtag campaign should increase audience engagement on Twitter. Hashtags have tremendous utility for connecting people who are conversing around the same topic but do not necessarily share the same networks. I may not follow you and you may not follow me, but if we are both tweeting about or following the same hashtag, we can connect with each other. By invoking popular hashtags, Twitter communicators can reach new audiences with shared interests and, ideally, pick up new followers as a result.

While all those potential outcomes of a hashtag campaign sound appealing in theory, this particular campaign presented a challenge: How would we get students to care? We had all seen hashtag campaigns that sounded great to librarians but never seemed to break through the noise and gain students' attention. Like #OpenAccessWeek, Wikipedia citations seemed to be one of these topics that excited librarians only. How could we approach this differently?

7.4.2 THE IDEA

By coincidence, the timing of #1lib1ref was set to line up with the moment when college basketball season—an all-consuming phenomenon at UNC—gains increasing intensity. The basketball rivalry between UNC and Duke is so heated that it merits an entire merchandise section in the campus bookstore, has been the subject of at least one book, and, critically for our purposes, has its own suite of hashtags.

To take advantage of the attention students devote to the UNC-Duke basketball rivalry, we initiated our own competition. We challenged the Duke Library to a contest to see which library could contribute more citations to Wikipedia during the #1lib1ref project. We planned to use not only the #1lib1ref hashtag but also #UNCvsDuke, in the hopes that we would appear on the radar of students who did not (yet) follow us on Twitter.

The practice of using a trending topic to draw attention to yourself is known as *newsjacking*. Perhaps the most famous example in recent memory was Oreo's famous tweet during the 2013 Superbowl blackout—a photo of an Oreo cookie carefully lit in a dark space, which appeared with the text, "Power out? No problem. You can still dunk in the dark."

For every clever example of successful newsjacking, it is easy to find several clumsy or tone-deaf examples. As a result, this practice should be undertaken with careful forethought and with alignment to a larger strategy. We decided, for example, not to tweet *during* any UNC versus Duke basketball game. Yes, using the #UNCvsDuke hashtag during a game would surely get our content in front of more eyes, but it would run the risk of alienating people who would likely see our game-time tweeting as irrelevant, and blatantly self-serving, noise.

7.4.3 THE EXECUTION

Before the #1lib1ref project began, we reached out to contacts at Duke Library to initiate the competition and establish terms, rules, and a timeline. We introduced the contest to UNC Library staff members during an all-staff meeting, during which we were pleased to find that the friendly competition with Duke appealed to many of our colleagues.

Then we created a loose content plan for the campaign. Because tweets with photos tend to draw more engagement than text-only posts, we planned to include photos of our librarians in the act of editing Wikipedia. But because a photo of a person sitting at a computer makes for a less-than-compelling Twitter post, we planned to create a side-by-side image for each photo post, pairing a photo of the librarian typing in her or his office with a screenshot of the Wikipedia article she or he edited.

We planned our content in advance so we could pace our posts throughout the campaign. Because a three-week campaign is long in social media time, we sought to strike a balance between keeping up the momentum and tweeting too much: We wanted to keep the project on our audience's radar, but avoid alienating them and risking unfollows. In our case, that meant tweeting with the hashtag on average once a weekday, although there were a few weekdays on which we did not tweet with the hashtag at all and a few on which we tweeted more than once.

Our core content themes were:

- The library's staff are interesting people with a wide range of interests and expertise.
- The library's staff are eager to share their topical knowledge and citation expertise.
- Librarians can support student work with citations and/or Wikipedia.
- The library is engaged with the larger campus community and has a stake in (friendly) intercollegiate rivalries.
- We take research and citation seriously, but we know how to have a good time.

We sent email to our staff throughout the campaign, inviting volunteers to appear in photo posts and updating them on the score as our citations added up. Many staff members demonstrated a willingness to participate in the social media aspect of the campaign, which gave us rich fodder with which to flesh out the details of our content plan (Fig. 7.4.1,7.4.2).

Our tweets included:

- Until 2/3, @UNCLibrary, and @DukeLibraries will compete to see how many citations they can add to @Wikipedia. Go Heels! #1lib1ref #UNCvsDuke.
- UNC librarians have added over 100 citations to Wikipedia so far during #1lib1ref. Proud to improve access to accurate information!
- If all this talk about Wikipedia citations has you eager to edit, we'll host at least 4 edit-a-thons this spring. Stay tuned! #1lib1ref.
- Anatomy of a Wikipedia citation. We do this for fun, and we can help you with all your writing and citing needs! #1lib1ref [This appeared with a screenshot of a Wikipedia citation (Fig. 7.4.3)].
- The series of side-by-side librarian and screenshot photos appeared with text such as:
  - Did you know there's a Wikipedia page listing state foods? Its citations are solid thanks to [librarian's name]. #1lib1ref
  - @Wikipedia page about the Nigerian city Abeokuta, now with better citations thanks to [librarian's user name]. The #UNCvsDuke #1lib1ref contest continues!

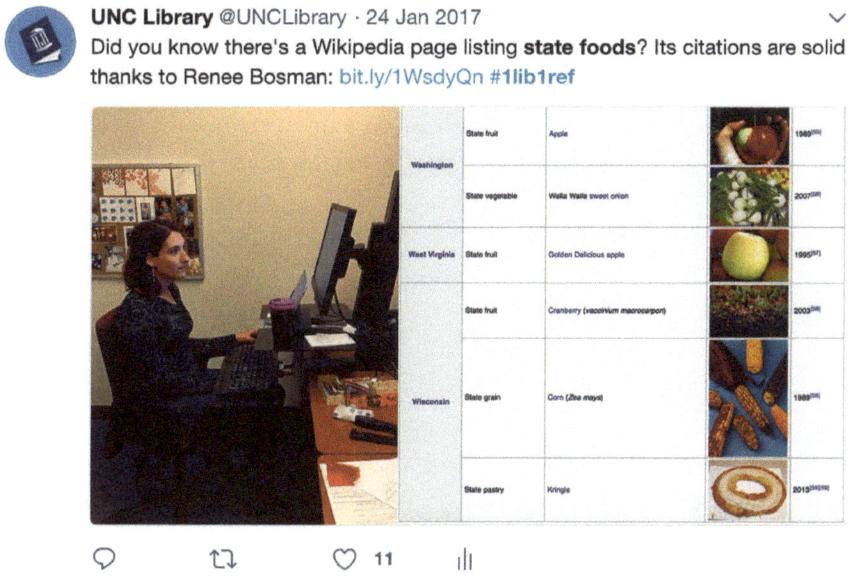

Figure 7.4.1 Several tweets throughout the campaign included photos of library staff.

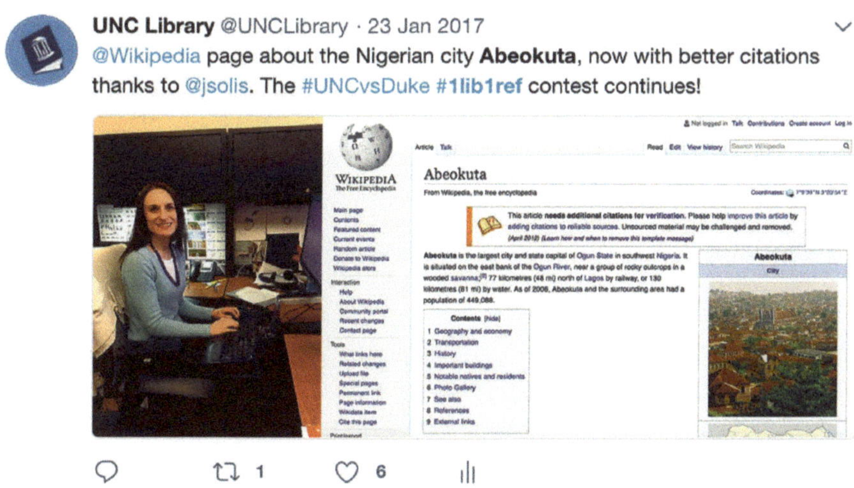

Figure 7.4.2 Side-by-side posts depicting librarians next to the articles they edited showed the range of interests and expertise among our staff, and were our most successful in terms of audience engagement.

- E-records archivist [librarian's name] updated the Wikipedia page on Margaret Warner Morley. B/c more citations = a better Wikipedia. #1lib1ref.
- Wikipedia article about fictional detective Phryne Fisher: Sources are no longer a mystery thanks to librarian [librarian's name]. #1lib1ref.
- The #UNCvsDuke Wikipedia citation battle continues: [librarian's user name] adds a citation to the page about electronic health records. #1lib1ref.
- [librarian's user name] found a German source for this article about Madeira and had to translate before citing. Above and beyond for #1lib1ref!.

As the campaign drew to a close, we posted two summary images: One, our most popular tweet during the campaign, was a "team" photo in which we asked a handful of willing library staff members to pose wearing UNC colors, holding books and computers, and glaring at the camera—a familiar style of team photo in the sports world. The tweet read, "#UNC librarians bringing their A game in a Wikipedia citation battle with @DukeLibraries. #1lib1ref #UNCvsDuke."

The second was a photo grid consisting of eight separate images of library staffers at their computers—photos we already had—with the Wikipedia logo in the center. This appeared with the text "The UNC Library had a great time improving Wikipedia citations during #1lib1ref. We will host several edit-a-thons in March & April. Join us!" (Fig. 7.4.4).

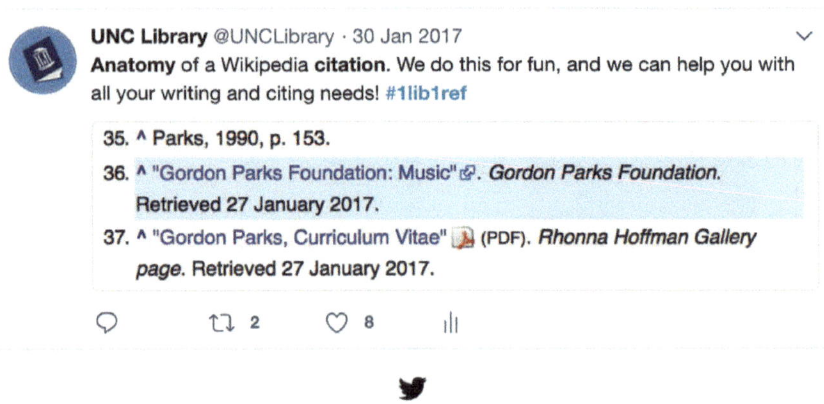

Figure 7.4.3 Tweets such as this promoted our staff's writing and citing expertise.

Figure 7.4.4 One of our summary tweets showed photos of librarians hard at work in a grid around the Wikipedia logo.

A few days after the #1lib1ref campaign ended, UNC's basketball team played Duke's. The day of the game, we tweeted, "In the Wikipedia citations battle, the score: @UNCLibrary 204, @DukeLibraries 29. Aiming for similar tonight. #UNCvsDuke #1lib1ref #UNC."

7.4.4 MEASURING SUCCESS

Aside from the challenge of getting librarians to put on a mean face for our team photo, the campaign was successful in achieving our primary goals:

7.4.4.1 Goal: To Increase Engagement With the @UNCLibrary Twitter Account

During the 22 days of the campaign, we posted 60 tweets, compared with 55 in the previous comparable 22-day period (a roughly comparable number). For the sake of comparison, we looked at November for a comparable period to avoid the winter holidays.

During the November period, we accrued 50.3 K total impressions. During the 22 days of #1lib1ref, we accrued nearly double that number, 101.3 K impressions. Our link clicks more than doubled, from 109 in November to 301 during #1lib1ref. So did our retweets, from 60 in November to 204 during #1lib1ref. Our likes were up from 120 in November to 397 during #1lib1ref. Our engagement increased from 0.9% in November to 1.6% during #1lib1ref. Isolating the numbers for tweets tagged with #1lib1ref only shows the success of the campaign even more starkly: The engagement rate for the 16 #1lib1ref tweets was 4.1%.

Table 7.4.1 shows our Twitter engagement during the campaign compared with the previous comparable period.

7.4.4.2 Goal: To Establish a New Identity and Voice for Our Twitter Account; to Show Librarians as a Useful Resource for Citation Help and to Model Good Information Literacy Practices in Unexpected ways

One of the goals of our newly expanded communications team was to highlight the human side of the library, which we did in this campaign. The data for these posts showed that this emphasis on people is a

Table 7.4.1 Twitter engagement during the #1lib1ref hashtag campaign compared with the previous comparable period

	Previous comparable period (Nov. 2 to Nov. 23, 2016)	Period of the campaign (Jan. 19 to Feb. 9)—all tweets	#1lib1ref tweets only (Jan. 19 to Feb. 9)
Tweets and replies	55	60	16
Impressions (K)	50.3	101.3	34.6
Engagement rate (%)	0.9	1.6	4.1
Link clicks	109	301	180
Retweets	60	204	91
Likes	120	397	210

successful strategy for our audience. Out of the 16 tweets we posted, nine included photos of library staff, and the engagement rate for those nine photos was 5.6%, even higher than our overall #1lib1ref engagement rate. Although this was not part of our initial strategy, tweeting photos of library staff members helped those tweets reach a wider audience because staff members with Twitter accounts retweeted the posts in which they appeared, which spread our content into new networks.

A few staff members tweeted about the campaign independently, including one who tweeted, "For my #1lib1ref #UNCvsDuke I added citations to the Frank Porter Graham entry, but it needs LOTS more work. Help me finish it!" Retweeting such tweets gave us an opportunity to show librarians' enthusiasm for this project through their own voices. This particular tweet also beautifully showcased the collaborative spirit of both Wikipedia and the library.

Anecdotally, while few people in our audience tweeted directly at us, colleagues within the library and across the UNC campus commented on how clever and entertaining they found the UNC versus Duke Wikipedia citation competition. While these offhand remarks are not hard data, they do suggest that the new identity and voice for our Twitter account had caught people's attention. And we did get a few direct tweets, including this one from an alumna:

"My husband's PhD is from Duke, mine is from UNC: we're cheering you both on!"

7.4.5 WHY IT WORKED

Several factors were instrumental in our success. First and foremost was getting buy-in from the library's administration and, by extension, library staff. Having the opportunity to present the competition in person at a staff meeting gave us a chance to build buzz around the project and to demonstrate how little time it would take to add a Wikipedia citation. This translated into a willingness on the part of 68 staff members to participate in the project, many of whom volunteered to support our content plan by appearing in photos.

The side-by-side posts depicting librarians next to the articles they edited worked incredibly well in helping us achieve our goal of showing the human side of the library. Most of our staff members edited articles on topics of personal interest, which enabled us to showcase the range of interests and expertise among our staff. Those posts proved to be our most successful in terms of audience engagement.

It is difficult to gauge the success of the newsjacking strategy of using the #UNCvsDuke hashtag along with #1lib1ref, because there is no way of knowing whether the people who engaged with our posts found them through the #UNCvsDuke hashtag. Anecdotally, we did receive numerous compliments on the cheeky approach of tying our citation rivalry to the basketball rivalry through the competition, hashtag use, and fierce "team" photo.

One of the final images we posted, the photo grid with the Wikipedia logo in the center, was retweeted by the official @Wikipedia account, which has a high followership. As a result, that tweet received 90 total engagements, among the highest for the entire campaign. The post likely got the @Wikipedia account's attention because it used their logo in a context that is consistent with Wikipedia's mission of a free, open encyclopedia in which people with expertise make frequent contributions. This can be a successful strategy if deployed carefully—the Wikipedia logo is open source and can be used and shared freely, which is not true of most other logos. But the same principle could be successfully applied in other ways.

7.4.6 THE BEST-LAID PLANS...

Of course, planning a social media campaign that depends in some way on another institution means losing some control. Our initial vision for our content plan had included some mock-hostile trash-talk between the two libraries, but the contest was a runaway. Trash-talking when you are up by dozens of points just comes across as gloating, and that was not the message we wanted to convey: At its heart, the broader #1lib1ref project is about collaboration, and the collective power of librarians everywhere working toward the same goal. We intend to invite more local libraries to participate in our competition next year, with the hope that more participants will ratchet up the competitive aspect of the campaign and provide more opportunity for lighthearted interlibrary Twitter taunts.

One other sticking point had to do with our analysis itself: in the end, it is difficult to determine whether we reached our target demographic of students, because Twitter's analytics tools are not granular enough to tell us *who* was liking and retweeting our posts.

7.4.7 WHAT WORKED

- Getting buy-in and support from the library's administration.
- Invoking a popular local hashtag to draw more attention.
- Connecting a phenomenon few people care about (bibliographic citation) to something many people care about (college basketball).
- Highlighting the human side of the library by posting tweets with photos of library staff.
- Retweeting #1lib1ref tweets by library staff members on their personal accounts.
- (Carefully) seeking retweets from accounts with high follower counts.

7.4.8 WHAT DIDN'T WORK

- Developing a content plan that anticipated a close competition (which ours was not).
- Trying to determine whether we had successfully reached our target audience using Twitter's analytics tools.

7.4.9 RECOMMENDATIONS

- Do not try to participate in every hashtag campaign. Choose strategically based on your goals.
- When engaging with a hashtag campaign that may have limited appeal to your audience, combine it with something that has broader appeal.
- Start with your communication goals (e.g., show librarians as experts and interesting people) and keep your content focused accordingly.
- Keep people front and center in your tweets to establish a unique identity. Show librarians' workspaces and what they do when they are not on the desk.
- Retweet from your librarians and staff when it is possible and appropriate; their voices are often more personal than the voice of the institution.
- Show the products of research—not just the raw materials that go into research.
- Use photo posts for higher engagement—and remember that high image quality is essential.
- Tag other Twitter accounts—especially high-profile accounts.

- Keep your content diverse to avoid boring your followers. During a hashtag campaign, be sure to tweet other, nonhashtag-focused content.
- Engage with other librarians and libraries.
- When engaging with a hashtag campaign that requires staff participation, it is essential to practice good internal communication throughout to keep up momentum and participation. Your library's staff are your greatest resources in a project like this one!

7.4.10 FINAL WORDS

Participating in hashtag campaigns can be exhilarating, but success depends on strategic participation. Start by establishing your goals, voice, and identity. Then creatively embrace hashtag campaigns that are a good fit for your unique presence, brand, and objectives.

The fundamental goal of a library's social media account should be to advance the mission of the library. In an academic library, that usually means a focus on research, teaching, and learning. Of course, on social media our content appears embedded in a steady stream of viral videos, celebrity selfies, and mesmerizing animated GIFs. This campaign demonstrated that it is possible to rise above the noise in a way that stays true to your institutional mission and communication themes.

CHAPTER 8
Facebook

8.1 CASE STUDY 1

Breaking Up Is Hard to Do: UAB Libraries and Facebook's Mis(sed)connection

Dana Hettich and Becca Billings
UAB Libraries, University of Alabama at Birmingham, Birmingham, AL, United States

Institution: UAB Libraries, University of Alabama Birmingham, Birmingham, AL, United States.

Campaign Purpose: To measure potential impact of marketing via different media channels on database usage.

Target Demographic: Students.
Measure of Success: Weekly increase in numbers of registered users. Looking for obvious spikes of registered users as the result of a particular medium.

Team: Marketing Committee comprised of four librarians and three library staff.

8.1.1 INTRODUCTIONS

I think I have to break up with Facebook. In the beginning, the adoption of the social media channel was easy. Some peers were even early adopters on a personal level and on a professional level knew that we needed to be out there. Unfortunately, they were also unwilling to discover where "there" was. Truthfully, it was difficult to discern what this channel would do. Now almost 11 years later, I am faced with possibility of letting this effort go. I remember when I had to have an .edu to access Facebook. I remember when I could insert boxes on a Page to write html. But now I wonder: Do I stay, or do I go? And if I go, who feeds the Pets virtual cat?

Social Media
DOI: https://doi.org/10.1016/B978-0-08-102409-6.00008-0

8.1.2 LOVE AT FIRST LIKE

8.1.2.1 First Dates

Like many, when we first met Facebook, my library was unsure exactly how to use the platform. A history of top-down approaches to marketing is just as pervasive in the academic world as it is in the commercial world. However, given the relationship-building potential of Facebook, there was the promise of something exciting and new in terms of how we might engage with stakeholders. So we plunged headlong into developing our Facebook page, pretending that our library was a person—strictly speaking, organizations were not supposed to have accounts—liking and friending everyone in sight, and giddy when someone returned the favor.

8.1.2.2 Facebook Meets Your Friends

Founded in 2004, Facebook was initially a platform to connect college students with other college students. As the site's popularity grew, librarians, like those at the Houston Cole Library at Jacksonville State University (JSU), found themselves tasked with helping packed computer laboratories of students edit Facebook profiles (Charnigo & Barnett-Ellis, 2007). Such experiences triggered the idea that maybe librarians and libraries could develop Facebook accounts to connect with their users.

My library had a "page" as early as 2005. But early adoption was a little lonely. While we prided ourselves on trying new things, it sometimes seemed as if we were waiting for everyone else to arrive. Students were participating, but the real growth would not really pick up speed until 2006. In addition, there were not that many other libraries on the platform. Both trends can be seen in Charnigo and Barnett-Ellis' 2006 study, when they surveyed 244 academic libraries to gain insight into Facebook usage. Of the 126 respondents, 60 confirmed that their institution was part of the Facebook directory. However, only 3% of respondents worked at libraries with an actual Facebook profile (Charnigo & Barnett-Ellis, 2007).

In 2006, Facebook began to garner attention outside of the college and university sphere. In March, *Business Week Online* noted that Facebook was "the seventh most trafficked website on the internet" (Rosenbush, 2006). Facebook then began to open up its membership, gradually including students in high school and members of the military. By the end of the year, the number of active users grew to 12 million, dispelling the idea that Facebook was just another passing fad (Morrissey, 2006; Lacy, 2006).

8.1.2.3 The Honeymoon Period

Social media changed the rules of marketing. With "opinion makers, journalists, seasoned practitioners and, of course, audiences" interacting, the goal was to create an organically evolving world of authentic social recommendation (Fernando, 2007). Anything was possible in this new environment, which harkened back to the 2004 film EPIC 2014, by Robin Sloan and Matt Thompson. This was a world where people could tell everyone about their day, their washing machine, and the puppy they found wandering in their neighborhood. The information moved so fast, that the puppy could be home by the next day. It was stunning. By the end of 2007, *Marketing* ranked Facebook among the Top 10 Media Brands of the year (Clark, 2007).

The potential for such organic growth emerging from recommendation and reference peaked library interest as well. If students could reach out to one another via Facebook to find puppies, then what could an academic library help them do with resources and research? Finding ways to connect with students using chat widgets and book recommendations seemed good places to start. In many ways, the waiting for the student to ask the question was no different from manning a reference desk; just more flexible in time and scope. With an increased focus on meeting students "where they are," reaching out through Facebook seemed like an opportunity not to be missed.

8.1.2.4 Moving in Together

With an average of 250,000 new registered users a day, Facebook's population soared to 57 million by the end of 2007. Suddenly we were all living, commenting, and liking together! And there is nothing like "togetherness" to test a new relationship. When in the fall, Facebook founder, Mark Zuckerberg, unveiled a new Facebook Ad system that married social recommendations to advertising campaigns, many Facebook denizens cried foul (Klaassen, 2007a). Still, opening up brand pages and matching personal data to marketing efforts knitted consumers and marketers closer together, creating a virtual cat's cradle out of this new evolving relationship.

Many of these changes made what our library was attempting to achieve a little easier. Even if you never purchased an advertisement, the likes and interactions with your patrons pulled you into conversations throughout the platform. When someone asked a question on our Page, the response would appear as a part of their newsfeed, to be liked and shared with their friends. The same could be said for unique content, like photos and videos from events. When we uploaded video from a Banned Books Week reading, friends of participants liked the content. This activity was then broadcast to others in their Facebook social circles. Reciprocity could also be utilized. If, as a Page, you "liked" what your patrons were talking about, your Page appeared among the list of people that their friends could see as active on any given post.

Functionally, it made advertisers of everyone. Your friends could not only see what you were interested in, but also see your purchases. Every "like" was a promotion. Every search was a potential piece of data that would shape what you would see in your News Feed, and what others would see about you. As Nick Carr, former executive editor of *Harvard Business Review*, noted on his blog, "First you [Facebook] get your users to entrust their personal data to you, and then you not only sell that data to advertisers, but you get the users to be the vector for the ads" (Klaassen, 2007b). In retrospect, this was a turning point for both marketers and consumers.

8.1.2.5 Communication Breakdown

Communication is a key to any relationship. Especially in a relationship that is, as Phillips (2011) pointed out, "fundamentally about relationships" (p. 512). Facebook's commitment to communication has been increasingly unpredictable. Arguably the most impactful change came in 2012.

In the fall of 2012, Facebook made substantial changes to EdgeRank, the algorithm that assembles the individual newsfeeds (McArdle, 2013). This change shifted how marketing content was selected for the NewsFeed. To make the content more "sticky," the consumer/user now had to continually engage with content from the marketer/friend. Not doing so made the content less "sticky" resulting in a decreased likelihood that the user would see future posts. At the same time, the addition of "suggested post" allowed marketers to pay to have their content fed directly into newsfeeds, increasing the likelihood that the customer would engage with the page, and thereby increasing the "stickiness" for those who paid (McArdle, 2013).

The following year, algorithms were adjusted to create new types of subfeeds, theoretically giving users more control over what they saw; such as posts from friends, the most recent posts, and posts focused around interests (Rusli, 2013). This new, constantly adjusting algorithm created a dynamic and uncertain environment, where communication was less predictable than ever. And despite Facebook's asserted goal to make the site "personal, relevant, and useful," additional changes continue to encourage an environment where it costs to communicate (Albergotti, 2014).

All of these changes actively worked against libraries, who were, as a whole, still recovering budget shortfalls from the financial crisis. At our library, we could not pay to have our content promoted. As a result, we saw a marked drop in interactions with what had been, if not a robust group of ever expanding patrons, a predictably active core of users. If our patrons were not actively tuning into, or calling up, our pages and theirs, we missed opportunities to connect.

The changes that seem to occur almost monthly with Facebook's algorithm have led to a type of fatigue among both those who use Facebook for marketing purposes and those who write about it. In May 2017, an article began "It's that time again, Facebook is changing its newsfeed algorithm, and online publishers and ad companies are trying to figure out who's in the crosshairs this time around" (Marshall, 2017). The core of all the changes continues to be EdgeRank, the algorithm Facebook uses, which first appears when you interact with an object. Three aspects of an object—affinity, weight, and time decay—are then measured to decide whether you will continue to see the object. *Affinity* refers to the relationship of the viewing user with the creator based on interactions like direct messages. The *weight* is connected to a post's popularity or importance, so the more likes or comments something gets, the longer it will appear in newsfeeds. The last is *time decay*. As you might imagine, the longer something is posted and inactive, the less likely it is to stay on the newsfeed. And while many are perhaps weary of all the algorithm talk, it remains important for marketers and consumers to understand the basics of the power of EdgeRank, especially because of the potential for invisibility.

In Fall semester 2015, UAB Libraries Marketing Committee went through a substantial change of its own, when our former chair retired. Our colleague's sole responsibility with UAB Libraries was marketing. When she retired, we not only lost her experience and leadership, but also on a more pragmatic level, her position was not replaced. Instead, her responsibilities were absorbed by a handful of UAB Marketing Committee members. These additional demands were not accompanied by a release from other responsibilities and encouraged us to consider how we might best prioritize the committee's efforts. The continued limitations of time and budget called into question our relationships with the available media channels.

8.1.3 THE TEST

In Spring semester 2016, the Marketing Committee at UAB Libraries decided to maximize our time by combining two different, though related, efforts. The first was to heavily promote Mango, a language learning product we had recently acquired. The other was to use the promotion as a way to test and see if any particular media created a spike in usage. Because it was hard to control for the expected fluctuations in hours spent using the platform throughout the semester, we decided to focus on increasing the total number of users registered on Mango weekly.

With a promotional period of 10 weeks long, we planned to use a different media, Facebook being one of them, each week in the hopes that we might have a clear winner in terms of a return on investment of marketing time and effort. The three biggest increases in the number of registered Mango user occurred in weeks six-eight (see Fig. 8.1.1).

On week six, the week we used Facebook as the primary promotion tool, we planned and scheduled a week's worth of posts at the rate of three to five per day. We chose the times of postings based on when more of our potential audience would be online. These posts included art provided by Mango that was edited as necessary by one of our committee members. The committee worked with liaison librarians to tailor language to the needs of specific groups on campus. Finally, we addressed different departments and student organizations directly in posts by using their handles. Despite these steps, a potential audience of over 2,000 via the UAB Libraries Facebook Pages, and the additional potential audience available from other departmental Facebook Pages, we only garnered 10 new registered users.

In contrast, the week we posted static flyers designed using similar art and tailored language throughout campus classroom buildings and other

	Registered users	Media	Change
Week 6	132	Student organization social media	10
Week 7	146	Flyers (around campus)	14
Week 8	163	Electronic signage	17

Figure 8.1.1 Change in registered users during weeks six through eight.

student spaces like the UAB Campus Recreation Center, we gained 14 new registered users.

Still, neither the Facebook pages nor the flyers proved to be the most successful. The committee was quite surprised when, during week eight, campus-wide electronic signage proved the most effective of all marketing media attempted.

We had not anticipated this. The use of the electronic signage included some inherent limitations. We could not tailor the language as specifically as we could for Facebook or even flyers that were easily directed toward specific subgroups. Furthermore, the electronic signage was primarily located in the lobbies of student dormitories. The small number of students living in campus dormitories meant a potential audience significantly smaller than that found in classroom buildings or indeed on campus-wide social media. In addition, locations where students might have come into contact with the signage in nondormitory locations were at a minimum, since neither the new campus student center nor library locations were viable options for electronic signage at the time of the test. Despite these limitations, we added 17 registered users that week.

We understand that none of these differences are statistically significant. In addition, we understand the impact of one media was not bound by our weekly change and some of the increase could have been influenced by a previous week. However, we were looking for a clear spike in registrants and that did not happen.

8.1.3.1 Couples Therapy

The unintended consequence of our test was that a few members of the Marketing Committee questioned the wisdom of continuing to use Facebook as a medium for marketing. They wondered if it would be better to focus our efforts instead on flyers, whose audience required less continual cultivation. They also wondered if perhaps the electronic signage, which was being expanded into other locations and managed centrally, might not be a better use of time.

In 1994, Marshall McLuhan "depicted media as an extension of the human central nervous system. In this way all technologies are instrumental extensions of our physical and nervous systems . . ." (Hess, 2014). It probably comes as no surprise, that while some were ready to stop using Facebook, others on the Marketing Committee had a visceral reaction to this idea of abandoning Facebook. The possibility was only brought back to the table for consideration when a Marketing student with whom we were later working pointed out that our ratio of Facebook fans to the increasing number of enrolled students—during Spring 2016 it was approximately 1:9—meant a progressively smaller potential audience.

In a 2017 article, Harrison, Burress, Velasquez, and Schreiner (2017) argued that a normative mechanism is pushing academic libraries onto social media, without regard for efficiency or efficacy. Certainly, those at UAB Libraries who are in charge of marketing and social media have experienced plenty of "push" to continue using Facebook as a communication outlet. What we have lacked is a mechanism to evaluate the effectiveness of what we are doing.

To that end, we developed a rubric of sorts based on the following considerations:

Audience—Facebook's audience is always changing. Currently 24–35 is the largest age demographic. Ask yourself if that is your audience. Who is your audience?

Reach—Ask if you are reaching your audience. Are they reaching back? More likes does not mean more engagement and engagement is what matters. If you know the approximate size of your audience, say the student population of an urban university, compare it to the size of your active fans. Is that good enough for you?

Goals/Purpose—Most academic libraries use social media to do some combination of the following: marketing, staff development, community connection. Which you are doing? Is it effective? How do you know?

Media—Facebook is a really good choice if you want to work with live video and do not have access to something like Citrix or Zoom. However, if you are curating a collection of images, Flickr with a Creative Commons license might be a better choice.

The rubric below can be used to justify leaving or staying with Facebook, and can be tweaked to evaluate other social media tools. There is no expectation that anyone would score 20 out of 20, which is the highest score possible using the rubric. We chose 12 as our "break even" point. Feel free to choose your own.

Keep in mind that for some libraries a lower score could indicate that it is time to say goodbye, while for others (especially those who have not been working with Facebook for very long) a lower score could just indicate a need to expand what they are doing with the platform. Indeed if a library is just beginning to use a specific social media tool, and its use of the tool

The Rubric:

	1	2	3	4	5
Audience	Audience is the whole campus	Audience is divided between undergrads and grads	Audience includes undergrads, grads, faculty, & staff	Previous + further divided into various subgroups based on major	Previous 2 + aware of several interest groups within campus population
Reach	People rarely comment, like, or share	People like posts, but only occasionally comment or share	People frequently like and share posts	There is a core group of followers who routinely engage with posts	People frequently engage with each other while commenting on posts
Goals	Promote services, content and/or space	Previous + routinely provide reference services and/or chat with patrons	Previous 2 + connect to and/or cultivate relationships with groups /communities on or off campus	Previous 3 + participate in staff development opportunities with groups like LMAO	Previous 4 + actively communicate with staff about library services, new content and events
Media	Never use media, only post status updates	Post status updates with the images and/or graphics	Previous + routinely share images from around the library and/or campus	Previous 2 + promote and/or deep link to our collections	Previous 3 + use Facebook live to meet with students/hold meetings

Figure 8.1.2 Rubric developed to evaluate Facebook usage.

scores close to 12 on the rubric, this might indicate continuing growth with your audience, requiring only a little more time to mature (Fig. 8.1.2).

8.1.3.2 Decisions

After evaluating our activity on Facebook using the Rubric, we found that we scored exactly 12. Weighing the score against the age of the Facebook pages, the Marketing Committee decided that the best course of action was a compromise. We had been negotiating the possibility of merging the two pages into one and so, decided to use the merger as an opportunity to do so while gauging campus interest in a continued UAB Libraries Facebook Page. To that end, we created and promoted a new page and selected a start date of April 1, 2018 to begin using the new Page exclusively. We also designated an end date for this new evaluative period and selected our minimum number of users by which we will judge success. We are currently in the beginning of this final effort.

8.1.3.3 Recommendations

- Establish an audience, then tailor posts to their wants and needs.
- Plan ahead and prepare posts with Facebook scheduling or another medium like Hootsuite. This will prevent burn out or time wasted worrying about what to post each day.
- Have a goal in mind. It is easy to get caught up posting just to post. This goal could be a number of followers, a specific level of interactions, or promoting a specific resource consistently. Goals keep priorities in focus.
- Measure usage through Analytics. Pay attention to users' interactions with the post beyond likes.
- Try different times of the day to post. Heck, let different people post! Different voices can keep things interesting and fresh. I asked a staff member to start posting on our Facebook page, and her post resulted in more likes than mine ever had!
- Test other mediums or channels against Facebook. Maybe Facebook is the best channel or perhaps it is not.
- Consult team members. Get multiple perspectives on what to post, how often, and if putting the energy into your channel is worth it. A student worker pointed out our low percentage of followers to student body on campus. It was eye opening and led us to our adjustment period.

8.1.4 FINAL WORDS

As of right now, whether you are a marketer or a consumer, if you are not a Facebook user who conforms to the algorithmic "ideal" by actively and frequently posting, liking, direct messaging, sharing, and chatting, you will gradually lose your voice. One of the core functions of media is to make someone or something more visible, not less (Bucher, 2012). Facebook's algorithm-mediated communication contributes to ongoing questions about not only Facebook's presumed mantel, but also what it means if we are entering a world where our voices are entirely constructed and mediated by a third party.

REFERENCES

Albergotti, R. (2014). Facebook says it will phase out companies' promotional posts. *Wall Street Journal - Eastern Edition.*, B3. Available from https://www.wsj.com/.

Bucher, T. (2012). Want to be on the top? Algorithmic power and the threat of invisibility on Facebook. *New Media & Society, 14*(7), 1164–1180. Available from https://doi.org/10.1177/1461444812440159.

Charnigo, L., & Barnett-Ellis, P. (2007). Checking out Facebook.com: The impact of a digital trend on academic libraries. *Information Technology and Libraries, 26*(1), 23–34. Available from https://doi.org/10.6017/ital.v26i1.3286.

Clark, N. (2007). Top 10 media brands of 2007. *Marketing, 19*. Available from http://www.haymarket.com/home.aspx.

Fernando, A. (2007). Social media change the rules. *Communication World, 24*(1), 9–10. Available from http://www.scirp.org/.

Harrison, A., Burress, R., Velasquez, S., & Schreiner, L. (2017). Social media use in academic libraries: A phenomenological study. *The Journal of Academic Librarianship, 43*, 248–257. Available from https://doi.org/10.1016/j.acalib.2017.02.014.

Hess, A. (2014). You are what you compute (and what is computed for you): Considerations of digital rhetorical identification. *Journal of Contemporary Rhetoric, 4* (1/2), 1–19. Available from http://contemporaryrhetoric.com/.

Klaassen, A. (2007a). People power. *Marketing Magazine, 112*(22), 13. Available from http://strategyonline.ca/issue/.

Klaassen, A. (2007b). Real revolution isn't Facebook's ad plan. *Advertising Age, 78*(45), 3, 61. Available from http://www.adage.com/.

Lacy, S. (2006). Facebook: Opening the doors wider. *BusinessWeek Online, 8*. Available from https://www.bloomberg.com/.

Marshall, J. (2017). Digital media world tries to decode Facebook's latest algorithm tweak. *Wall Street Journal (Online)*. Available from https://www.wsj.com/.

McArdle, M. (2013). How to get ahead on Facebook without really trying. *Newsweek Global, 161*(10), 1. Available from http://www.newsweek.com/.

Morrissey, B. (2006). Facebook Gives New Face to Online Ads. *Brandweek, 47*(35), 11.

Phillips, N. K. (2011). Academic library use of Facebook: Building relationships with students. *The Journal of Academic Librarianship, 37*(6), 512–522. Available from https://doi.org/10.1016/j.acalib.2011.07.008.

Rosenbush, S. (2006). Facebook's on the block. *BusinessWeek Online, 16*. Available from https://www.bloomberg.com/.

Rusli, E. (2013). Facebook unveils changes to its news feed. *Wall Street Journal - Eastern Edition*, B4. Available from https://www.wsj.com/.

FURTHER READING

Fowler, G. A. (2010). Facebook unseats algorithm as boss. *Wall Street Journal - Eastern Edition.*, B1–B7. Available from https://www.wsj.com/.

8.2 CASE STUDY 2

Buying Likes: How Our Library Jumped From 200 to 1000 (Student) Likes in 5 Months

Nina Verishagen[1] and Ann Liang[2]
[1]Saskatchewan Polytechnic Library, Saskatchewan Polytechnic, Saskatoon, SK, Canada
[2]Saskatchewan Polytechnic Library, Saskatchewan Polytechnic, Moose Jaw, SK, Canada

Institution: Saskatchewan Polytechnic Library; 27,897 (2016–17) students across four campuses, five library locations (Saskatchewan Polytechnic, 2017).

Campaign Purpose: To attain and retain as many student Facebook likes as possible during their career at our institution.

Target Demographic: Students.

Measure of Success: Increased student engagement with the page (liking, sharing, commenting on posts); 1000 student likes by 2016, retained until Spring 2017 (end of academic year).

Team: Two librarians, two library technicians, one library clerk (for half the campaign), support from library staff and the institution's Communications and Marketing department.

8.2.1 THE SITUATION

In 2016, our Facebook page was not working. We had 200 likes on the page and very little engagement—a few comments, likes on posts, and user posts (usually complaints from the same user).

We started collecting informal information about which social media platforms our students were using in 2013. That year we distributed a survey to students at our annual Welcome Day event, asking them if they had a Facebook or Twitter account (these were the two platforms our library was using at the time). Eighty six percent (609 of 708 students surveyed) indicated that Facebook was the *only* social media platform they engaged with. Thirty two percent indicated they used a Twitter account, and nearly all students who had Twitter, were also using Facebook (226 of 229 Twitter users). Forty eight percent of surveyed students said they would follow or like us, if presented with our pages.

In spring of 2016, we asked our library advisory councils (62 student and faculty participants across four campuses) which platforms they engaged with, 77% ($n = 48$) reported that they were active Facebook users. Although this data only represents a portion of our community, it is meaningful. Every time the question has been posed, which social media platform do you use, Facebook is the overwhelming answer.

8.2.2 THE IDEA

Since taking over the page as admins in 2013, we had not been posting strategically. Every day or so we would post about an electronic resource, or a book hoping one of our followers would share or like it. When we finally began to think about it, we were not sure if our followers were a part of our current academic community. At some point they might have been, but there had been very little movement in over three years and we are an institution that offers certificates, diplomas, and *some* four-year degrees. Most of our students are with us for one or two semesters (sometimes only weeks). So even if those who were following us were students, it was unlikely that they were currently enrolled.

Our goal became twofold, get the likes, and keep the likes, for as long as a person remains a student. We had learned from our only previously successful campaign that to grab the attention of our user and get them to commit to liking our page, we had to offer incentive. We also understood that gaining a page like does not necessarily mean retention of the like or engagement from the like-ee. As such, the monthly contest was born. Rather than one big promotion with one large prize, we told our users to like our page, then watch for upcoming contests in hopes that we could retain the like and increase overall follower engagement.

8.2.3 SO IT MOSTLY WORKED! HERE'S HOW

8.2.3.1 Step 1: Make a Plan, But Remain Flexible

As with any major project at our library, we developed a plan. This document resided in a folder saved on SharePoint—our communication sharing site, along with other important contest information. The plan included:

- **Budget**
  - We utilized our social media management budget ($1000 for prizes, post boosts [which we did not end up doing], and a Hootsuite subscription which is a social media management platform that allows for advanced scheduling and coordinating of social media posts). We also utilized certain budgetary lines set aside for events to do contest promotions, for example, money for prize giveaways, as additional means to promote the contest.

- **Logistics**
  - Facebook requires users who are holding contests to include a *disclaimer*, which releases them from any connection to the contest and requires those who are holding the contest to link to an official rules page (Facebook Advertising Policies, n.d.).
  - *The Contest Rules* were crucial and detailed, outlining how the contest works and providing the appropriate information to entrants. We adapted a rule page created by our institutions Communications and Marketing (C&M) department for a contest they had previously held. We posted it on our library's homepage, as we were not able to post this information on Facebook, as per their Advertising Policies (Facebook Advertising Policies, n.d.). Every post related to the contest had a link to this page: http://library.saskpolytech.ca/news/posts/2017/Library-Facebook-Contest-Rules.aspx.
  - We developed a plan for *choosing winners*, which ensured they were selected at random and that they had liked our page. This section also included instructions on how to notify winners.
- **Timelines**
  - A projected timeline of the contest was outlined on this page. Ours would be held on the third Monday of each month, and winners would have two days to claim their prize (this, like many other pieces in the plan would be modified as needed throughout the year).

Another key planning document was our Promotion Plan, which guided the branding and marketing strategy for the contest. The plan included things like: library staff education, events we planned to advertise at, promotional materials for librarians to utilize in their teaching sessions, signage, and ideas for giveaways (for more on this, see Step 3: Promote, Promote, Promote).

When we originally envisioned the contest, we had each monthly activity mapped out, down to the contest question, prizes, and dates. Here are two examples:

8.2.3.1.1 Launch—September

- Prizes: Four $25 Prepaid Gift Cards–institution-wide.
- Runs: 20 days—Tuesday, September 6th–Monday, September 26th.
- Purpose: A big kick off to garner as many likes as possible.
- Requirement: LIKE the page to enter.
- Result: Success (# of likes).

8.2.3.1.2 Regular Monthly—Ran November, December, March, April

- Prize: Gift card of some sort, usually a denomination below $25 and for popular store or service, Starbucks, for example.
- Run: six days
- Purpose: Usually a tie in with something happening at the library or on campus, for example, in March the contest tied in with Intercultural Week.
- Requirement: Engage with post as indicated in contest directions—this could be a like, share, comment or a combination.
- Result: Some monthly contests were very successful, some were not.

It should be noted that the January and February contests were canceled because the social media team felt like there was contest burn out. In November there was no up-take from students, even a generic $25 prize did not seem to appeal.

Over time we realized that contests would need to be altered. We came to understand that they could not be too detailed (as many of our planned contests were), and we had to make room for unplanned targeted contests. For instance, after the low participation with a selfie contest, we developed a new idea for a photo contest using a photo booth manned by a library staff member who would engage with the participants, sign the appropriate forms, and take the photo with fun props and backgrounds. This opportunity for face-to-face interaction with students also allowed us to ask questions about our services. Anyone who participated in the photo booth was automatically entered into the contest. This was so successful that our Institution's C&M department did this exact same photo booth idea for their Welcome Week activities months later. The next time we do this, we have invested in a mobile photo printer (Sprocket) and we will see if providing students with the instant gratification of a photo will increase participation and interest.

8.2.3.2 Step 2: Ask for Help From the Big Guys

We worked with our Institutional C&M department to develop a look for the contest. The look fell into a new visual image for the entire institution and the library, which had been developed earlier in the year. They created a PowerPoint slide, table toppers (that were placed in student lounges or hubs), and web images to promote the contest (Fig 8.2.1).

Developing a relationship with this department was especially helpful in getting advice, as they had run similar contests in the past. It was also a

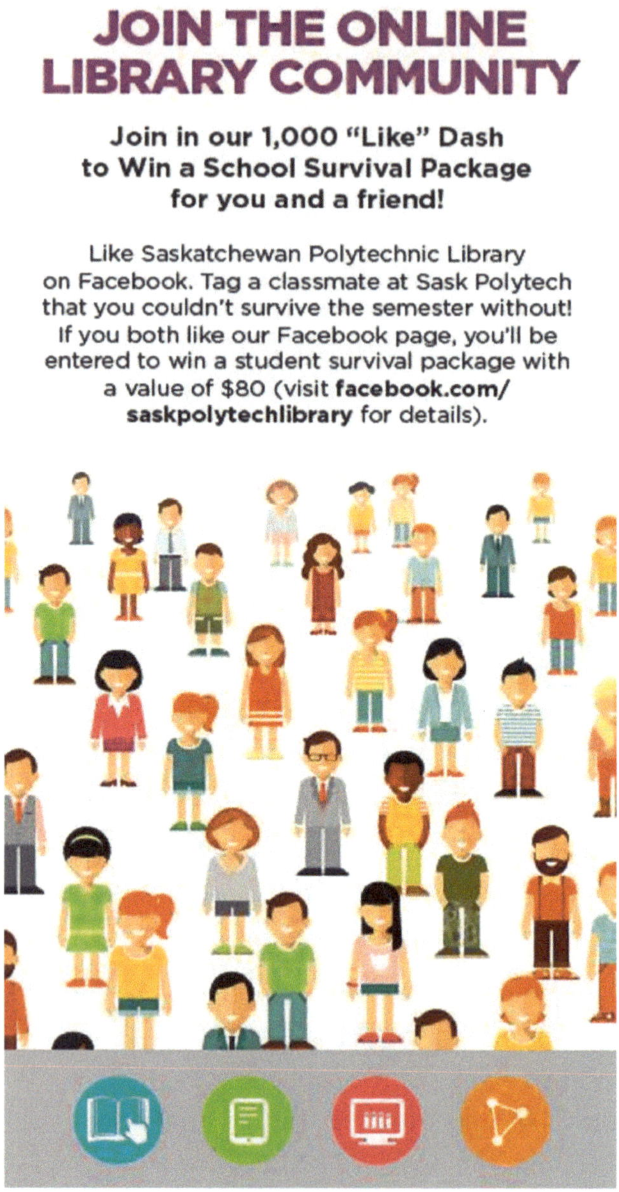

Figure 8.2.1 An original promotional piece, developed by the Institution's C&M department.

way to ensure that our schedules for online promotions did not conflict with theirs. For instance, at the beginning of the year they had run a very successful selfies contest, which we did not want to compete with.

In some instances we requested that the C&M department share our Facebook posts to their page (which has over 30,000 likes), in others we would simply tag their page in our post. We would also tag other active institutional Facebook pages, for example, the International Students page. This would give the administrator of the page a notification and would often trigger a "Share" or "Like" of the post. These shares helped us to reach students that were a part of the Sask Polytech community, but who may not have joined our page yet.

8.2.3.3 Step 3: Promote, Promote, Promote

8.2.3.3.1 Inform Your Staff, They Are Your Most Valuable Asset

It was crucial that library staff understood the contest. Being that our libraries are spread across four campuses in four different cities, it is easy for information to fall through the cracks. If a project lead does not communicate something effectively, it can be quite damaging, especially for a campaign such as this.

In mid-August, approximately two weeks before the contest launch, we hosted miniature Skype for Business (our video conferencing system) meetings to inform staff about the contest. All library staff were required to attend. These informational meetings took only 5–10 minutes of their time. We used a short PowerPoint to describe the contest.

These meetings were valuable in informing staff, but they were also an opportunity for the staff to provide feedback, showcase interest and ask questions. For example, we put together a document of talking points for front-end staff because a staff member suggested it in one of these meetings.

8.2.3.3.2 Tell Your Students

The main promotional effort for this contest involved Word of Mouth Marketing. As indicated in the previous section, staff members were armed with contest details at the front desk, so they could respond to student questions with ease.

In addition, a very large point of contact between students and library staff occurs during Library Orientations. In September 2016, 3332 students had face-to-face contact with one of our 13 Librarians at all campus locations. We created a PowerPoint slide (describing the contest) and

Figure 8.2.2 Contest PowerPoint slide.

asked all of the librarians to include it in their orientation materials (Fig. 8.2.2).

Initially we suggested they add it to the end of their slides, but after teaching a few classes ourselves, we realized it was more effective to have the slide up when the students entered. Since they often show up early, log on to the computers or fiddle on their smartphones waiting for other classmates to arrive, it is a great opportunity to tell them about the contest.

We noticed significant spikes at times when orientations were occurring, sometimes 10 or more likes within a 5-minute period. See Appendix A for the full breakdown of the changes in our "Likes" as we progressed through different promotional efforts. The Likes data indicates that our most effective promotional effort occurred within the library classroom.

8.2.3.3.3 Utilize Every Face-to-Face Opportunity

Each Fall semester there is a Welcome Day at each campus. Student Services, including the library, set up booths in high traffic areas and most use incentives to facilitate informal conversations. In 2016 the library booths hosted prize wheels, one of the prizes was a candy bag with a label that described the contest. The candy and materials were purchased in bulk, making them very cost-effective, and they were extremely popular. We also plastered the booth with information about the contest and encouraged the staff working at the booth to promote it. Of note, 147 likes were gained during this event, due to the combination of promotional candy bags, signage, and the staff's vocal encouragement.

8.2.3.3.4 Keep It Simple

We originally planned to work with our Institution's C&M department to brand the campaign with specific visuals and use them throughout. However, we found that the design was very text-heavy and ineffective (see Fig. 8.2.1). Over time, we discovered that having library staff working directly with an online design tool (Canva.com) allowed for a quicker turn-around. We could decide on a contest on a Monday, and throw something unique and appealing together to be posted on Tuesday. Whereas, when working with our C&M department, we would often have to wait a number of days (sometimes weeks) to move up in their queue and see a design (see Fig. 8.2.3). In the social media environment, waiting often is not an option. Our designs often used only an image, or very straightforward instructional text. Fig. 8.2.3 is an example of a simple graphic created for our most successful contest. This post reached 10,411 people, had 269 Likes, Comments & Shares, and 800 post clicks.

This workflow change was a blessing in disguise as we would later discover that Facebook updated its Ad Approval process to stipulate that text-heavy images would be shown to less followers and cost more to run (Facebook Advertising Policies, n.d.). It is very possible that by the time you are reading this the Ad Approval Process will have gone through another round of changes, as we are aware of the approval process having changed twice since we began this campaign.

Figure 8.2.3 Simple contest design created by library staff.

8.2.3.4 Step 4: Selecting Winners

Since this was a first try at contests, we opted for a low tech solution for randomly selecting winners. We collected entrant's names in an Excel spreadsheet and used a randomization formula (=INDIRECT (CONCATENATE ("A(column)", RANDBETWEEN (1, end number)))) that would select one name from the list entered. However, as our contest gained more exposure and more entrants, this method became time consuming. We found a free solution on a website called "The Good Luck Fairy" by fanpage karma (http://www.fanpagekarma.com/facebook-promotion). We would enter the URL of our post, then the site would sift through the comments and likes and select a random winner (Fig. 8.2.4). To find the URL for the specific post, you can click on the date/time stamp (this is located below your Facebook username) and it will bring you to that post's URL to copy and paste it.

In addition, we needed to confirm that the winners had in fact liked our page and were current students.

In order to confirm if a participant has liked the page, visit your page's *Settings* and select *People and Other Pages* on the left-hand side. Here you are able to search for people who like the page. One important note is that if someone has incredibly restrictive privacy settings for their Facebook profile, they may not show up in this listing.

To confirm that the potential winner was a current student, we consulted a student directory. However, a problem emerged in situations when a student used a pseudonym on Facebook. In this case we would contact the student first via Facebook Messenger (if their profile allowed others to contact them), if they entered the contest by commenting on the post, a message button will appear under their comment. We would inform them that they had won the contest, but that we needed their full name and campus location. We then confirmed that the student was in our directory and proceeded with awarding the prize. Since we are across multiple campuses, the prizes needed to be mailed via interoffice mail, and the student would get a follow up message alerting them of when the prize has arrived and when they could pick it up. We also had each winner sign a receipt of prize.

8.2.3.5 Step 5: Announce the Winners

Early in the planning process, the team discussed the many social media contests we, as social media users ourselves, had entered throughout the

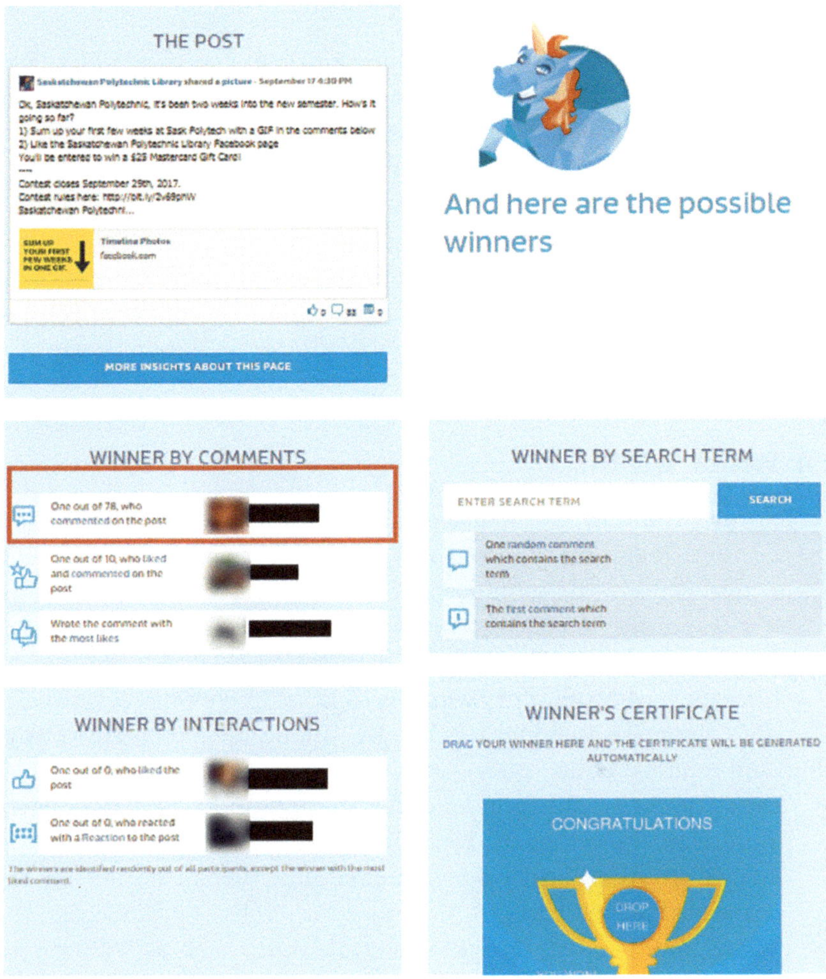

Figure 8.2.4 Good Luck Fairy.

years. Many of us were unable to pinpoint who had ever won these contests, all we could say for certain was that it had not been us. We wondered: Did anyone win? Were the prizes even real? Therefore, we decided to show our followers that our prizes were real and our winners did exist. When the winner came to pick up their prize, we asked for consent (vocal and written) to pose for a picture. Most winners were happy to pose for a photo, and the posts that resulted were among our highest performing for the year.

8.2.3.6 Step 6: Assess

Pay attention to the information made available via Facebook's Post Details. Click on the hyperlinked number of people reached (below each post) to view the *Performance of Your Post*. This will provide you with the good (likes, comments), the bad (hide posts), and the ugly (unlike page). You can also do this by clicking on *Insights* then *Posts*. This will provide a list of All Posts Published and include details like *Reach* and *Engagement*. Use this information to assess. Why did six people unfollow our page after that post? How can we avoid this in the future? Then, dust yourself off and try again.

8.2.4 WHAT WORKED

- Unplanned Contests targeting specific groups.
  - Contests that were targeted toward specific school-related events or groups were the most successful. For example, contests directed at our nursing students, which offered a specific academic prize (an online password for an exam prep resource).
- Collaborating with other departments to develop contests.
- Simplified contests (see Fig. 8.2.3)—gifs, asking their program, engaging, and minimal effort.
  - Each contest would include, at the absolute most, two tasks, listed in numerical order at the top of the post so participants would see them first. Additional rules or information would be left for the second half of the post.
  - Asking more casual, less academic questions, such as "What program are you in?"
- Using online graphic design software.
  - We recommend Canva.com; vecteezy.com (for free copyright cleared clipart); paint.net (for free open source photo editing).
- Using a Third Party scheduling system to plan and schedule posts across multiple platforms, we used Hootsuite (for pricing information, see Chapter 5: Using Scheduling Apps to Streamline a Social Media Workflow).
- Face-to-face promotion or in-person contests (photo booth example).
- Posting images of winners.

8.2.5 WHAT DIDN'T WORK

- Heavily detailed signage and web images (see Fig. 8.2.1).
- Complicated contests.
  - If a contest required too much thought or effort, students simply would not participate.
  - It was also difficult to garner student interest in the selfie contests with an associated hashtag, or to post them on the contest post on our Facebook page. The one time we attempted this we had only one entrant.
- Advertising in high traffic areas.
  - We placed table toppers (tents) in high student traffic areas such as the student lounges, cafeterias, and computer laboratories and utilized our institution's digital signage that appears in hallways and congregation areas. However it is difficult to establish if this promotion worked. Assessments could be done in the future.

8.2.6 RECOMMENDATIONS

- Ensure you are running your contest on the platform of choice for the majority of your target demographic.
- Make a plan, but be ready to adjust it based on successes and failures.
- Follow the platform's rules for contests.
- Utilize your most vital asset, your people.
- Take advantage of every face-to-face opportunity with your target demographic.
- Partner up with departments that can help you via cross posting and shares.
- Use the data made available by the platform.
- Keep it simple.

8.2.7 WHERE ARE WE NOW?

So we accomplished what we had set out to do. We reached 1000 likes by the Spring of 2017 and our engagement has never been higher. We have also learned a lot in the past two years, but not so surprisingly things have already started to change. Those who have already liked our page are engaging with posts like never before. A post from October 2017, that our Institutional Facebook page did *not* share, asking followers to "tag a friend you're thankful for" reached 10,410 people, had 799 post clicks and 235 comments. With only five followers hiding that specific post, and two hiding all of our posts. These are numbers we would have never dreamt of in early 2015.

We still do contests, but not under a specific campaign and not every month, and we have noticed that our overall followers have stagnated since the end of the original contest. This could be attributed to the lack of a specific contest campaign, or maybe it is a sign that the Facebook landscape or our student's social media preferences are changing. What is this telling us? it's time to assess.

8.2.8 FINAL WORDS

It has been interesting to complete this chapter almost a full two years after its original conception, and amidst an ever changing social media world. We ourselves, are Millennials, and avid social media users and we have personally pulled away from using Facebook. With the rising popularity of other platforms, we wonder, are our students still using this platform? Should we be continuing with these efforts? We realize that there is a constant need to assess our target user groups and ensure that the social platform we are utilizing is not only in the palm of their hands, but also that they actually want us participating on that platform. Our next step will be to assess the continual usage of Facebook, or consider incorporating a new platform. We want to be critical of Facebook in particular in light of the changes coming that will prevent "Engagement Baiting" posts targeted at users; which means we will no longer be able to ask users to comment, vote, react, share, or like a post (Silverman, 2017). One thing we can say with confidence is that the points laid out in the recommendations section, unlike social media platforms themselves, will remain effective and constant for libraries or similar institution looking to build a social media contest. This campaign was a definite success and an educational experience for those of us on the Social Media committee.

APPENDIX A: COMPARISON OF "LIKES" BEFORE AND AFTER AN EVENT OR CONTEST

Event	Initial likes	Likes after event	Change in likes
Initial likes as of Sep. 1, 2016	315		
Orientations period, Sep. 6–26, 2016	325, Sep. 5, 2016	696, Sep. 26, 2016	+371
Welcome Day activities, Sep. 6–9, 2016	325, Sep. 5, 2016	472, Sep. 9, 2016	+147
September contest, Sep. 13–26, 2016	482, Sep. 12, 2016	696, Sep. 26, 2016	+214
October contest–1000 like dash, Oct. 4, 2016–Feb. 24, 2017	711, Oct. 3, 2016	1005, Feb. 24, 2017	+294
NCLEX, Nov. 6, 2016–Nov. 14, 2016			
December Contest, Dec. 15, 2016; Stress Better Related to Dec. 21, 2016	897, Dec. 14, 2016	914, Dec. 21, 2016	+17
March Contest Intercultural week selfie, March 21–24, 2017	1011, Mar. 20, 2017	1018, Mar. 24, 2017	+7
April Contest Stress Better, Apr. 10–13, 2017 comment	1023, Apr. 20, 2017	1038, Apr. 13, 2017	+15
1000 Like photo booth contest, Apr. 12–13, 2017	1029, Apr. 11, 2017	1038, Apr. 13, 2017	+9
May 1–7, 2017, mental health week contest self care package provided by nursing	1036, Apr. 30, 2017	1041, May 7, 2017	+5

REFERENCES

Facebook Advertising Policies. (n.d.). Available from https://www.facebook.com/policies/ads/#

Saskatchewan Polytechnic. (2017). *Impact that matters: 2016–2017 Annual report*. Available from http://saskpolytech.ca/about/about-us/reports-and-statistics/annualreport/documents/2016-17%20Sask%20Polytech%20Annual%20Report.pdf

Silverman, H. (2017, December 18). News feed FYI: Fighting engagement bait on Facebook | Facebook newsroom. Available from https://newsroom.fb.com/news/2017/12/news-feed-fyi-fighting-engagement-bait-on-facebook/

8.3 CASE STUDY 3

So You Have Been Given the Social Media Passwords. Now What? A Trial-by-Fire Case Study in Facebook Marketing

Molly Marcusse
American Heritage Center, University of Wyoming, Laramie, WY, United States

Institution: American Heritage Center (AHC), University of Wyoming; 12,397 students (September 2017). University of Wyoming is the only 4-year degree-granting school in the state of Wyoming.

Campaign Purpose: Facebook engagement, knowledge of resources and archives, grow institution's online audience, and generate potential in-person users. Ongoing campaign.

Target Demographic: Residents of Wyoming.

Measure of Success: Increased followers, increased and sustained engagement (likes, comments, and shares), and increased and sustained number of reference requests from Facebook.

Team: AHC website/marketing committee; currently two archivists and one office associate, with support from other archives employees. At start of campaign committee was comprised of two archivists, one graphic designer, and one photographer; all but myself have left the AHC. I take primary responsibility for Facebook management.

8.3.1 THE SITUATION I INHERITED

The American Heritage Center (AHC) is the archives at University of Wyoming. The AHC holds approximately 75,000 linear feet of material in collecting areas that include Wyoming and the West, the University of Wyoming archives, mining and petroleum industries, the entertainment industry, environmental conservation, and a range of other topics. Holdings include materials on local history from across Wyoming, state and regional history, national history in some areas, and international history in other areas.

A previous archivist launched the AHC's online marketing in 2011 by creating and maintaining a Wordpress blog, a Facebook page, and a Twitter account. She was passionate about maintaining the social media presence for the archives but found it difficult to balance with other responsibilities. She left for another position in September 2015, and the AHC's existing website committee was tasked with this responsibility. Simultaneously, I was assigned to join the committee. The website committee had previously been responsible only for the institution's official university webpage but was excited to take on social media management. My first meeting with the committee consisted of a training session on each of the social media platforms and a gift: the social media passwords! And ta-da! Social media was suddenly part of my job.

My experience with these platforms was not extensive. I had used Twitter only in graduate school when it was required for a course; I had never used Wordpress. I was at least a proficient Facebook user. The other committee members were also most comfortable with Facebook. We began experimenting with this weird, new job responsibility as a group. Quickly, we saw an issue with the Facebook page. When we took over in September 2015, we had about 450 followers but these followers were rarely engaging with our posts in any way. In fact, committee members' parents were among the only followers that were liking posts consistently; the gesture was appreciated, but not our goal. In addition to the lack of engagement, our number of followers had remained stagnant for some time. This was an opportunity to experiment with the Facebook page and figure out how to grow and engage the audience.

8.3.2 THE FIRST FACEBOOK EXPERIMENT: #FOOTBALLFRIDAY

My first experiment with Facebook posting for the AHC focused on one of my interests: college football. I knew from my investigations into other institutions' experiences that having a regularly occurring themed post had been successful for other cultural heritage institutions on social media and decided to launch a series for the fall that I called #FootballFriday (Hager, Daniel, Nash, Norling, & Crilly, 2015). College football games are typically on Saturday, and my hope was that by posting the day before, people getting excited about the upcoming football game would engage with the posts through likes, shares, and comments and become regular followers. Each Friday during the 2015 football season, I posted a historical tidbit from the AHC's holdings to the Facebook and Twitter pages. In choosing materials, the following were some of my criteria:

- materials related to a previous game against the week's opponent (Fig. 8.3.1);

Figure 8.3.1 An example of a #FootballFriday post from November 2015 that gives the history of a tradition with longstanding rival, Colorado State University. The post did not receive much engagement.

- materials related to a previous game on the same date; or
- if neither of those were available, I would choose something fun that I found interesting.

The campaign ended with University of Wyoming's football season in November 2015. Even though the topic and content were rich in potential, the #FootballFriday posts rarely performed well. The posts typically reached 100–300 people, received a few likes, and sometimes were shared or commented on by one person. I examined the results of this campaign to figure out what had gone wrong:

- I did not sponsor any of the posts and instead expected a new audience to discover the posts on their own. Sponsoring some or all of these posts would have helped the posts receive more engagement.
- Football was an interest of mine but possibly not an interest of the existing audience. I found the content interesting and expected a new audience to find the posts and become followers.
- If football was of interest to individuals in the existing audience, the 2015 season was not particularly good for University of Wyoming. By writing about undefeated seasons and bowl game wins from the 1950s and 1960s, I failed to see my audience's perspective of the present and was reminding them of a renowned past that had seemed to disappear.
- I missed opportunities to promote this campaign to the audience that would have been interested. A partnership with the University of Wyoming football Facebook page would have been beneficial. I also could have sponsored posts to increase the number of people that saw them.

Throughout the fall 2015 #FootballFriday campaign, I had one truly successful post. It was my post related to the homecoming game. For this post, instead of focusing directly on football, I found a great photo of the University of Wyoming marching band majorettes from the 1941 homecoming parade. Over homecoming weekend, the post was shared by a large number of people, received a large number of likes, and reached over 10,000 people (Fig. 8.3.2). This post immediately became the most successful post to the AHC's Facebook page up to that time. I think this post was successful because the focus on the homecoming parade seemed to resonate with my current group of followers more than the posts focused solely on football. I also think this post was more successful than others in the #FootballFriday campaign because it was posted during homecoming week when alumni and the university community are most engaged with campus. This post received a high number of shares that led to nonfollowers seeing the post and engaging with it by liking, commenting, or sharing. Although the #FootballFriday posts did not receive much engagement when I posted them, I have found that the posts featuring video of old games have been successful over time. I think that these videos have seen long-term success because Facebook puts videos near the top when people are viewing the AHC's page, tempting them to click and watch.

Figure 8.3.2 #FootballFriday post for the week of Homecoming. This post was an immediate success and outperformed any previous posts to the AHC's Facebook page.

In trying to determine what did not work in the #FootballFriday campaign, I turned to the data provided by Facebook (called "Facebook Insights") to learn more about the current followers, what might resonate with them, and future areas for growth.

8.3.3 USING THE DATA TO DEFINE MY AUDIENCE

After this experiment, I needed to learn more about my existing followers in order to increase engagement with them. I also needed to learn more about them to identify areas for audience growth and pockets of potential followers that I should cater to (Watson, 2016). In using Facebook Insights, I gathered that of the existing 450 followers, almost all of them lived in two cities. First was Laramie, WY, the home of University of Wyoming and the AHC. Second was Cheyenne, WY, the state capital, largest city in the state, and the only city within an hour of Laramie and the AHC. Those 450 followers were split fairly evenly between men and women (the only gender data that Facebook gives). Those 450 followers were also fairly evenly split among the age groups delineated by Facebook (13–17, 18–24, 25–34, 35–44, 45–54, 55–64, and 65 +), with 13–17 being the smallest group.

I had learned through research that having a narrow focus in social media for archives can increase success, and I chose to focus on Wyoming residents as my target audience, using Wyoming history as the primary content (Hager, 2015, pp. 34–35). Why focus on the residents of Wyoming? The simplest reason is because this incorporated and built upon my existing audience. I also wanted to focus broadly on the residents of Wyoming instead of just a narrow focus on the campus community because University of Wyoming is a land-grant university, making outreach to the state an important function of the university and its units.

I also felt that the general nature of Wyoming made this a natural fit. Wyoming is one of the largest US states in terms of physical land but has the smallest population of all states with a little under 600,000 people (U.S. Census Bureau, 2017). This means the population is spread out and the entire state has a small-town feel. Due to the physical size of Wyoming, many state residents are not able to visit the AHC in person. Facebook provides an opportunity to reach those residents and show them some of the holdings and what the archives can do for them. I particularly wanted to increase the number of followers from across the entire state. Laramie and Cheyenne are among the largest cities in Wyoming and contain about one-third of the state's population, making them important audiences. I wanted to reach the residents of Wyoming's smaller towns as well. Through Facebook and other marketing efforts, I want Wyoming residents to see the AHC as a potential resource that they can ask questions of without having to be in the physical building in Laramie (Theimer, 2011, pp. 335–336).

Another unique aspect of Wyoming is that the Wyoming State Historical Society does not collect or maintain an archives of their own, one of the few state historical societies that does not provide this service.

The AHC has a strong relationship with the Wyoming State Historical Society and fills much of the void of collecting, preserving, and providing access to local and state historical materials. Facebook is one way to spread the word about local and state records available for research. The AHC's holdings related to Wyoming history are extensive and provide a seemingly endless supply of content for Facebook posts, while Facebook provides a cheap and easy-to-use platform for shining a light on that content.

8.3.4 GOALS

Once my target audience was defined, I set goals for the Facebook page based on my own research and discussions with the committee. The goals for the Facebook page are as follows:

- Grow an audience of users and potential users across all of Wyoming.
- Increase general awareness of the AHC and what services we can provide to the state's residents.
- Increase the number of potential and actual users, both online and in person.
- Generally increase the online presence of the AHC.

8.3.5 #WYOWEDNESDAY CAMPAIGN

Armed with lessons learned from the #FootballFriday campaign, a defined audience, and goals, I was ready to move forward and try my next experiment. I began looking for interesting tidbits of Wyoming history within the AHC's digital collections. I used the digital collections because I did not have to scan materials myself, searching was faster than finding nondigitized materials, and access was easier because I can download items from the digital collections while connected to campus internet. Because Facebook marketing is an additional responsibility on top of my regular duties, these time-saving advantages of the digital collections are vital for allowing me to create posts efficiently and move on to other tasks. When I began posting these tidbits, I did not have an actual campaign formulated or follow any sort of schedule; I would simply post something interesting from Wyoming history when I had downtime. This slip-shod approach resulted in five total posts between January and May 2016. All of these posts received a fair amount of engagement and one post did exceedingly well (Fig. 8.3.3). The number of followers to the

Figure 8.3.3 A Facebook post from March 2016 showing aerial photos of Cody, Wyoming, that I had download from the AHC's digital collections. This was an early post in what became the #WyoWednesday campaign.

page grew from 553 on January 1, 2016, to 931 on May 31, 2016. Most of the new followers were from a variety of cities and towns in Wyoming, fitting my goal of growing the statewide audience. While I was seeing results from these posts, I was also noticing that simply posting a random tidbit when I had time was not sufficient in order to achieve sustained results and accomplish my goals.

In June 2016, I finalized this into a weekly campaign that I decided to call #WyoWednesday. I knew from other institutions that having regular postings helped grow the audience base and encouraged user engagement (Hager et al., 2015); I also hoped that this weekly structure would fit my schedule and help me incorporate Facebook posting as a regular part of my routine. I tried to be flexible in my approach to social media outreach and decided to continue #WyoWednesday for as long as users were engaging with the campaign posts. People continue to engage with the posts, and I have been posting almost every Wednesday since launching the campaign.

As I have continued to write #WyoWednesday posts, I still utilize the AHC's digital collections for easy content, especially during busy weeks. I have also worked to include content from portions of the holdings that have more barriers to access, primarily photo files that are not cataloged and collection material that is not digitized. My early posts typically focused on specific towns within Wyoming, but I have expanded to include other locations, like ghost towns and historic forts, and events that happened in the past on specific dates. A colleague knew of an Excel file that was created by an intern many years ago of "historic events" in Wyoming. Each date has between four and six events ranging from the miniscule and ridiculous (September 21, 1888: Pig stuck in barrel behind Douglas newspaper office died) to the profoundly important (September 30, 1889: Constitutional convention unanimously adopted Wyoming constitution). This calendar has become my first step when choosing the focus of my next post; if there is anything worthwhile for the date of the post and I can find related material for that event within the AHC's holdings, I use that as my post (Fig. 8.3.4). What makes an event worthwhile?

- It was important to the development of Wyoming.
- It is interesting to me.
- It relates directly to a collection at the AHC.
- It relates directly to the mission of the AHC.

If there is nothing worthwhile on the calendar, I will go to the photo files and look in random files until I find something interesting, or I will

Figure 8.3.4 A #WyoWednesday post about the history of Old Main, a building on University of Wyoming's campus. The photographs show Old Main being constructed in 1886 (top), c.1912 with the original tower in tact (bottom left), and sometime in the 1920s after the tower had been removed (bottom right).

choose a town in Wyoming to highlight first and then find material related to that town. I keep a running list of the content used in each #WyoWednesday post and the date of posting to help me avoid highlighting the same area or topic too frequently and to avoid posting the same material multiple times.

I have found this rather loose approach to be useful for a few reasons. First, I have a lot of content available at my fingertips that can be used for #WyoWednesday posts. Although I work at a very large archives, small university and college archives and special collections also contain a large array of content that could make for interesting social media posts. I find it more interesting to create the posts if I am looking at a variety of content, material types, and access points, and I think that offering a variety to the audience keeps them interested and engaged. This loose approach to the #WyoWednesday posts also helps me learn a little bit more about Wyoming history every week, which is beneficial in my day-to-day work as a reference archivist. There have been many times where I have been able to help a researcher in the reading room more efficiently and effectively because of information that I had learned while creating a #WyoWednesday post.

When I started the formal #WyoWednesday campaign in June 2016, the AHC Facebook page had 935 likes. As of September 1, 2017, the page had 1343 likes. The level of engagement with the AHC's Facebook page has also increased since launching this campaign. The number of likes per each post has gone up. The number of shares that each post gets has increased substantially. Posts now get shared by other state agencies, organizations, businesses, and a wide range of individuals. The number of comments that posts receive has also increased. Not every post receives comments, but many of the #WyoWednesday posts do. These comments come in three types:

- People sharing their memories that relate to the post. These are the most common.
- People tagging other people that they think would enjoy the post too. This is the second most common type of comment. These often lead to follow-up comments from the people tagged.
- People asking questions related to the post. These are the least common but occur regularly. I always answer these questions and I try to do so quickly and publicly.

I respond to the substantive comments that are received on the AHC's Facebook posts. I like the comments that tag other people, I like and say thanks to the people that share memories, and I always respond to any questions. With questions, I respond directly on the comment as much as possible; if I feel that a private response is needed, I still leave a publicly visible response to the comment and send the individual a more complete, private answer. It is important to show an active presence and engage with the comments that appear on your posts (Haydon, 2016). Since I have launched the #WyoWednesday campaign, the AHC Facebook page has also seen an increase in the number of questions sent as Facebook messages. When users ask reference questions over Facebook, I see that as a success in bringing more users to the archives.

In addition to the #WyoWednesday campaign, the committee also decided to try sponsored advertisements through Facebook during this time period. We decided to pay $15 (US) per month and ran five sponsored advertisements that rotated randomly. Facebook provides options for targeting specific audiences based on facets including gender, age, and interests, but we opted for our advertisements to appear in Facebook news feeds of any users in our area because our target audience is defined geographically; we wanted to reach a wide variety of people locally. Instead of sponsoring specific posts, we chose five eye-catching images from the archival collections or of the AHC building that we had previously posted and included open hours for the reading room and rare books library (Fig. 8.3.5). These advertisements contributed to the increased engagement and bringing in new followers, but the increased engagement was possible because the AHC's Facebook page regularly posts new content. The sponsored advertisements and the #WyoWednesday campaign and other postings of the page all must work together in order to achieve the desired results from paying for the advertisement.

8.3.6 FUTURE PLANS

The #WyoWednesday campaign and Facebook page are just a part of a larger marketing strategy and are influenced by that overarching strategy and available resources. The website committee has been given an expanded charge that includes all marketing and has experienced a complete turnover in members since I launched the #WyoWednesday campaign. The #WyoWednesday campaign has remained a stable marketing strategy, and I intend to continue it for the foreseeable future. In order to measure progress and set new goals for growth and development, I need to implement metrics for measuring success with this campaign and all Facebook efforts of the AHC.

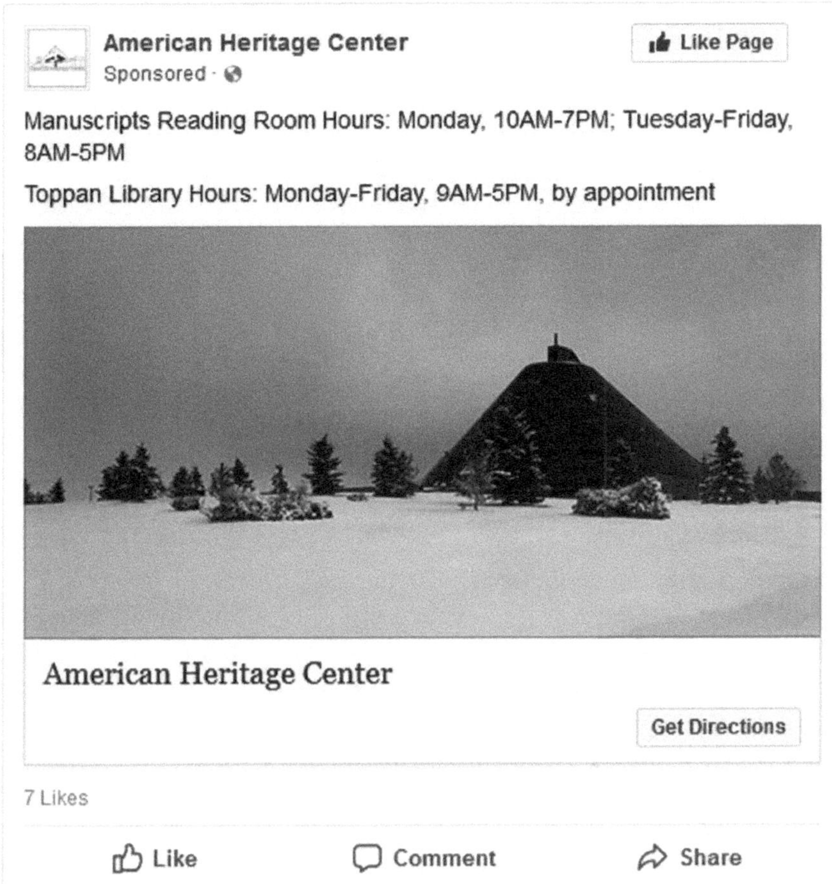

Figure 8.3.5 Sponsored advertisement featuring a photo of the Centennial Complex, where the AHC and University of Wyoming Art Museum are located.

I became chair of the committee in August 2017 and am now more focused on the bigger picture of marketing for the AHC. One of the committee members added in July 2017 discovered that he enjoyed the Facebook marketing and requested to take over as lead administrator of the page. His ideas of what should be marketed and how to do it on Facebook are broader than mine, and this change has been a positive one. I am expecting that this change will give me more ability to focus on the #WyoWednesday campaign. I am also looking to launch one or two other ongoing campaigns for the AHC's social media in the near future to continue building on the success that I have found with #WyoWednesday.

8.3.7 WHAT WORKED

- Experimenting and being flexible.
- Utilizing easily accessible content for postings.
- Using Facebook Insights to understand my followers (#WyoWednesday campaign).
- Having a defined audience and goals.

8.3.8 WHAT DIDN'T WORK

- Not being familiar with my followers (#FootballFriday campaign).
- Expecting new followers to find the page on their own.
- Not having a posting schedule.

8.3.9 RECOMMENDATIONS

- Have a posting schedule for regular campaigns.
- Utilize the systems in place at your institution to simplify your process for finding content and creating posts.
- Stay organized about your posts and campaigns. Create and use any documentation needed to stay organized.
- Do not be afraid to try new things and evaluate the results. Figure out what works for you and your audience, then do it.
- Engage with the people that engage with your Facebook page.
- New followers are unlikely to discover your page on their own. Sponsored advertisements help bring in new followers. Tagging other relevant Facebook pages in your posts can bring in new followers. Think of ways to make your Facebook page and posts more visible to nonfollowers.
- If you think something is interesting and fun for a post, other people probably will too!
- Know your audience and use that knowledge to determine what might be impactful with that audience.
- Set clear goals and use those goals to guide what you post.

8.3.10 FINAL WORDS

Posts about history have longevity on Facebook. People can and do engage with these posts long after they are posted. The special collections or archives staff at your institution can help find content and provide contextual information for a regular Facebook campaign. Your special collections or archives have engaging content within their collections that can be the basis of a successful Facebook campaign.

REFERENCES

Hager, J., Daniel, D., Nash, K., Norling, S., & Crilly, M. (2015, August). Narrowing the focus of digital and social media outreach. In: *Session presented at the Society of American Archivists annual meeting, Cleveland, OH.*

Hager, J. D. (2015). To like or not to like: understanding and maximizing the utility of archival outreach on Facebook. *The American Archivist, 78*(1), 18–37. Available from https://doi.org/10.17723/0360-9081.78.1.18.

Haydon, J. (2016, November). Embracing patrons: shifting your communication strategy from interruption to invitation. In: *Keynote session presented at the second annual Library Marketing & Communications Conference, Dallas, TX.*

Theimer, K. (2011). Archivists and audiences: new connections and changing roles in archives 2.0. In K. Theimer (Ed.), *A different kind of web: New connections between archives and our users* (pp. 334–346). Chicago, IL: Society of American Archivists.

U.S. Census Bureau (2017). *Annual estimates of the resident population for the United States, Regions, States, and Puerto Rico: April 1, 2010 to July 1, 2017.* Available from https://www.census.gov/data/tables/2017/demo/popest/state-total.html.

Watson, A.M. (2016, November). Manage your social media in 5 minutes a day. In: *Session presented at the second annual Library Marketing & Communications Conference, Dallas, TX.*

CHAPTER 9

YouTube

9.1 CASE STUDY 1

Thousands of Views: Why Three Simple Library Videos Have Done So Well

Dan Sich
Western Libraries, University of Western Ontario, London, ON, Canada

Institution: Western Libraries; total of 38,335 (2016–17) Full Time Equivalents (FTE), with 32,529 (2016–17) FTE on our main campus (Office of Institutional Planning & Budgeting—Western University, n.d.); 8 library locations; and 4 affiliated university college libraries.

Campaign Purpose: To create and market Information Literacy instruction videos that address frequently taught concepts.

Target Demographic: Students.

Measure of Success: Lifetime number of views in YouTube; 221,000 + , 58,000 + , and 23,000 + views as of April 2018.

Team: Three librarians.

9.1.1 THE OPPORTUNITY

Along with two other librarians, I was tasked with creating a small number of video tutorials to teach Information Literacy concepts. We chose three topics and worked together to brainstorm ideas, script, develop illustrations, and narrate. The three videos, which are the primary focus of this case study, have had tens of thousands of views to date:

- "Evaluating Sources" (Western University, 2012a) (i.e., the CRAAP Test, 221,000 + views),
- "How to Read a Scholarly Article" (Western University, 2012b) (58,000 + views), and

Social Media
DOI: https://doi.org/10.1016/B978-0-08-102409-6.00009-2

- "The Peer Review Process" (Western University, 2011) (23,000 + views).

This case study will provide advice on the successful use of YouTube. My recommendations are based on my years of experience producing over 40 videos and supplemented by specific examples from the most successful three.

9.1.2 THE APPROACH

We created the three videos in response to an expressed need for ready-made, self-serve bits of Information Literacy instruction that most of Western Libraries' instruction librarians have taught many times over. From the start, there was the sentiment that teaching Information Literacy concepts rather than tools (e.g., a specific database) would give us a greater return on investment. The topics we covered included source reliability, reading a scholarly article, and the peer review process. These were chosen because they were identified as three of the most commonly taught concepts from our units' Information Literacy instruction sessions.

Each video presents concept with broad academic appeal. We have received several requests from library staff at other institutions to use/embed our "Evaluating Sources" video (our most highly viewed video). This video was also featured in a blog post (A Media Specialist's Guide to the Internet: UPDATED POST: Do Your Students Know How to Evaluate a Website?, 2015), which was linked from American Libraries Direct (AL Direct 12/4/2015, 2015). By focusing on topics with mass appeal (where not already covered adequately by others), we have encouraged more views of these videos.

The following covers the steps we took to create the videos, everything from developing learning outcomes to file storage.

9.1.2.1 Develop a Single Learning Outcome

The obvious first step in instructional video creation is to develop learning outcomes. When drafting the learning outcomes for our videos, we found it useful to do the following:

- Write a proper learning outcome using Bloom's taxonomy. For example, "After watching this one to two-minute video, viewers will be able to apply the CRAAP test to evaluate information sources."
- Aim for a maximum duration of two minutes.

- Limit to one learning outcome per video. If it is determined that a larger topic must be addressed via video tutorials, this content can be presented in a series of short videos. For example, "How to cite a journal article using APA 6th edition" could be part of a series of videos on APA 6th edition citation style.
- Refer to the learning outcome when developing an outline for the video. Reflect back at appropriate intervals (e.g., after drafting an outline, after drafting a script) to ensure that the video fulfills its intent.

9.1.2.2 Brainstorm

Brainstorming is a helpful step that can occur at any point between developing learning outcomes and finalizing the script and images. We did our brainstorming in MS Word and included the video outline, point form notes on what the script should cover, and our image ideas (described in words). Rough sketches were sometimes created on the spot with pen and paper.

In these three videos, we used static, hand-drawn (with pencil, paper, and Sharpies) images, which we then scanned. Our approach of using drawings and humor was modeled on S Peter Davis's "Three Minute Philosophy" videos (CollegeBinary, n.d.).

9.1.2.3 Scripting

With the learning outcomes and outlines in hand, the next step is to create and edit scripts. When scripting a video, it is useful to do the following:

- Make a good "pitch" within the first 10 seconds of the video.
- Leave out the "welcome" and/or "brought to you by" statements. These only serve to make the video longer, at the risk of decreasing viewer retention. Introductions are unnecessary as the topic/title and creators of videos are self-evident from YouTube.
- Use a conversational (Q&A) format.
- Time the script, aiming for two minutes.
- Include only essential details that serve the learning outcome.
- Vet scripts to colleagues for editing; this will result in more concise, logically ordered content.
- Describe services rather than using library jargon or the services' branded names, which are prone to change and not very user friendly.

For example, use "course-specific library guides" rather than "program guides" or "LibGuides."

- Change the script while rehearsing the narration, to ensure that it flows.
- Actually have a script and stick to it. While unscripted videos can feel more "authentic," they require more work in the editing room.

9.1.2.4 Exclusions (or Things Readers Might Want to Include, But Shouldn't)

Many things on the web, for example, a website name or URL, are subject to change with short notice, if any. Showing or describing these in a video means that the video is more likely to go out-of-date. As such, we omitted the following visuals and details from our videos, unless absolutely necessary:

- the library website,
- online resources,
- navigating through web pages, and
- institution-specific details.

An added benefit to omitting the library website and institution-specific details is that such videos can be (and have been) useful to an audience beyond Western.

We also chose not to show the narrator, as it would only have served to detract from our visuals. Videos without much in the way of visual content might benefit from showing the narrator. In addition, we left out any sort of background music on these three videos. If music is used in Information Literacy instruction videos, it should be Creative Commons (with re-use allowed), and attribution should be provided in the video's credits or description.

9.1.2.5 Audio-Visual Technology

I recorded audio using an Apogee MiC and GarageBand on an iMac. GarageBand (Mac only software) provides excellent audio editing capabilities and was the audio recording and editing software with which I was most familiar. Background noise was avoided by recording in a quiet environment where I would not be interrupted. Further measures could have been taken to reduce background or white noise (e.g., recording at the campus radio station).

Audio and scanned images were imported into Camtasia, a robust software with a wealth of features beyond what was required for these three videos. We used Camtasia to adjust the relative timing of audio and visuals, and for minor zooming-in on images. Although Camtasia has a bit of a learning curve, it is excellent software that we have used for many other videos. It also enables the capture of screen animation.

We have also used other video creation software and hardware. Snagit is effective at creating quick videos that one might expect to have a short lifespan. PowToon enables the inclusion of cartoon animation. iMovie has been used for "live action" video footage. A "lightboard" was used to provide stimulating visuals for a dull topic (Boolean operators). Each tool has its strengths and should be chosen according to the desired presentation style.

9.1.2.6 Narration

Narration is one aspect of video production where the video creator has more freedom. In my experience with these and other videos, viewers are less forgiving of poor narration as compared to unprofessional-looking visuals. The latter can be charming while the former can be irritating. Having experience as a campus radio station announcer, I elected to narrate the videos myself. I put no small amount of effort into:

- focusing on pronunciation, pace, tone, emotion, pitch, and variation of pitch;
- avoiding "white noise" and other auditory distractions;
- editing out breathing and other distracting noises (hiring a professional voice actor can negate the need for this);
- timing the narration with the visuals; and
- ensuring there were no distracting words on the screen (i.e., words that do not match the narration).

9.1.2.7 Utilize Skills and Outsource When Necessary

Luckily, among the three members of our group, we had experiences with:

- teaching Information Literacy instruction,
- drafting succinct scripts (a skill similar to that for writing for the web),
- brainstorming image ideas,
- drawing,

- voiceover,
- recording and manipulating audio, and
- producing videos.

Readers who do not have these necessary video creation skills should consider outsourcing certain aspects. We outsourced pieces of some of our later videos to technology-savvy student staff at our institution's Information Technology Resource Centre (ITRC). These videos were generally more polished and professional-looking when compared with library staff output, though sometimes at the cost of control over the final result.

9.1.2.8 Style Considerations

Some institutions may pursue having a consistent style for all of their videos. This is only important if there is a desire to establish an 'authoritative' voice or visual style. Our three videos had a consistent style in that they used:

- drawings by the same artist,
- the same sense of humor,
- the same narrator,
- the same title page format, and
- the same 'outro' page.

This consistent style may have had something to do with the three videos' success. At the same time, this style would not be have been appropriate for all of our subsequent videos.

The initial 5–10 seconds of the video, during which viewers are making a decision about whether or not to watch it, are extremely important. Title pages and "welcome" messages are unimportant, given that video title and description are provided in YouTube.

After the important video content has been delivered is a fine time to present the viewer with video credits, copyright or Creative Commons, and contact information. This poses no risk of losing viewers early.

9.1.2.9 Gather Feedback

In terms of obtaining feedback, the three initial videos were vetted to colleagues. We now typically vet video ideas, scripts, and draft videos to colleagues. Seeking feedback early in the process helps identify potential problems early on, when they are easier to fix. At one point (for another video project) we held a "screening party" (with popcorn) for other staff in the department. This experience provided feedback regarding the clarity and content of videos that was useful in making changes before the videos went live.

9.1.2.10 File Storage

We keep all 'production files' on a shared drive. These files include learning outcomes, outlines, scripts, closed captions, images, audio, and software (e.g., Camtasia) specific files. We have learned that when it is time to upload a video to YouTube, it is handy to already have created a 'metadata' file containing the video's title, description, tags, category (likely "Education"), and license and rights ownership. The video description which appears in YouTube (Fig. 9.1.1) should include:

- authority information, for example, "[Title of video] was created/uploaded by [name of library],"
- copyright and Creative Commons information (if applicable),
- a description of the content,
- any additional links (e.g., to resources or services mentioned),
- encouragement for viewers to provide feedback or new video suggestion, and
- contact information.

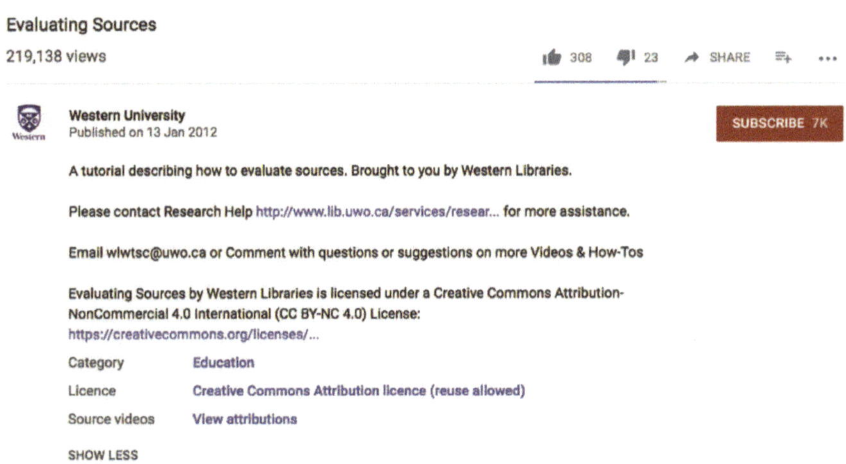

Figure 9.1.1 Sample YouTube video description.

9.1.2.11 Licensing

The license and rights ownership options in YouTube are currently limited to "Standard YouTube license" and "Creative Commons—Attribution." This information may be expanded upon in the video's description by including a Creative Commons license (Choose a License, n.d.), permitting others to re-use and re-mix a video for noncommercial use, for example. Not all viewers are familiar with Creative Commons licenses, and we are occasionally contacted by other libraries or institutions for permission to embed specific videos.

9.1.2.12 Accessibility

In Ontario we are governed by the AODA (Accessibility for Ontarians with Disabilities Act, 2005, S.O. 2005, c. 11, 2014) requirements. AODA requires that institutions do the best they can with available time and resources to make videos accessible. Note that this does not mean that all videos must be "fully AODA compliant" in order to fulfill "the spirit of the legislation" (Oldham & Doan, 2015). We provide accurate closed captions (in YouTube) and scripts (on the library website) for all of our videos. There are various ways to create closed captions files. We upload our scripts to YouTube and use YouTube's closed captions editing interface to produce accurate, properly timed closed captions. This is nitpicky work, but is an easy way to add a little polish to videos. YouTube's automatically generated closed captions (included by default) are often inaccurate, but do provide a starting point with good 'time stamps.'

If we had more resources, we could enhance accessibility by providing text explanations of the visuals in the video. However, this would be quite labor intensive for videos showing screen activity, so we have not pursued this.

9.1.3 DISSEMINATING AND PROMOTING VIDEOS

Videos are only useful if our users know they exist and have some reason for watching them.

We have a few YouTube playlists related to library videos, one specifically for "Western Library Tutorials." These can help viewers find their way to our other videos, aiding in promotion. Over the years, we have created other playlists, such as one containing a series of seven APA videos.

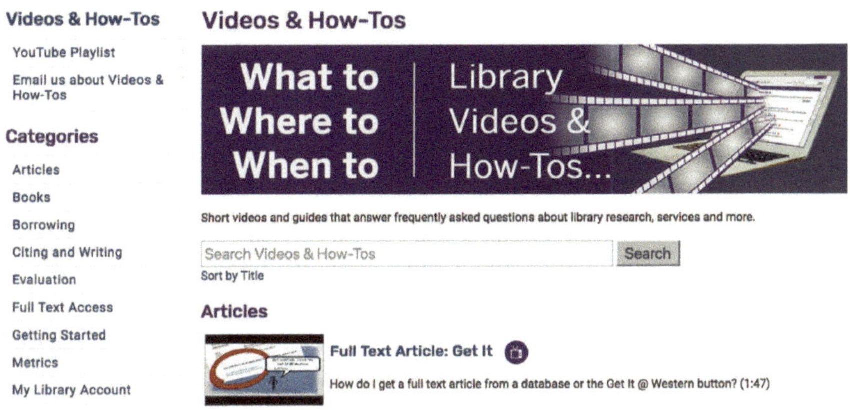

Figure 9.1.2 Videos & How-Tos mini site.

In addition, we have a "Videos & How-Tos" mini site on our library website (see Fig. 9.1.2). Videos are organized in categories on this mini site's homepage, with a thumbnail image and brief description provided for each video. We embed our YouTube videos on subpages, using the YouTube-supplied embed code. (Our YouTube video settings enable others to embed them as well. This encourages re-use by other library staff and by those beyond the library.) We place the video script under the embedded video.

We promote our video tutorial to library staff and users in several ways. On a monthly basis we email library staff regarding our "Video Tutorial of the Month," which is often chosen based on what is going on with the students at that point (e.g., just getting started with the library, writing essays), what video content is new, or what video content has received too few views. A thumbnail of this video appears in a 'spotlight' section of our library's homepage, which links out the video on YouTube.

These Video Tutorials of the Month and other videos are promoted via Twitter and Facebook as well, at least once per month. Facebook encourages users to upload videos directly to Facebook rather than linking to YouTube videos. They do this by making linked YouTube videos appear in 4–5 times fewer feeds than videos uploaded directly to Facebook. We note that videos uploaded directly to Facebook begin playback immediately (no click required), but lack closed captions and do not link viewers to our YouTube playlist. They are also not easily found in facebook when repeat viewing is desired. To compensate, while we have switched from including YouTube URLs in Facebook posts to uploading videos directly to Facebook, we accompany these uploads with text and links directing users to our other videos. Our Twitter posts include YouTube URLs.

We encourage librarians to embed these and other appropriate videos in their library subject guides and course guides, and in pages in our institution's Learning Management System. Embedding can be done in such a way that video playback starts (and ends) mid-video, in order to take viewers directly to the instruction they require. The three videos in our case study are the ones most often embedded in such guides or pages by instruction librarians.

We ask librarians and other library staff to use our videos during Information Literacy instruction classes and reference interactions (in person, chat, or email). Information from librarian colleagues involved in instruction indicates that these three videos are the ones most often featured in such classes. Given that these three videos have the most views, this sort of 'marketing' may be one of the best approaches. We make sure that the videos are prominent on a page we have created for chat reference service providers from other libraries in our corsortial chat reference service, which includes many other Ontario university libraries.

9.1.4 ASSESSMENT AND RENEWAL

We review our videos on an annual basis to ensure that they are current and relevant. One benefit of teaching Information Literacy concepts rather than specific tools (e.g., databases) is that the videos rarely require updates. When assessing a video, we try to answer the following:

- Is it delivering what its title and description promise?
- Is it still accurate enough to be of some use? If not, can it be salvaged? If not, delete it!
- Is it (still) visually appealing or does it look dated?
- Is video still the best way to deliver this content, or would a web page (potentially with images) do a better job? Web pages are easier to update.
- Is the video being watched?
- Do the closed captions require any corrections?

To facilitate our annual review, we maintain an up-to-date 'inventory' spreadsheet of current tutorials. It includes their title, creator(s)/owner(s), URL, creation date, view statistics, date last reviewed, name of reviewer, decision at time of review (e.g., keep, update, or delete), and comments

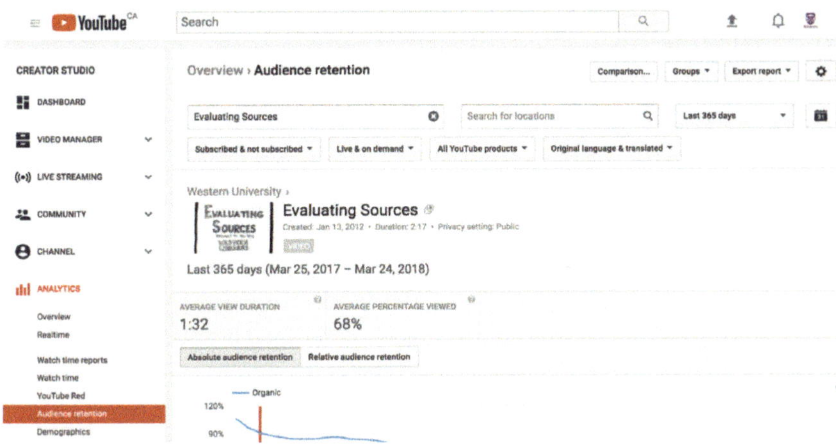

Figure 9.1.3 Sample YouTube Analytics.

(e.g., required updates). We pull YouTube Analytics and Google Analytics (for the website pages that 'host' these videos) on an annual basis. These statistics help to identify both successful videos and those requiring more promotion. Pulling YouTube Analytics "average percentage viewed" has provided us with some indication of which videos are doing a good job of keeping viewers' attention (see Fig. 9.1.3).

Unsurprisingly, there seems to be a rough correlation between high views, high "average percentage viewed" and short video length. Note that a low number of views alone do not indicate that a video is unsuccessful; videos with low views but high "average percentage viewed" show us where additional marketing may be in order. On the other hand, a high number of views accompanied by a low "average percentage viewed" show us which videos may have missed the mark, but does not tell us why.

What dates a video the quickest is the inclusion of images or footage of the library website or database interfaces, names of library services, and other things subject to change. Avoid referring to anything as "new," because that newness does not last for long. Because these three videos teach Information Literacy concepts rather than specific tools, they will never go out-of-date for this reason. At one point, one of our videos shows a drawing of an abstraction of the Ulrich's Periodicals Directory search engine. When Ulrich's changes its interface, we will not have to change our video, because we have used a drawing rather than a capture of the website itself.

While most video creators are excited about creating new videos, they are less enthusiastic about updating these videos. If a lot of work has gone into creating a video, and it is only slightly out-of-date, then it may be better to try to salvage that video. Such changes can be commented upon in the video's closed captions, script, and/or description.

If an 'interface specific' video has become too out-of-date to salvage, consider replacing it with a more 'interface agnostic' video. For example, it may be possible to speak to a database feature in general without referencing a specific database or interface. We have done just this in our video "Two Ways to Search a Databases" (Western University, 2016). If showing a specific interface (website, database) is required, consider creating a quick-and-dirty, unedited, 'disposable' video (meaning that not much effort has been spent when it comes time to delete it) using software such as Snagit.

Updating a video requires uploading a new video file and results in a new YouTube URL. This can result in broken links, making it necessary to update links to the video on the library website. Updating, let alone identifying, any links to videos from outside of one's institution may be near impossible.

When a video must be deleted, we ensure that we have archived everything available. If the MP4 is not already archived, it can be downloaded from YouTube. Such content can come in handy when creating future versions of the video.

9.1.5 WHAT WORKED

What led to these videos receiving so many views? We believe several factors contributed. All three videos

- have a narrow focus and brief duration;
- teach concepts with broad appeal;
- retain currency, due to their content;
- have reasonable quality audio (narration) and visuals;
- favor images over text;
- use humor; and
- were promoted to library staff and users prior to publication.

9.1.6 FINAL WORDS

These three videos got a relatively high number of views considering that they are Information Literacy instruction videos. Other librarians (outside of Western Libraries) have asked us for permission to use our videos. The videos are posted in library course guides and in our Learning Management System.

When we have stuck to the idea of teaching Information Literacy concepts rather than specific tools, our videos have received more use, and have not gone out-of-date.

Along the way we have built expertise in creating, delivering, assessing, and renewing videos. We have developed and documented (on our staff intranet) local best practices in a 'toolkit' for our staff. We also provide Western Libraries colleagues in our eight physical library locations with as much (or as little) support as they need at any point in their video creation and renewal process.

We have not yet broken the 10,000 views threshold with any of videos beyond these initial three. Many of our videos teach specific interfaces (such as the library catalog) and just do not have the same broad appeal. Others may teach concepts that do not provide library instructors (our best marketers) with the same "bang for their buck" and do not merit inclusion in guides or other pages.

The real reason for high or low views and "average percentage viewed" may be near impossible to determine. In any case, along the way we have learned something about what makes a good Information Literacy instruction video. We are continually trying out new approaches to video creation in our ongoing attempt to provide excellent service to our users.

REFERENCES

A Media Specialist's Guide to the Internet: UPDATED POST: Do Your Students Know How to Evaluate a Website? (2015, December 4). Retrieved September 15, 2017, from http://mediaspecialistsguide.blogspot.ca/2015/12/updated-post-do-your-students-know-how.html

Accessibility for Ontarians with Disabilities Act, 2005, S.O. 2005, c. 11. (2014, July 24). Retrieved September 15, 2017, from https://www.ontario.ca/laws/statute/05a11

AL Direct 12/4/2015: Do your students know how to evaluate a website? (2015, December 4). Retrieved September 15, 2017, from http://ala-publishing.informz.net/informzdataservice/onlineversion/ind/bWFpbGluZ2luc3RhbmNlaWQ9NTIwODk4NCZzdWJzY3JpYmVyaWQ9MTA1ODM1NTEwMQ==

Choose a License. (n.d.). Retrieved September 15, 2017, from https://creativecommons.org/choose/

CollegeBinary. (n.d.). Retrieved September 15, 2017, from https://www.youtube.com/user/CollegeBinary

Office of Institutional Planning & Budgeting - Western University. (n.d.). Western Facts. Retrieved September 26, 2017, from https://www.ipb.uwo.ca/facts.php

Oldham, R., & Doan, A. (2015, September). *AODA: Enabling Innovation*. Presented at the Access, Toronto, Ontario. Retrieved from http://accessconference.ca/2015-toronto-on/program/archived-presentations/

Western University. (2011). *The Peer Review Process*. Retrieved from https://www.youtube.com/watch?v = MLGp7LC2Nbw&list = PLBC826C3769B18E1F&index = 1

Western University. (2012a). *Evaluating Sources*. Retrieved from https://www.youtube.com/watch?v = EyMT08mD7Ds&index = 3&list = PLBC826C3769B18E1F

Western University. (2012b). *How to Read a Scholarly Article*. Retrieved from https://www.youtube.com/watch?v = 3SmOq6gENPM&index = 2&list = PLBC826C3769B18E1F

Western University. (2016). *Two Ways To Search a Database*. Retrieved from https://www.youtube.com/watch?list = PLBC826C3769B18E1F&v = s4gHgx7gSrg

9.2 CASE STUDY 2

Show Me: Getting YouTube Videos to Your Students Through SEO

Lauren Valentino Bryant
Shoreline Community College, Shoreline, WA, United States

Institution: Shoreline Community College, Ray W. Howard Library.

Campaign Purpose: Increase views of our instructional videos on YouTube.

Target Demographic: Students at Shoreline Community College, members of any academic institution are a bonus.

Measure of Success: Increase number of views of YouTube.

Team: One librarian.

9.2.1 BACKGROUND

During my time as webmaster for Shoreline Community College's sole library, I have observed that students' information-seeking behavior is largely dependent on search engines like Google and Bing. I have conducted several usability studies on the library's website in which students were instructed to browse for topics in any way they desired except using the website's search box on the library homepage. The intent of these studies has been to refine the navigation menu I designed for the website, a navigation bar with buttons and drop-down menu choices. Whether they were looking for food rules for the library or a tutorial on how to create an annotated bibliography on the library's website, students would turn to a search engine within 30 seconds, even if they were instructed to use the site's navigation menu. Seeing this trend repeatedly made it clear to me that affecting search engine results was the key to meeting students' information-seeking needs. Therefore, rather than attempting to train each student to find resources through the library's website, we needed to make said resources more visible on search engines.

When I first took my position in 2015, the library had already developed a wealth of resources on YouTube. I saw an opportunity to reach students through the social media platform. I took a close look at the library's YouTube account and began making changes to improve findability. As a result the channel saw a gradual increase in views. The procedures I used may be helpful as a template for other professionals looking to improve their YouTube viewership. Utilizing this step-by-step approach will provide readers with a suite of organized videos and improve content quality, which will contribute to overall findability.

Search Engine Optimization (SEO) is the practice of designing a web resource to be easily indexed and then findable through search engines such as Google or Bing. By using SEO practices when creating YouTube videos, a person can produce a resource that is more discoverable. The connection between videos, specifically YouTube videos, and search engines is important because YouTube content popularity can influence search engines to boost the ranking of associated web content as well. So, if your library's YouTube channel sees an increase in popularity, your library's website will also see an increase in traffic. YouTube videos are a particularly flexible form of media because they can be embedded into other social media such as Facebook, be linked to from static sources such as PDF documents or websites and embedded into dynamic formats such as LibGuides, the content management system for my library's website, or Canvas, the learning management system (LMS) for my campus.

At Shoreline I used YouTube's Analytics tool to track traffic sources to determine changes in our videos' popularity. The Analytics dashboard shows the increase in video views in response to the SEO tactics I had employed. Since SEO is a strategy that must be applied to a channel as a whole, the total views of all of our videos is most illustrative of our success. Our statistics show an increase in views while also revealing our most viewed videos, telling us which videos were working well with our students and faculty (Fig. 9.2.1).

9.2.2 EVALUATING TRAFFIC

Before making changes to your YouTube channel, there must be a way to measure and assess your progress. The standard way to measure the popularity of web content is site hits or, in this case, video views. The built-in analytics section of a YouTube channel illustrates the channel's progress clearly and may reveal interesting information about viewers.

YouTube's Analytics section shows views per video, popularity, and some viewer demographics. This tracking is applied both directly on YouTube as well as on embedded videos. Once your first video is posted, YouTube starts collecting statistics through its own YouTube Analytics dashboard. Access to more detailed information can be achieved through

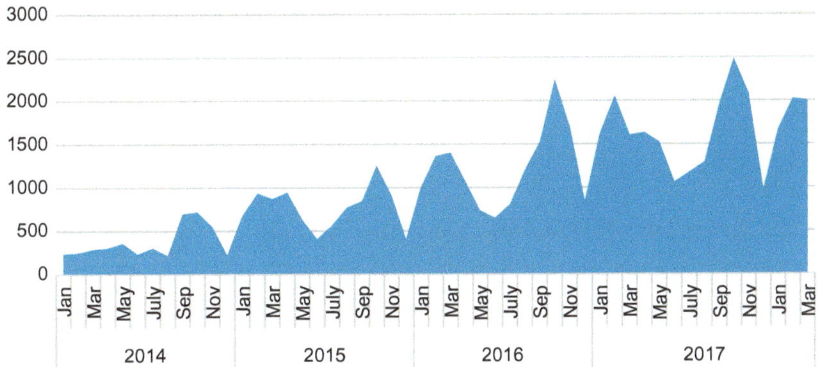

Figure 9.2.1 Video views. Source: *Data taken from YouTube analytics*

Google Analytics, which can provide age range, gender, location, and device used to view the videos.

To set up Google Analytics, insert the tracking ID from a Google account into the YouTube interface. Setting up a tracking code that connects this data with Google Analytics will ensure that the data will be available when you wish to view it. Having this data is helpful for assessment, tracking progress, popularity, and growth. At Shoreline Library, we found it helpful in establishing the age ranges of those watching our videos. Having those age ranges was useful because our students' overall demographics varied from this data, we found that younger students were more likely to turn to YouTube for assistance. We were also able to verify that most views were coming from our students, since traffic was overwhelmingly coming from nearby geographic locations.

9.2.3 INCREASING TRAFFIC

9.2.3.1 Via Search Engine Optimization

We used Google's Search Engine Optimization Starter Guide to improve our YouTube traffic findability. Traditional search queries have always been able to latch onto keywords, but over time search engines algorithms have evolved to prefer "compelling and useful" webpages that provide "quality content" (Google Search, 2010). Therefore, search engine queries can be improved through a campaign that targets keywords and key phrases (Google Search, 2010). The guide recommends strategic use of keywords in titles, descriptions, and tags. It also suggests the use of keywords in uploaded file names. For example, the thumbnail image for a video about narrowing a research paper's topic could be topic_narrow.jpg which would insert additional keywords into the HTML markup of the page that were unnoticeable to the video's viewer. Finally, the SEO guide suggests promoting the videos by linking them elsewhere on the web which boosts their visibility in search engine results (Google Search, 2010).

Our library uses LibGuides to provide information literacy content to our students and we include links to our suite of YouTube videos within these guides where appropriate. Our Graphic Novels guide is a good example of effective use of SEO. Because the Graphic Novels LibGuide has ranked among our top five most visited pages, it has been known to appear on Google results pages in unexpected ways. When a user searches for 'Ray Howard Library' the Graphic Novel page appears under the results as a subpage in the same manner as a general information page such as mission statement, contact page, or hours. Additionally, if a user's browser is set to indicate that their location is in the Shoreline area of Washington, the page ranks high in a general Google search for 'graphic novels'. The guide stands out from our other pages because it features a set of YouTube videos called *Books for Busy Students*, a series of videos I created in partnership with another librarian. While the videos themselves are not popular, they mirror the keywords from the graphic novel guide and each video includes a link to the guide, pointing it out as a related resource. Having user created content on YouTube takes advantage of backlinking, when the video links to the web page and vice versa, it follows the search engine optimization model of connecting similar content to each other across web platforms.

9.2.3.1.1 Staying Current Through SEO

YouTube suggests newer videos to users on both the search results page and the website's navigation menus. For this reason, it is important to design a video's channel as a stream of newly generated content that stays relevant and up-to-date. By creating new videos, the overall content of the channel becomes larger while also keeping content fresher and newer. The *Books for Busy Students* series provides a good example of a project that has potential for growth. SEO strategies encourage YouTube creators to branch out and broaden the number of topics covered on the channel. We see it as important to create video tutorials for databases, but we have increased our scope to include other relevant and timely topics such as the campus Community Read, a book club we have at Shoreline that includes staff, students, and faculty.

YouTube restricts video replacement. This can be a problem when content becomes outdated, incorrect, or obsolete. Channel reputation is affected by 404 errors, the error that occurs when a link sends a user to a video that is no longer there. Once you share a link to a video that could become outdated, that link will be in circulation long after you intend it to be. In our case, instructors were leaving links to deleted videos in their syllabi, causing a lot of broken links on our channel. The old videos should be set to "unlisted" under the video's Info & Settings, which will prevent it from appearing in the list of the channel's videos to the public but will allow access through a direct link. YouTube has many tools to help users find the latest version of your video from the old one. Providing a link in the old, unpublished video's description box is helpful, but also using the YouTube's integrated referral tools such as annotations or cards will help send users from the old linked video to the new updated one.

9.2.3.2 Via Profile Optimization

SEO involves setting up the information in such a way that allows it to be collected and repurposed in search results. Accordingly, metadata is critical because it identifies the information to the search engine and allows it to display the text, video, or image appropriately. The best way to identify the overall message of a YouTube channel is through the About tab. When a description is added in a YouTube profile, it is wrapped in a description metadata tag. The Google SEO starter guide mentions that, "description meta tags are important because Google might use them as snippets for your pages" (Google Search, 2010). This information tells us that Google's algorithms are not only able to read meta description tags, but also they use them to deliver content identified with those tags through Google search results.

There is a maximum of 5000 characters to describe intent, purpose, and qualify credentials of the video's authors. Avoid filler words like 'basically' and words that have empty meanings like 'elucidate.' Load this area with keywords that students might use to search for videos such as database provider names and words common in assignment prompts.

If you qualify for a custom URL, customize the URL for the whole channel and use that when linking because that URL will never change or expire. To qualify for a custom URL, you must have 100 or more subscribers, "be at least 30 days old, have an uploaded photo as channel icon, and have uploaded channel art," which would display in a browser's bar as "youtube.com/yourcustomname" (Get a Custom, 2017). Our library has the custom URL https://www.youtube.com/RayHowardLibrary, which makes it easier for search engines to associate our content with anything that includes the phrase, Ray Howard Library, and furthermore, identifies our channel as a library. This kind of URL is recommended by Google's SEO guide, which explains that, "if your URL contains relevant words, this provides users and search engines with more information about the page than an ID or oddly named parameter would" (Google Search, 2010).

9.2.3.3 Via Content Rich Descriptions

Each YouTube video has its own description box. YouTube's algorithms cannot access the actual video or transcript but it does pull information from the video's tags and the description. YouTube's description box is the perfect place to include a summary full of key phrases and illustrate the proper use of citations. By inserting links to related content, you can implement backlinking, the SEO strategy of connecting one web resource to another. It creates a connection between the video's content and the linked content, which helps search algorithms determine the topic of your video and aids findability. The Search Engine Optimization Starter Guide has more information about backlinking and mentions that, "effectively promoting your new content will lead to faster discovery by those who are interested in the same subject" (Google Search, 2010).

Many popular YouTube personalities have set a precedent for using the YouTube description box for bibliographies and abstracts. The channel vlogbrothers has a habit of providing sources in the description box and some standout examples include "What Is the Real Unemployment Rate?" and "Is Obamacare Working? The Affordable Care Act Five Years Later" (vlogbrothers, n.d.). YouTube audiences expect informational videos to include links to each source mentioned in the video and including the full APA or MLA citation is going a full step further. Many of the videos on the Ray Howard Library's channel have this, but the best example is the *Books for Busy Students* series of book talk style videos where titles such as *Drowned City: Hurricane Katrina and New Orleans* and *Thor: Goddess of Thunder* are cited in the description box (Ray W. Howard Library at Shoreline Community College, 2016).

9.2.3.4 Via Channel Introduction Video

An introduction video declares the focus of the channel's videos and operates as a welcome message for visitors. This video can be set to autoplay for first time visitors. Set this video as the channel's trailer on YouTube by turning on channel customization, then click the "for new visitors" tab and choosing the introductory video. It can be a variety of things, such as: a virtual tour of the physical space, an introduction to the library's website, or a description of the library's resources. YouTube is more likely to suggest other videos from the same channel to a visitor who has watched the introductory video. This means that users who watch it while signed into their Google account are more likely to find more videos from your channel while browsing and clicking through the YouTube navigation menus. At Shoreline Community College, many instructors include the introductory video in their online syllabus. It is important to keep this video up-to-date. Almost every year, our introduction video must be changed when the online tools illustrated in the video are replaced or removed. By importing the mp4 of the previous year's video into your video editor, creating a new video is as easy as slipping in screencast clips that replace outdated information then rerecording the voiceover. The current introductory video covers the online collections at the Ray Howard Library and introduces our new, inclusive discovery tool that allows users to search many of our databases and our catalog at once.

9.2.3.5 Via The Library Website

YouTube content does not have to be viewed at YouTube.com. YouTube videos can be inserted into any HTML environment. They can be embedded into a webpage, a blog, a post on a social media platform, or an online class. Since YouTube viewership is measured by number of views, not visits to the channel, the flexible nature of these videos is an opportunity to reach more users.

Shoreline Community College uses the Canvas learning management system (LMS) for its online classes. To make it easier for instructors to find applicable library videos and include them in the LMS, we create easily findable modules that include the ideal video content. This type of backlinking, between a YouTube video and the Canvas module, is not very helpful to SEO because the Canvas module is not public on the web. Nevertheless, it does provide some one-way traffic which boosts the video's visibility. For instance, I work frequently with a Communications instructor who teaches exclusively online. We worked together to make a module on the Canvas Commons called Mind Mapping, which includes an embedded video called *Learn to Make a Mindmap with MindMup* (Bryant, 2017). Other librarians later used the same video and Canvas module with other Communications classes, which increased the video's views. Most LMS environments are compatible with embeddable YouTube videos and this strategy can be applied at other institutions.

9.2.4 VISUAL INSTRUCTIONAL DESIGN OR HOW TO MAKE THE VIDEOS CHECKLIST

The intent behind Google's conception of SEO is to connect users with the highest quality content that matches the search terms. Adjusting settings and refining technical aspects of web content can only go so far. The SEO guide published by Google reminds us that, "creating compelling and useful content will likely influence your website more than any of the other factors discussed here" (Google Search, 2010). Keeping all the channel's videos on par with a quality standard can be difficult, especially when more than one creator is making the videos but having a checklist that fulfills the following categories will help.

9.2.4.1 Item 1: Start With a Learning Objective

To start your instructional video outline, design a learning objective phrase using action verbs from Bloom's Taxonomy of the Cognitive Domain (Bloom, 1956). For an introductory lesson, the lower level of Bloom's taxonomy is appropriate, applying words like 'remember,' 'define,' 'duplicate,' 'repeat,' or 'state.' A learning objective from one of our videos at this level might be something like, 'Define the difference between a primary source and a secondary source.' The instructional verbs toward the top of the pyramid are challenging, requiring student engagement and critical thinking. More advanced learning objectives use terms such as 'interpret,' 'experiment,' 'critique,' and 'construct.' Defining a learning objective for a video is important because it ensures the message has a focus and stays with that purpose. Include the learning objective in the video's script within the first 10 seconds (Fig. 9.2.2).

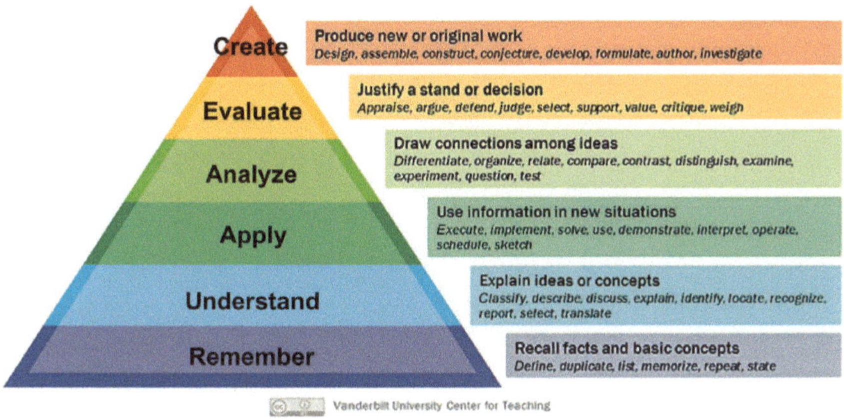

Figure 9.2.2 Bloom's Taxonomy.

9.2.4.2 Item 2: Write a Script

Writing a script is helpful because editing a text version of a script is easier than editing the audio and video once it has been recorded. There are times when a combination of words works well on the page but sounds awkward or strange when spoken aloud. During the editing process, it can be helpful to read the script aloud before setting up the voice recording equipment. Structuring the script to define the topic in the beginning can be helpful to the browsing viewer. This is a good opportunity to include facts and statistics that endorse or explain the purpose of the video. Tutorial videos for academic databases are a staple at academic libraries and we often define the scope of the database at the beginning of such a video. Certain information will help the user decide whether they want to watch the rest of the video. For example, student viewers will want to know if the database has a specialty subject matter, contains primary sources, or peer-reviewed journals. I often include an estimate of how many articles are in the database because they are often overlooked as an invisible resource, since students cannot see the physical, printed journals that are contained.

9.2.4.3 Item 3: Screencast

Video-editing software is necessary for video creation. Most software uses a timeline representation of the video that will allow users to clip, stretch, add, or speed up sections of the timeline. This software can be used to take screencasts that illustrate the video's topic. Set your screencast area to be 1280×720 and carefully position your recording area only on the relevant section of your screen. You may have to change the resolution of your monitor if 1280×720 is too large or too small. Connect the video together and edit it to be three minutes or less. Techsmith Camtasia is a popular software and it is the one we use to create videos.

9.2.4.4 Item 4: Voiceover

If you are using voiceover, record once the video's visuals play smoothly and have logical transitions. Speak slowly and clearly. A smile will come through in the audio and can be very effective at the right moments. If there is dead air, increase the speed of the video to avoid having silence during the video. If you are using Camtasia, isolate the section of the video you want to speed up by clipping either side of it and change the percentage based on how fast it needs to be to remove the silence. The final part of the video should include a way to contact the library or follow up. Every one of our videos ends with the library building hours, our contact email address, and phone number, and informs the viewer that we have a 24-hour chat service.

9.2.4.5 Accessibility Issues

The Shoreline Community College campus is undergoing an overhaul of all electronic sources that do not fit the standard of web accessibility according to Web Content Accessibility Guidelines (WCAG). Aside from the obvious importance of ensuring content is viewable to those with disabilities, WCAG standards are a way to measure the overall quality of a web resource. Google mentions that, "the WCAG is one of the most widely-accepted international standards for accessibility." (Initiatives and Research, n.d.). There are many benefits to web accessibility that go beyond inclusivity. The World Wide Web Consortium (W3C) states on their website that, "Accessibility overlaps with other best practices such as mobile design, device independence, multi-modal interaction, usability, design for older users, and search engine optimization (SEO)" (Accessibility, 2017). To fit WCAG standards (Henry, 2005), videos must:

- provide text alternatives for nontext content,
- provide an alternative to video-only content,
- provide captions for videos with audio,

- have a second alternative if it has audio,
- not communicate meaning solely with color, and
- not play audio automatically.

9.2.5 FINAL WORDS

As organization professionals well versed in taxonomies and proper referencing, librarians are ideal web content creators. Just as a librarian must curate a collection that caters to the unique patron base of their library, so must a video creator consider the needs of its viewers. Strategies such as SEO can be misinterpreted as a set of technical checkboxes, but at heart of these practices is the goal of delivering quality resources to information-seekers.

REFERENCES

Accessibility. (2017). Retrieved from W3C website: <https://www.w3.org/standards/webdesign/accessibility> Accessed 05.04.18.

Bryant, L. (2017, February 21). *Learn to make a mindmap with MindMup* [Video file]. Retrieved from <https://www.youtube.com/watch?v = w1Uj_aeqLHM >

Get a custom URL for your channel. (2017). Retrieved from YouTube website: <https://support.google.com/youtube/answer/2657968?hl = en> Accessed 28.09.17.

Google Search Engine Optimization Starter Guide. (2010). Retrieved from Google website: <https://static.googleusercontent.com/media/www.google.com/en//webmasters/docs/search-engine-optimization-starter-guide.pdf>.

Henry, S.L. (Ed.). (2005, July). *Web content accessibility guidelines (WCAG) overview.* Retrieved from W3C Web Accessibility Initiative website: <https://www.w3.org/WAI/intro/wcag> Accessed 28.09.17.

Initiatives and research. (n.d.). Retrieved from Google Accessibility website: <https://www.google.com/accessibility/initiatives-research.html> Accessed 05.04.18.

Ray W. Howard Library at Shoreline Community College. (2016, August 3). *Books for busy students* [Video file]. Retrieved from <https://www.youtube.com/playlist?list = PLI-TctEQirT_TIRjk1v82pKpUIbEKY2kN&disable_polymer = true>.

Vlogbrothers. (n.d.). Retrieved from YouTube website: <https://www.youtube.com/channel/UCGaVdbSav8xWuFWTadK6loA>.

FURTHER READING

Bryant, L.V. (2016, June 29). Video (instructional) checklist. Retrieved from Google Drive website: <https://goo.gl/vdtQxH >

Center for Teaching Vanderbilt University. (2016, September 6). *Bloom's taxonomy [Infographic].* Retrieved from <https://www.flickr.com/photos/vandycft/29428436431>.

Sorkin, A.R., & Peters, J.W. (2006, October 9). Google to acquire YouTube for $1.65 billion. *The New York Times*. Retrieved from <http://www.nytimes.com/2006/10/09/business/09cnd-deal.html>.

Traffic Sources Report. (n.d.). Retrieved from YouTube website: <https://support.google.com/youtube/answer/1714921?hl = en> Accessed 28.09.17.

Wooshue, K., & Makani, J. (2006). Information seeking behaviours of business students and the development of academic digital libraries. *Evidence Based Library and Information Practice, 1*(4), 30–45, Retrieved from DOAJ database.

CHAPTER 10

Snapchat

10.1 CASE STUDY 1

Snapchat in Academic Libraries: We Ain't Afraid of No Ghost

Nicole Maddock[1], Monica Fazekas[1] and Kevin Tanner[2]
[1]Western Libraries, Western University, London, ON, Canada
[2]Reg Erhardt Library, Southern Alberta Institute of Technology, AB, Canada

Institution: Western University, Western Libraries, 23,139 (2016/17) undergraduates served by 8 library locations.

Campaign Purpose: Our purpose was twofold: (1) To explore storytelling as a useful method for engaging with our undergraduate student population using the Snapchat "My Story" feature; (2) to work collaboratively with departments across Western's campus to develop and post creative content to a single shared Western University Snapchat account.

Target Demographic: Undergraduate students.

Measure of Success: Maximum impressions per snap per story, viewer retention throughout the story, subscriber acquisition and retention. Stories are benchmarked against previous stories and other institutional stories at Western.

Team: Four-member team of three librarians and library staff and one student Snapchat Research Assistant.

10.1.1 INTRODUCTION

When Evan Spiegel created Snapchat as a way to send disappearing pictures to friends on the Stanford campus (Colao, 2012), little did he know that his college app would skyrocket to fame and become one of the

Social Media
DOI: https://doi.org/10.1016/B978-0-08-102409-6.00010-9

most popular social media platforms among 18–24-year olds (Statista, 2017). Since then, brands, celebrities, news outlets, and even Prime Minister Justin Trudeau and other heads of state, take advantage of Snapchat to reach out to the younger generation. Western Libraries quickly recognized that Snapchat has the potential to be a powerful tool for engaging with our undergraduate students in a new and unique way. This is our Snapchat story.

10.1.2 TO SNAP OR NOT TO SNAP?

When Snapchat first emerged as a social media platform in 2011, the newly minted app was used at Western Libraries primarily by our student library assistants, much like Evan Spiegel originally intended, to send informal and ephemeral snaps to friends and fellow employees. As Snapchat's popularity grew on Western's campus, Western Libraries began to consider the feasibility of adding Snapchat to our roster of social media engagement tools; however, Snapchat was a personal communication channel among friends and we felt uneasy infiltrating our students' private spaces.

In 2013, Snapchat added the "My Story" feature, broadening the scope of possibilities for the app's use. Snapchat describes My Story as "a collection of Snaps that play in the order they were taken. You and your friends' Stories cover the last 24 hours, so you can see the day unfold" (Snapchat, Inc., n.d.). Taco Bell, McDonald's, and Acura—early adopters of the app—introduced interesting possibilities for storytelling and engaging with Snapchat "My Story." These trailblazers lent the app an air of legitimacy and turned Snapchat from a personal and private platform to an effective social, promotional, and engagement channel.

After other major brands established a track record for using the platform for promotional instead of personal engagement, Western Libraries' social media team met to explore how we might use Snapchat in an academic library. Still we hesitated; too many questions remained unanswered. How would we sustain an active Snapchat account? What type of content would resonate with undergrads? Would students even follow a library on Snapchat? Our instinct told us to put Snapchat on hold for a little while longer.

In spring 2016, Western University's Communications and Public Affairs' (C&PA) social media team invited other departments on campus to collaborate on a central Western University Snapchat account. The excitement at Western Libraries was palpable. Contributing to a shared account, managed by C&PA, not only provided us the space and time needed to develop unique and meaningful Western Libraries content for Western's account, it also allowed us to leverage the well-established audience of Western's Snapchat followers. The time had finally come: we put together a Snapchat team, hired a student Snapchat research assistant, and set out to conquer our fear of ghosts.

10.1.3 WE AIN'T AFRAID OF NO GHOSTS

When we began developing our Snapchat strategy in spring 2016, few educational institutions, let alone academic libraries, were using Snapchat. Universities and colleges with Snapchat accounts used the app mainly to promote events or to market the institution to prospective students. Some public libraries were experimenting with Snapchat, but their marketing strategies and audience were different from ours. While we discovered a small number of academic library Snapchat accounts, it was unclear if these libraries' promotional efforts were successful.

Snapchat in academic libraries was in its infancy; the scholarly literature explored only the behaviors of users themselves but not user's perceptions of brands on the platform, while trade articles mostly described basic app functionality (Bayer, Ellison, Schoenebeck, & Falk, 2016; Piwek & Joinson, 2016; Vaterlaus, Barnett, Roche, & Young, 2016). As a result, for inspiration we turned to nonprofit organizations, popular users with a wide reach of followers termed "social media influencers," and brands. We followed trendy Snapchat accounts such as Taco Bell, General Electric, NPR, Los Angeles County Museum of Art (LACMA), and even DJ Khaled. These accounts gave us an inside look into what was current on the platform, and key success strategies from observing popular Snapchat accounts emerged right away: good Snapchatters are young, creative, and fun, and the best accounts use a narrative arc to turn multiple snaps into an interesting story. With these three things in mind, our Snapchat team began to develop a Snapchat strategy that prioritized storytelling as an effective method for engagement. Our goal was to create disappearing stories that would make a lasting impression on our undergraduate student population.

10.1.4 TELLING LIBRARY STORIES WITH SNAPCHAT

So, how does one tell library stories that resonate with undergraduate students? The best and most successful Snapchat posts have a few things in common: they are usually creative, candid, and comedic. When creating content, we try to think like an undergrad and often consult our student library assistants. What lingo are students using? What is trendy in popular culture and on campus this year? The beauty of Snapchat is the in-the-moment ephemeral nature that allows us to produce experimental content that may fall flat on another social channel. With Instagram and Facebook, viewers expect quality images and videos or well-written text. In Snapchat, we doodle, post awkward photos, and have fun with emojis, whereas we tend to choose more professional content for Facebook and Instagram. We try to instill comedic flair into our stories and are not afraid to poke fun at ourselves or libraries in general. Most importantly, we try to make sure our snaps are candid and genuine, or we risk sounding insincere and embarrassingly out of touch.

When a story idea starts to percolate, we begin the essential planning stage, which is key to the success of a Snapchat story. Our Snapchat Research Assistant, Kevin, developed a very helpful and simple storyboard tool that we use as a framework to develop and outline our content (Fig. 10.1.1).

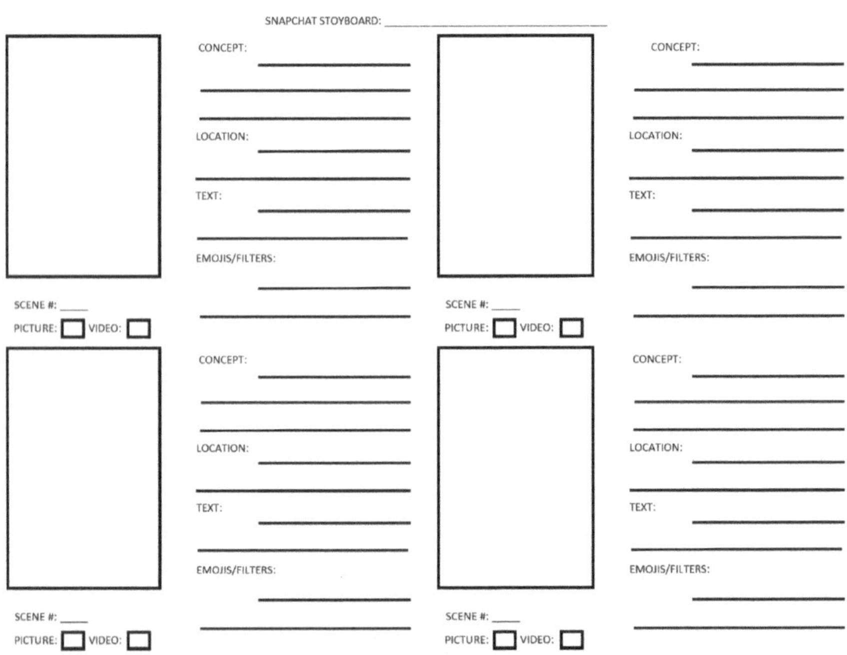

Figure 10.1.1 Storyboard tool, developed by Kevin Tanner.

Storyboarding is a great way to organize the details of each snap, including images, stickers, locations, and text. Snapchat stories take time to create. Working out the small details during the storyboard stage, rather than while "snapping," is preferable. Planning every snap works well for many types of stories; however, the exception to this rule is live events where it is impossible to anticipate every shot in advance and still get that live-action flavor. When snapping live events, flexibility is important, as is the ability to nimbly change direction when something unexpected happens during a live Snapchat story.

To hold an audience's attention, stories must be engaging from start to finish. Individual snaps are up to 10 seconds long and stories are comprised of a series of these "snaps," which post in the order in which they are captured. Viewers have the option to tap to skip individual snaps or to swipe to skip the whole story. The story as a whole must captivate our students' attention throughout; or, out of boredom, they may not continue watching after the first snap or two and miss the message we are trying to convey. Snaps at the beginning of a story generally get the highest number of views, with views for each subsequent snap decreasing as the story progresses. To ensure as many students as possible see the most relevant content, we emphasize important information at the beginning and post less engaging snaps at the close of a story. For example, when external video or music is incorporated, it is necessary to credit our sources. Those music, image, or video credit snaps, while required to meet copyright compliance, receive fewer views and we place them strategically at the end as a way to address the gradual decrease in viewership for each snap in a story. Another way to keep students engaged to the end is to limit stories to about 6–8 snaps with a maximum of 12 snaps. With Snapchat, brief and succinct is the way to go.

One of the strategies we use to incorporate preplanning into our Snapchat story is to use airplane mode. Before we begin creating our story, we place the device we will be using in airplane mode, allowing us to take multiple snaps of each image or video and then review the story as a whole, choosing the best snaps and deleting any we do not like. Once we have narrowed it down to a few key snaps, we take the device out of airplane mode and tap each snap again to upload the final completed story. By using airplane mode, individual snaps all post at the same time so our audience sees the story in its entirety, instead of one snap at a time. Using airplane mode gives us more control over our image and videos and an opportunity to review content that we would lose if we posted live in the moment.

Our approach to Snapchat is unique in academic libraries. Each Western Libraries' Snap is an individual story, with a beginning, middle, and end. Storytelling is an extremely effective way to engage with an audience: stories elicit emotion, change minds, and warm hearts (Holliman & Rowley, 2014; Pulizzi, 2012). After research into the literature and an in-depth investigation into a multitude of popular Snapchat accounts from libraries, post-secondary institutions, museums, nonprofits, and even brands, we succeeded in developing a collaborative Snapchat strategy focused on storytelling.

10.1.5 OUR FAVORITE STORIES

Booky—One of our favorite stories features our character Booky McBookface and his search for love in the library catalog: the Tinder for books. This Valentine's Day love story was planned in detail using our storyboard tool (Fig. 10.1.2).

London Comic Con—Western Archives holds an extensive comic book collection that was displayed at the 2016 London Comic Con. The Western Libraries Snapchat team was there to capture it all. We went in with a plan and layout but noise in the venue prompted a complete change of direction in our story. We were able to meet the challenge head on and created another of our favorite stories to date (Fig. 10.1.3).

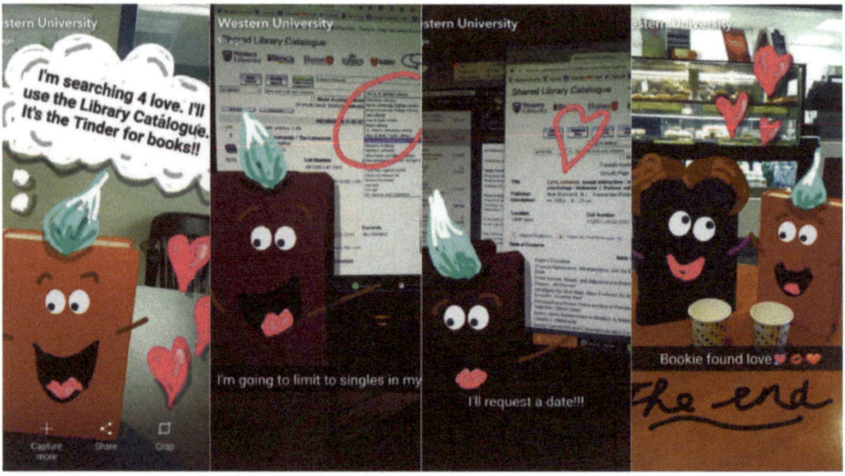

Figure 10.1.2 Booky McBookface Valentine's Day snapchat story.

Figure 10.1.3 Snapchatting live from London Comic Con.

24/7 Extended Examination Hours—Western Libraries is open 24/7 during the December and April exam periods. To gain entrance to the library, students show their university IDs to security. Every year we get complaints from students who forget their ID and claim they did not know about the requirement. We posted a fun Snapchat story that reminded students of this condition of entry, and for the first year ever, we did not receive any complaints (Fig. 10.1.4).

Figure 10.1.4 24/7 Examination period Snapchat story.

10.1.6 OTHER WESTERN LIBRARIES STORIES

Book Face Swap—Mini book reviews using the face swap feature where two faces swap places. We swapped our faces with those on the book covers we were reviewing.

5 fast facts—Five interesting facts about Western Libraries—Our snap that received the most screenshots was from this story and displayed the URL for our student job postings.

Booky McBookface's Search for Great Grandpa—Introducing our character Booky as he tours the Western Archives and Special Collections in search of his long lost ancestor.
Western Libraries Wonders—Western Libraries Snapchat spokesperson asks random students on campus, "How many libraries are there at Western?" The answers from students were all over the map.
O-Month tent—Highlights from our Orientation Month Western Libraries tent. Students interacting with giant games, making buttons, and speaking with library staff about our services.
Space Master Plan—Short Snapchat story to promote the Western Libraries Space Master Plan to the campus community.
Weldon Wellness Station—Weldon Library collaborates with Western's Wellness Education Centre to support students during the stressful exam period. This story introduced the friendly and knowledgeable staff from the Wellness Centre and Psychological Services staffing the Weldon Wellness Station.

10.1.7 WHAT WORKED

- Using stories with a beginning, middle, and end.
- Storyboarding, planning, and scheduling stories in advance.
- Featuring students in our Snapchat stories and trying to present the student voice.
- Keeping stories candid, comedic, and creative.
- Working with a team of library staff personally experienced with Snapchat.
- Including music, video captures from YouTube, and other media in our stories.
- Including a URL in a snap—our snap that included a URL had the most screenshots of any of our stories.
- Using Snapchat's ability to track the number of views and screenshots as an analytics tool to measure the success of our stories.
- Sharing one campus Snapchat account.
    - The greatest benefit to a shared account is inheriting all of the university's Snapchat followers. Undergraduate students are more likely to follow a university Snapchat account than they are a library account.
    - Successful Snapchat accounts provide regular content. We can spend time developing quality and timely content to contribute to

the shared account. We do not need to worry about sustaining an individual library account or developing daily posts.
  - The library is integrated as an important voice in the university's social media fabric, both from the student perspective and as campus partners working together to offer diverse and interesting stories about life on campus.
- Using Slack (a communication app for teams) to coordinate logging in and out of the shared Snapchat account.
- Cross-promoting stories on other social media platforms using screenshots from our snap stories.

10.1.8 WHAT DIDN'T WORK

- Shared account does not allow students to send snaps back in reply.
- No current opportunity for contests or other two-way engagement with the app.
- More than one campus department posting different stories on the same day.
  - Since stories last for 24 hours, sometimes two stories will overlap on the same day. The department with the second story will get far fewer viewers than the first.
- There is no opportunity for Western Libraries to schedule stories during campus-wide events and initiatives, such as Homecoming, International Week, Convocation, etc., as the account is already reserved by C&PA.

10.1.9 RECOMMENDATIONS

10.1.9.1 Planning

- Brainstorm story ideas and map out a schedule a few stories at a time—we planned all our stories for the fall semester in the summer.
- If you share an account, schedule your stories in advance to be sure to secure the best dates and times for your stories.
- Use a storyboard tool to plan your stories in detail.
- Save time by choosing your filters, stickers, and text in advance.
- If appropriate, find music and video clips to use.
- Credit and cite content that is not yours (e.g., YouTube clip).
- Post citations on the last slide.
- Scout locations in advance to ensure optimal lighting and sound.

- Track your views—login at the 23rd hour, before your Snapchat story disappears, to screenshot and record the number of views and/or screenshots received by each snap in your story. This way you ensure you record the maximum impressions per snap per story and can use these analytics to measure success.
- Follow a variety of popular Snapchat accounts to stay current with the app and see how others are using storytelling to their advantage.
- Share an account. What worked outweighs what did not work.

10.1.9.2 Storytelling

- Use an opening snap that clearly identifies your library and a closing snap that marks the end of your story.
- Place important information at the beginning of your story.
- Consult and/or involve students in your stories to get student voice and perspective.
- Make note of the language students use and make sure you use it in a genuine way.
- Plan stories that are candid, comedic, and creative.
- Don't be afraid to draw on your snaps, use silly filters, or add video features such as slow motion, reverse, etc.
- Use airplane mode to curate your story by choosing the best of each image and video snaps.
- Allow for flexibility when Snapping live events.

10.1.9.3 What to Snapchat

- Anything that happens in the library that might interest undergraduate students. For example:

  Snapchat events in your library or hosted by your library, that is, author talks, concerts, GIS Day, etc. Snapchat can be a window into what is happening for those unable to attend (NPR and other news channels Snapchat accounts are wonderful examples for this).
- New and exciting items in your collection relevant to your audiences' interests.
- Behind the scenes work in the library (e.g., how a book ends up on the shelf or a database in the catalog).
- Highlight new books (can do book face swap or regular book talk).
- Contests—If your library/institution allows followers to respond to your snaps, hold a contest.

10.1.10 FINAL WORDS

Western Libraries' Snapchat strategy is successful for two reasons. Our collaboration on a shared Western University account with an already established audience makes it easy to contribute quality and timely content to students who otherwise might ignore a library Snapchat account. Our use of storytelling as an effective engagement tool sets our Snapchat stories apart from other academic accounts. Storytelling is a timeless technique that can be used to any library's advantage on a range of communication and social media platforms. Instagram, for example, launched their own stories feature in August 2016, almost identical to that of Snapchat (Constine, 2016). All the storytelling techniques outlined earlier can be used to develop Snapchat or Instagram stories; the key is not the platform that is used but the story that is told. With a year of snapping stories under our belt, we are excited to explore new and exciting opportunities to tell Western Libraries' stories with Snapchat.

REFERENCES

Bayer, J. B., Ellison, N. B., Schoenebeck, S. Y., & Falk, E. B. (2016). Sharing the small moments: Ephemeral social interaction on Snapchat. *Information, Communication & Society, 19*(7), 956–977.

Colao, J.J. (2012). *Snapchat: The biggest no-revenue mobile app since Instagram.* Retrieved from <https://www.forbes.com/sites/jjcolao/2012/11/27/snapchat-the-biggest-no-revenue-mobile-app-since-instagram/#4925a9b47200> Accessed 26.09.17.

Constine, J. (2016). *Instagram launches "stories," a Snapchatty feature for imperfect sharing.* Retrieved from <https://techcrunch.com/2016/08/02/instagram-stories/> Accessed 30.01.18.

Holliman, G., & Rowley, J. (2014). Business to business digital content marketing: Marketers' perceptions of best practice. *Journal of Research in Interactive Marketing, 8*(4), 269–293.

Parker, R., Jr. (1984). Ghostbusters. On *Ghostbusters: original Soundtrack Album* [Motion picture soundtrack]. US: Arista Records.

Piwek, L., & Joinson, A. (2016). "What do they snapchat about?" Patterns of use in time-limited instant messaging service. *Computers in Human Behavior, 54*, 358–367.

Pulizzi, J. (2012). The rise of storytelling as the new marketing. *Publishing Research Quarterly, 28*(2), 116–123.

Snapchat, Inc. (n.d.). *Snapchat support about stories.* Retrieved from <https://support.snapchat.com/en-US/a/about-stories> Accessed 12.12.17.

Statista (2017). *Most popular social networks of teenagers in the United States from Fall 2012 to Spring 2017.* Retrieved from <https://www.statista.com/statistics/250172/social-network-usage-of-us-teens-and-young-adults/> Accessed 26.09.17.

Vaterlaus, J. M., Barnett, K., Roche, C., & Young, J. A. (2016). "Snapchat is more personal": An exploratory study on Snapchat behaviors and young adult interpersonal relationships. *Computers in Human Behavior, 62*, 594–601.

10.2 CASE STUDY 2

Snap to It: Reaching Users Where They Are With Snapchat Geofilters

Laura MacLeod Mulligan[1] and Alexander S. Di Iorio[2]
[1]Head of Access Services, Ball State University Libraries
[2]Panel Research Coordinator, Simmons Research

Institution: Ball State University: 22,513 total students as of Fall 2017 (Ball State University website, 2017). On-campus population: 16,825 (15,379 undergraduates). Off-campus population: 5,688 (4,670 online students).

Campaign Purpose: To have a University Libraries-owned Snapchat geofilter serve as both a tool to increase engagement among library users and a product of students' direct requests.

Target Demographic: Undergraduate and graduate students.

Measure of Success: Anecdotal evidence, cross posts with geofilter on other social media platforms.

Team: One librarian (also social media coordinator); one graduate assistant; support from Information Services unit, Assistant Dean for Public Services, and Dean of the University Libraries.

10.2.1 BACKGROUND

Ball State University Libraries' main campus library is formally known as the Alexander M. Bracken Library. It opened its doors on September 9, 1975, and contains hundreds of thousands of volumes; over 200 subscription databases; 100 staff employees and at least as many student assistants; and five floors with discipline-specific collections, equipment, spaces, and personnel. Centrally located on campus, it serves as a well-respected and oft-used resource for on-campus and distance education students, faculty, and community members.

In the eyes of some of its more frequent users, however, for many years Bracken Library has been lovingly dubbed "Club Bracken." While there is no doubt that it provides invaluable academic resources for its users, it is also a social hub. Library users visit the library to do work, of course, but they also come to see friends, grab a coffee or a sandwich from the Bookmark Cafe, and participate in activities sponsored by the Libraries and other campus entities. Even Happy Friday Guy (an unofficial university mascot in a blue suit) makes the effort to dash through the library lobby at the end of every week, reminding everyone within earshot that it is, in fact, Friday. The Libraries encourage new visitors and help to continually engage repeat visitors by hosting sponsored activities such as "Friday Night Cardboard," the annual "Catan-ament," and the "No Work Zone" stress-relief event. Importantly, the hope is that students will feel welcome enough after partaking in these events to take advantage of the academic resources the library has to offer. Outreach is an important factor in keeping the library fun and relevant for the community it serves.

10.2.2 THE IDEA

On a daily basis the Libraries' social media accounts—including Facebook, Twitter, Instagram, and Pinterest—receive engagement from students, faculty, community users, and campus groups. Types of engagement vary widely. It could be a compliment, a complaint, or simply a like.

Early into the Fall 2016 semester, a simple request came through via Twitter from a returning Ball State student (see Fig. 10.2.1).

Thirty of the student's followers liked the tweet, backing up the student's sentiment and request.

Although Ball State itself is represented by several Snapchat geofilters, at that time, the Libraries were not. We take library user suggestions seriously and consider ourselves responsive to their needs. Considering the idea to branch out to uncharted waters was directly tweeted to us by one

Figure 10.2.1 Tweet from a returning Ball State student, asking us to create a Bracken Library Snapchat filter, Fall 2016.

of our student users, we decided to try our hand at an exclusive Bracken Library geofilter.

While we had never entertained the idea of a Snapchat geofilter before, we immediately began to research what it took to create one. In Snapchat's own words on their website, "Geofilters are creative overlays that capture where you are or what you're up to in a Snap! Create your own, and surprise Snapchatters in the locations you choose." We discovered before, during, and after the design process some important factors to consider when creating geofilters:

- You do not have to have a Snapchat account to create a geofilter.
- They are not permanent, unless you want them to be.
- They cannot use official logos or designs—they must be completely original.
- You must indicate the geographic coordinates where the geofilter will be active.
- The geofilter must not take up more than ⅓ of the screen, and it must be transparent.
- It is completely free, and as long as you have a compelling reason for making one available (and make your case), the Snapchat geofilter gods will typically allow it.
- As of September 2016, not many libraries had ventured into this realm.
- Due to the very private nature of Snapchat snaps, there are barriers to finding out how much reach a geofilter (or any post to Snapchat, for that matter) has among a community of users.

10.2.3 MEASURE OF SUCCESS

At the time this geofilter was launched, we did not have an active Snapchat account, so there was not a way to see how many users were engaging with us on that platform. Even if we had a Snapchat account at that time, there would not have been a way to know how many users were making use of the geofilter. Snapchat provides a private and fleeting way to snap photographs and communicate between friends. Consequently, it does not report engagement analytics in the way that our Facebook, Twitter, and Instagram accounts do.

Our best way to know how far reaching the geofilter had become was to gather anecdotal evidence in casual conversation with library student assistants (some of whom had been using the filter but did not realize we created it ourselves) and occasionally library users. Some library users cross-post to different applications, and we noticed several public posts with the geofilter overlaid to Instagram and Twitter (sometimes mentioning or tagging our account, sometimes using "Bracken Library" as the location or using keywords that made the post more discoverable in advanced social media searches). The response was overwhelmingly positive. We did not receive any criticism regarding the effort.

10.2.4 TECHNICAL ASPECTS

The first element that was considered for the design was the building's distinctive architecture. After hours of brainstorming and sketching, the second design tactic considered was to dig deeper into the club aspect of Club Bracken. Some audio systems and audio visualization programs use vector bars that correspond to the rhythm and volume of music. Bracken's towering structures seemed the perfect space in which to incorporate these vector bars. Thus a geofilter was born (see Fig. 10.2.2).

Snapchat will not accept any submitted artwork that is not optimized for web, does not have a 1080 × 1920 pixel resolution, or has a file size greater than 300 kilobytes, among other criteria that are listed on their website. "Optimized for web" means that the file must be in a PNG format with transparency to allow the users to take "snaps" that can rest in the background with a geofilter overlay. Although Adobe Illustrator and Photoshop were both used to create the design, we recommend using Photoshop to compile all design elements into a final piece. Photoshop is often used to create image files for the web (PNGs), so it has easily accessible options for saving the design in the proper format. We also recommend that care is taken to test the appearance of graphics and text on a variety of backgrounds; the nature of a geofilter is to appear in front of anything the individual's smartphone camera picks up.

10.2.5 WHAT WORKED

- Making a geofilter available to primarily students as well as other visitors to our physical space was a way for us to connect with them on a deeper level by means of an application on which we had not been active prior to the creation of the geofilter.

Figure 10.2.2 Bracken Library Snapchat geofilter, Fall 2016. *Credit: Photograph by Laura MacLeod Mulligan. Geofilter design by Alexander S. Di Iorio.*

- Generating a geofilter as a product of a student's request shows that we are responsive to the interests of our students, which subsequently bolsters their level of engagement with the Libraries.
- The nature of the design appeals to students, especially those who are familiar with the main library's nickname: Club Bracken. Our graduate assistant played off the club aspect by creating a design in the same vein as a nightclub's logo. The sound vector bars typically seen on many audio visualization programs—otherwise colloquially known as the sound lights that go up and down when the music gets louder and softer—were integrated into the geofilter to convey Bracken as a lively

and desirable place to be. Indeed, Bracken is a popular meeting spot on campus.
- The nature of the design also maintains the University Libraries' long-standing effort to be known as a destination for research, learning, and friends.

10.2.6 WHAT DIDN'T WORK

- The first submission of the geofilter was not accepted by Snapchat, and in the boilerplate rejection email, no reason was provided besides the standard list of criteria by which Snapchat geofilter submissions are judged in general. By all accounts, it met the technical criteria of the submission process; the only aspect we thought might not have passed muster would have been our argument for the relevance/applicability to the community. Without implementing any design or technical changes, our resubmission of the geofilter involved writing a short justification memo explaining why the image design was relevant to the students who would eventually use it—that the distinct architecture of the building and the "Club Bracken" reputation would both be evident. The geofilter was subsequently approved as is and became immediately usable within 24 hours.

10.2.7 RECOMMENDATIONS

- The design process can often be highly subjective, and one team member's helpful criticism to the designer could potentially challenge another individual's thoughts of how the design should look.
- Goals should be agreed upon at the beginning. Although we did not run into this issue, we recommend that before any design is made, meetings with senior staff members take place in order to make sure everyone's goals are consistent.
- We recommend working with library administration on drafting the design, making sure that the ultimate product reflects the mission of the library. Library administration was supportive of our using work time for the effort and gave useful feedback along the way. Upon acceptance of the geofilter by Snapchat, library administration was enthusiastic and understood the great effort involved in making the geofilter available for library users.
- Keep in mind that what worked for us may not work for all—so local considerations would have to be made.

10.2.8 FINAL WORDS

With the success of the Snapchat geofilter project of Fall 2016, the Libraries are excited to announce that as of September 2017 we now have additional geofilters to serve the branch campuses: Science-Health Science Library and Architecture Library. We have also received approval from library administration to create a full Snapchat account with capabilities to post photographs and videos (i.e., Snapchat stories). In addition, as a freelance project in summer 2017, our then-graduate assistant designed another geofilter for the Raymond H. Danforth Library on the New England College campus.

When the Club Bracken geofilter first became live, we loved seeing students' affection toward the geofilter on our social media sites and in person. Now, it is over one year old, and the initial excitement among staff has waned, but it remains a way for new and returning students to express their love for the Libraries. The geofilter has become part of the daily life of any Snapchatting student who sets foot in Bracken Library.

FURTHER READING

Ball State enrollment largest in university history (29 August, 2017). Retrieved from <http://cms.bsu.edu/news/articles/2017/8/ball-state-enrollment-largest-in-university-history>.

Snapchat geofilters (n.d.). Retrieved from <http://www.snapchat.com/geofilters>.

CHAPTER 11

Pinterest

11.1 CASE STUDY 1

Extending the Library's Presence Into the Virtual Space Using Pinterest

Brandy R. Horne
University of South Carolina Aiken, Aiken, SC, United States

Institution: Gregg-Graniteville Library, University of South Carolina Aiken, 3548 students (2016).

Campaign Purpose: To extend the reach of the library's displays into the digital space.

Target Demographic: The campus community—students, faculty, and staff.

Measure of Success: The successful creation and deployment of digital displays for maximum visibility.

Team: Instruction/Reference Librarian responsible for marketing and promotion.

11.1.1 PINTEREST IN LIBRARIES

Pinterest describes itself as "the world's catalog of ideas" ("About," para. 1, 2017). Users can create boards to which they "pin" images and other content that appeal to them. A well-populated board looks like a digital collage, and the overall effect is similar to that of a designer's inspiration board (Mikos, Horne, & Weaver, 2015). Due to the attractiveness of its display and relative ease of use, millions of people use Pinterest to collect all sorts of things, such as decorating ideas, recipes, and crafting projects.

Libraries are often enthusiastic adopters of technology and tools that allow them to be where their users are. Pinterest not only facilitates that goal, but also the curation aspect of the tool can be especially appealing

Social Media
DOI: https://doi.org/10.1016/B978-0-08-102409-6.00011-0

to librarian sensibilities. Libraries have come up with several creative ideas for using Pinterest to curate content for library patrons. Lofland (2012) describes several of these ideas, which include creating reading lists, sharing new acquisitions, highlighting library staff members, running book clubs, and providing access to digital collections.

As the librarian responsible for marketing and promotion at the Gregg-Graniteville Library, I had the idea to use Pinterest to create digital versions of the library's physical displays in order to expand the reach of those displays. According to Severson (2014), "the easiest form of outreach is to get your collections visible in as many places as possible" (p. 15). I saw Pinterest as a tool that could facilitate such efforts.

11.1.2 BACKGROUND

The Gregg-Graniteville Library is fairly small with 13 full-time employees, several student assistants, and the occasional intern. Of the 13 full-time staff, there are six faculty librarians: two Instruction/Reference Librarians, the Government Documents Librarian, the Instruction Coordinator, the Collections Coordinator, and the Library Director. Due to the library's relatively small staff, each person wears many hats. While both librarians and staff participate in providing reference assistance, four of the library faculty teach the vast majority of the library's 250 + library instruction sessions annually. In addition to their substantial teaching loads, each librarian is primarily responsible for specific aspects of the library's operation. For example, one of the Instruction/Reference Librarians is also the library's instructional technology administrator, and she is also the archivist for the Graniteville Archives. As the other Instruction/Reference Librarian, I am the reference desk coordinator, and I am also responsible for spearheading the library's marketing and promotional efforts. Add to these roles the expectations of the tenure track, such as committee work and scholarship, and it is easy to see how the librarians can become overwhelmed.

Because everyone shoulders so many different responsibilities, creating library displays is often not prioritized. While I am ultimately responsible for the displays, the librarians and staff take turns creating displays as their schedules allow. Creating these displays requires a lot of time, work, and creativity, but they are fleeting and ultimately do not seem to attract much attention.

The Gregg-Graniteville Library has one display case that remains locked and is located in the building's foyer. Students, faculty, and staff walk past the display case as they enter and exit the building, but they rarely ever stop to actually look at it. While the area is one that gets a lot of traffic, it is not a space where people stop to linger. In addition, the display case competes with several signs, a rack of campus newspapers, and a drink vending machine. When patrons do stop, the locked case prevents them from actively engaging with the materials on display. While some patrons do occasionally ask if they can check out items in the case, many might assume they cannot check out the items, or they just decide it would be too much hassle to ask. If the point of a display is to highlight library collections for circulation, then keeping them in a locked case in a high traffic area defeats that purpose (Fig. 11.1.1).

Obviously, there are several issues that hinder the effectiveness of our displays, and addressing these issues has required a multipronged approach. I began creating displays in an open space near the reference desk using folding tables so that patrons could browse and engage with the items being displayed, addressing the issue of unnecessary barriers. In the vein of meeting patrons where they are, online content is curated and created in LibGuides to supplement the physical displays, and often this content is advertised via Facebook and a banner on the Library's homepage. LibGuides is a content management system and curation platform created specifically for libraries. In LibGuides, it is possible to create lists of books

Figure 11.1.1 Locked display case in the library's foyer.

Figure 11.1.2 Banned Books Week display set up on a folding table in an open area near the reference desk.

that link directly to the library's catalog, but this function is not practical for more than just a few books. A limitation of the platform is that these lists run straight down the page, so even just 10 books require a lot of scrolling long past the point where the rest of the page's content has ended. There is a scrolling gallery, but again, this is not optimal when trying to display more than just a few items (Fig. 11.1.2).

11.1.3 ENTER PINTEREST

This is where Pinterest proves especially useful. The layout of a Pinterest board, in addition to being visually appealing, allows for easy browsing and exploration. A quick glance at a Pinterest board can convey extent and scope of the materials available. In addition, one can easily share boards via email or various social media platforms, and widgets of functioning boards can be created and embedded where needed, like in a LibGuide (Fig. 11.1.3).

In the Gregg-Graniteville Library, Pinterest is primarily used to create digital versions of physical displays. The librarian responsible for marketing and promotion creates a board for a particular display, and each pin represents an item included in that display and links to the corresponding item record in the library's catalog. These displays can be augmented by

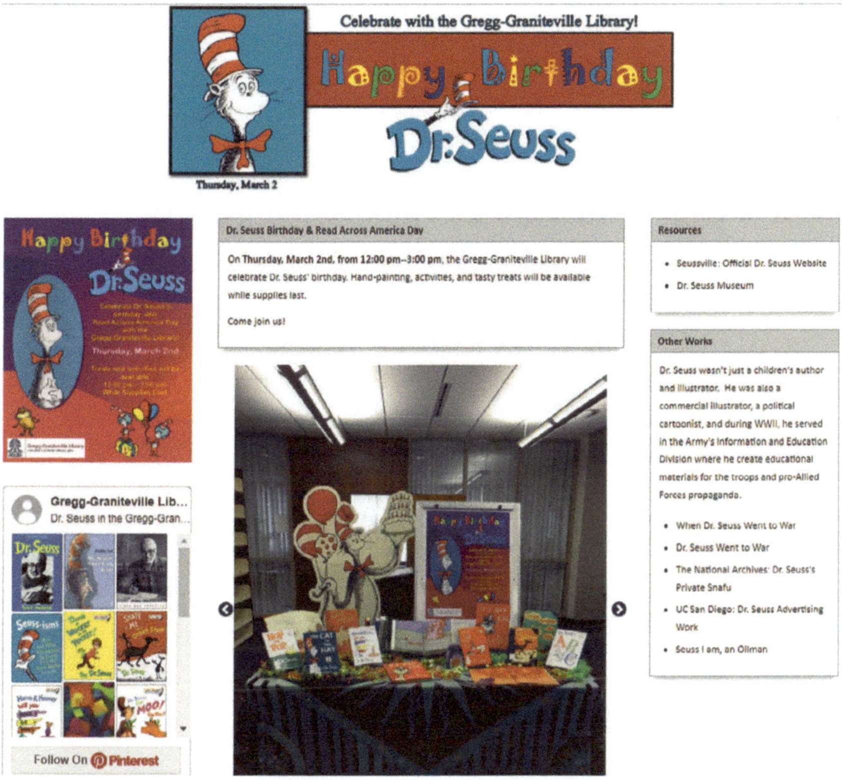

Figure 11.1.3 Screenshot of LibGuide created for Dr. Seuss event, including an image of the physical display and an embedded Pinterest widget. Dr. Seuss Properties™ & © [2019] Dr. Seuss Enterprises, L.P. All Rights Reserved.

adding relevant digital items not available in the library's collections, such as photos and online images, videos, or informational webpages (Fig. 11.1.4).

The library has also used Pinterest to curate material not contained within the collection. Leading up to graduation one year, a Pinterest board was created that contained links to famous commencement speeches. It could be reached by clicking on the "Congratulations Graduates" banner on the library's homepage. Another board was created as a virtual read-out for Banned Books Week, and it featured videos created by members of the campus community reading from banned books. A link to this board was provided in a LibGuide created for that year's Banned Books Week, which was accessed via a banner on the library's homepage (Fig. 11.1.5).

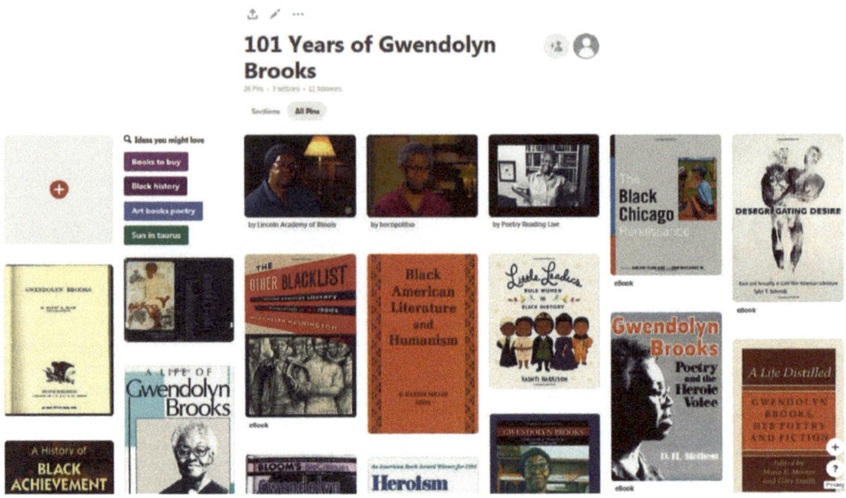

Figure 11.1.4 Screenshot of a Pinterest board created to accompany a physical display in the library, including books contained within the collection, as well relevant web content.

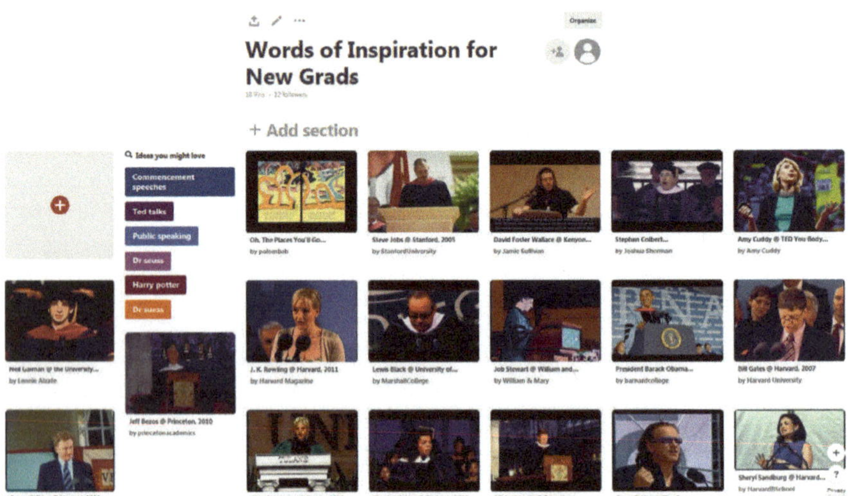

Figure 11.1.5 A Pinterest board populated by videos of iconic commencement speeches.

11.1.4 CREATING DIGITAL DISPLAYS USING PINTEREST

When using Pinterest to create digital displays, it is important that the pins lead patrons to the library or the library's catalog. When pinning books from your library's collection, it may be possible to pin the book cover image directly from your library's catalog. It is worth a try. However, in many cases, the resulting pinned image will be of poor resolution. If that does not work, Pinterest gives you the option to upload an image from your computer, so you can save the image then upload it. Once you have successfully uploaded the image to the board, click on it, and look for the pen icon. This will allow you to edit the pin. On the edit screen, you will have the opportunity to add a description and a website URL. For the description, I generally use a phrase like "Find this item in the Gregg-Graniteville Library." For the website, I paste the permanent URL for the item's record in the catalog. Do this for each item you want to include.

You can also pin images directly from a web search. Just remember to edit the pin, and change the description and website. Otherwise, you will be directing your patrons to whatever random website supplied the image.

11.1.5 SHARING PINTEREST DISPLAYS

There are several options for sharing Pinterest boards. You can invite individual people to join boards, or you can send boards directly from Pinterest to Facebook or Twitter. 'Send board' also provides the option to copy a shortened link that can be sent out or posted wherever needed. There is also the option to create a widget that can be embedded in webpages and LibGuides. The 'Make a widget' function gives you some options for formatting the size and shape of your board, including the ability to set your own parameters, along with a preview so that you can see how it will look. Pinterest will then generate a code that can be used to embed the widget where it is needed. In LibGuides, for example, there is a 'Media/Widget' option when adding content, so embedding a Pinterest board into a guide is very simple. Once embedded, patrons can browse the Pinterest board without leaving the library's webpages.

11.1.6 LIMITATIONS

You cannot rearrange pins. The items appear in the order in which they were pinned, with the most recent appearing at the top of the board. If the order in which the pins appear is important, then you will need to plan out your order before starting. If you have neglected to do this, one potential work-around is to pin all of your items onto a draft board and then create and title another board that will be the official board for the display. Once you have done this, go back to the draft board with all the pins. Thinking in terms of bottom to top, select pins to add to the official board in the order you would like them to appear.

11.1.7 WHAT WORKED

The Gregg-Graniteville Library has created several digital displays using Pinterest, but the most successful was a crowd-sourced display where we asked the campus community to share with us memories of their favorite childhood books (Mikos et al., 2015). We used this input to select items to highlight from our Juvenile collection, and the items were displayed along with the quotes and anecdotes provided. Over the course of this effort, we were also able to identify and address gaps in the collection. In addition to the physical display, the anecdotes were shared via Facebook, and a digital version of the display was created in Pinterest. The memories and anecdotes were posted as comments under each item on the Pinterest board. While the success of this display was not specific to the use of Pinterest, the creation of the digital display endures even though the physical display was eventually taken down, and we are still able to share what turned out to be a beautiful display with our campus community.

Because digital displays endure even after the physical displays are taken down, they can continue to grow over time and be reused when appropriate. Our Banned Books display, for example, is redeployed each year, and it is a bit more inclusive each time.

11.1.8 WHAT DIDN'T WORK

While the displays created in Pinterest do serve their purpose, it is difficult to assess their actual impact. The Gregg-Graniteville Library's Pinterest account has only 18 followers, but the ways in which we deploy our digital displays are often somewhat removed from Pinterest itself. Embedded widgets, for example, can be browsed from the webpages in which they are embedded. We have received countless notifications that various pins from our boards have been repinned, but there is no way to know if these notifications are being generated by activity within our campus community. If the Pinterest displays are not garnering, the views we would hope for, then the issue likely has more to do with a lack of marketing than the use or effectiveness of the Pinterest platform.

When the library first began using Pinterest to create displays, it was possible to pin the cover image directly from the library's catalog. However, issues within the catalog itself, along with updates in Pinterest have complicated that process. Now, in order to guarantee the pinned image is of good quality, it is almost always necessary to download the image and then upload it.

The Pinterest website can be quirky. Newly created boards often do not appear either on the library's Pinterest page or in the list of available boards. Also, when in the process of creating a display, new pins do not display immediately. Refreshing the page is sometimes necessary to make sure a pin looks good and so that you can click on it to edit the description and website information.

The Banned Books Read-Out board has only seven patron-created videos, but the live read-outs we have staged have consistently drawn healthy participation. Perhaps our campus community is camera shy, or perhaps the initiative has not been marketed effectively. So while Pinterest would be a good place to collect such videos, it is possible that members of our campus community would prefer not to have these videos saved in perpetuity.

11.1.9 RECOMMENDATIONS

Build boards/displays over time. This is especially good advice for boards where it makes sense to feature a lot of items, like a Banned Books Week display. The process of creating these displays is not difficult, but it is time-consuming and can be frustrating if done at the last minute. If possible, plan displays in advance and work on them throughout the year. If more than one person is available to create the Pinterest displays, assign each person specific displays to focus on, and make it a group effort.

Advertise your displays every way possible. Email links to your campus community, share via your chosen social media platforms, and embed widgets into your webpages and/or LibGuides pages. These are quick and easy steps to make sure that your community have the opportunity to engage with and appreciate your hard work. This is not something we have done consistently but plan to do going forward.

When sharing patron-generated content, make sure they understand how and where it will be shared. For the Banned Books Read-Out, we sent out a call for video submissions. In that call, we made it clear that the videos would be posted on the library's Facebook and Pinterest pages. When we asked for memories regarding favorite childhood books, we wanted to share the anecdotes along with the books in both the physical and digital displays. As these submissions came in, I followed up with each person via email to make sure they were okay with us sharing their words via Facebook and Pinterest.

11.1.10 FINAL WORDS

Often when it comes to social media, what you get out of it depends on what you put into it. When it comes to Pinterest displays, however, this relationship is not necessarily readily clear. As is the case with physical displays, it can be difficult to measure the actual impact. However, if the goal is to create a digital version of a display that is enduring and that can be shared far and wide, Pinterest is an excellent platform from which to do that.

REFERENCES

About Pinterest. (2017). Retrieved from <https://about.pinterest.com/en/press/press>.

Lofland, L. (2012). 20 great ways libraries are using Pinterest. Retrieved from <https://www.leelofland.com/20-great-ways-libraries-are-using-pinterest/>.

Mikos, I., Horne, B., & Weaver, K. (2015). Library display 2.0: Evolving from monologue to dialogue. *Library Philosophy and Practice*. Retrieved from <http://digitalcommons.unl.edu/libphilprac/1283>.

Severson, S. (2014). Moving beyond the display case: Getting your (digital) collections out there. *Argus*, *43*(1), 15–19.

INDEX

Note: Page numbers followed by "*f*" and "*t*" refer to figures and tables, respectively.

FSC
www.fsc.org
MIX
Papier | Fördert
gute Waldnutzung
FSC® C083411

Kolibri 360 GmbH
Ferdinand-Jühlke-Straße 7
99095 Erfurt, Deutschland
produktsicherheit@kolibri360.de